SHE COULD FLY

Volume Three

SHE COULD FLY

writer
Christopher Cantwell

artist
Martín Morazzo

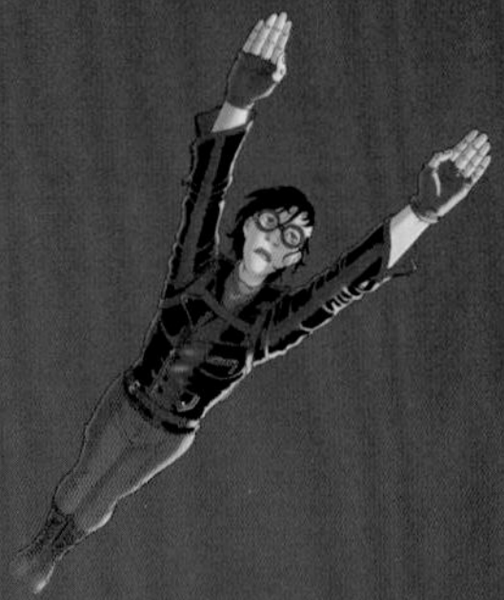

Volume Three

FIGHT OR FLIGHT

colorist

Miroslav Mrva

letterer

Clem Robins

Karen Berger
Editor

Rae Boyadjis
Associate Editor

Richard Bruning
Logo/Book Designer

Adam Pruett
Digital Art Technician

Mike Richardson
President & Publisher

First Edition: October 2021
ISBN: 9781506725635
Digital ISBN: 9781506725642

13 5 7 9 10 8 6 4 2

Printed in China

Published by Dark Horse Books
A division of Dark Horse Comics LLC
10956 SE Main Street, Milwaukie, OR 97222

SHE COULD FLY Volume Three: Fight or Flight

Library of Congress Cataloging-in-Publication Data
Names: Cantwell, Christopher, writer. | Morazzo, Martin, artist. |
Mrva, Miroslav, colourist. | Robins, Clem, 1955- letterer.
Title: The lost pilot / written by Christopher Cantwell ; art by
Martin Morazzo ; colored by Miroslav Mrva.
Description: First edition. | Milwaukie, OR : Dark Horse Books/Berger
Books, 2021. | Series: She could fly ; volume 3 |
Identifiers: LCCN 2021021817 (print) | LCCN 2021021818 (ebook) | ISBN
9781506725635 (paperback) | ISBN 9781506725642 (ebook other)
Subjects: LCSH: Comic books, strips, etc. | LCGFT: Comics (Graphic works)
| Science fiction comics. | Graphic novels.
Classification: LCC PN6728.S464 C34 2021 (print) | LCC PN6728.S464
(ebook) | DDC 741.5/973--dc23
LC record available at https://lccn.loc.gov/2021021817
LC ebook record available at https://lccn.loc.gov/2021021818

1.

superman
the wright bros
howard hughes
amelia earhart
wonder woman
archangels frm bible
elijah
lindbergh
rocky the squirrel
dumbo
mary poppins
peter pan
tinkerbell
Jean-François Pilâtre de Rozier
Jacques charles
mighty mouse
underdog
space ghost
yuan Huangtou
rocketeer
kyrpto
superwoman
hawk man
ultraman
john alcock and Arthur Brown
Giueseppe Cei
Charlie in Charlie and the chocolate factory and
uncle joe from the fizzy lifting drinks
Christa McAuliffe
Sally Ride
Neil Armstrong
Buzz Aldrin
The third guy on Apollo 11

The other Apollo guys
Jim Lovell was one of them
the little prince
Evel Kneival
the character you're supposed to be I
nthat old game Pilotwings whover that is
supposed to be
is supergirl the same as superwoman?
shazam
doctor doom
iron man
howard hughes
tom cruise whenb he was filming top gun
Sir Thomas Sopwith
Aldasoro bros
harry potter I guess and hios friends
James stewart in the movie about glenn
miller
Glenn Miller
Richie valens Buddy Holly Big Bopper (but
not Waylon Jennings)
jim croce too
silver surfer
All commercial airline passenngers ever
and the crews
Mario with a cape
Somewhat Mario with the leaf and the
racoon tails & ears
faeries
Charlie again in the glass elevator
Maybe Jesus not sure
All World War I and II pilots
All war pilots

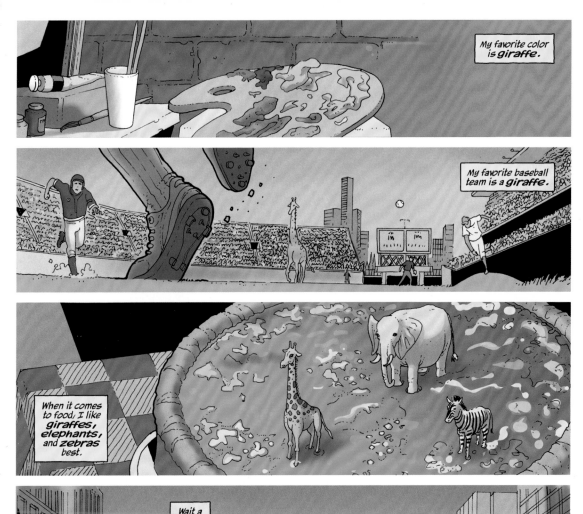

My favorite color is *giraffe.*

My favorite baseball team is a *giraffe.*

When it comes to food, I like *giraffes, elephants,* and *zebras* best.

Wait a minute.

What was I just doing?

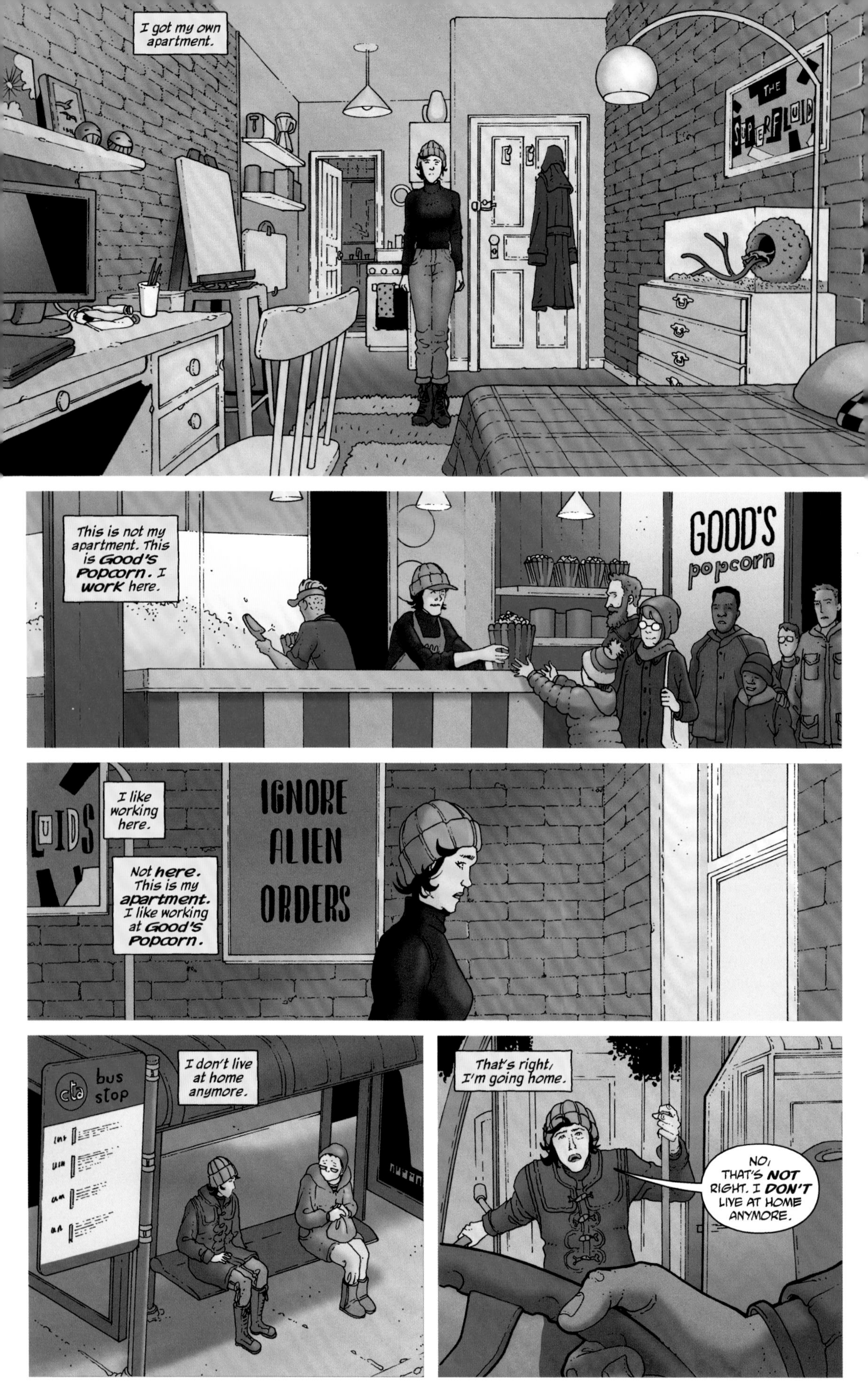

I got my own apartment.
THE SUPERFLUID
This is not my apartment. This is Good's Popcorn. I work here.
GOOD'S popcorn
I like working here.
Not here. This is my apartment. I like working at Good's Popcorn.
IGNORE ALIEN ORDERS
cta bus stop
I don't live at home anymore.
That's right, I'm going home.
NO, THAT'S NOT RIGHT. I DON'T LIVE AT HOME ANYMORE.

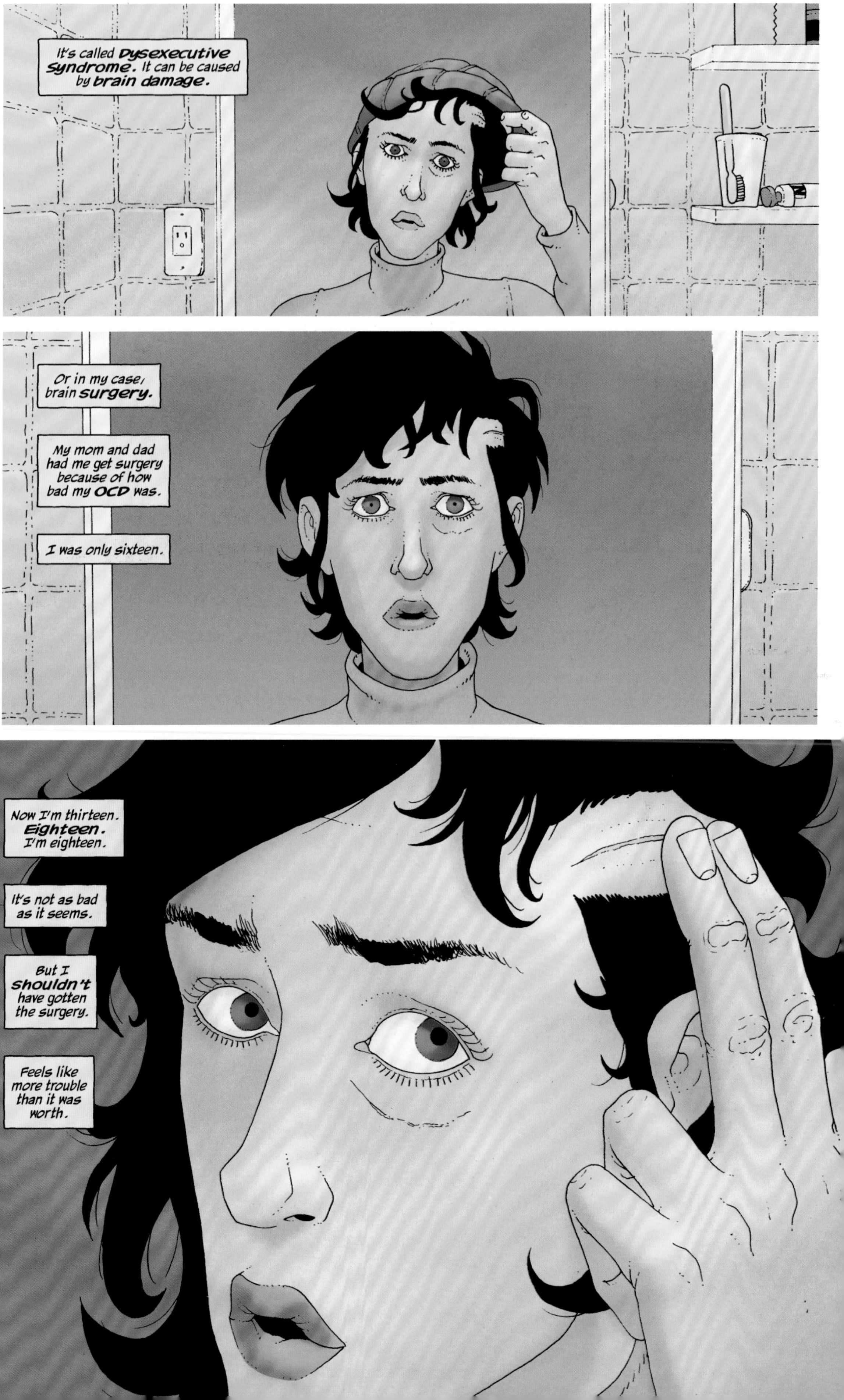
It's called Dysexecutive syndrome. It can be caused by brain damage.
Or in my case, brain surgery.
My mom and dad had me get surgery because of how bad my OCD was.
I was only sixteen.
Now I'm thirteen. Eighteen. I'm eighteen.
It's not as bad as it seems.
But I shouldn't have gotten the surgery.
Feels like more trouble than it was worth.

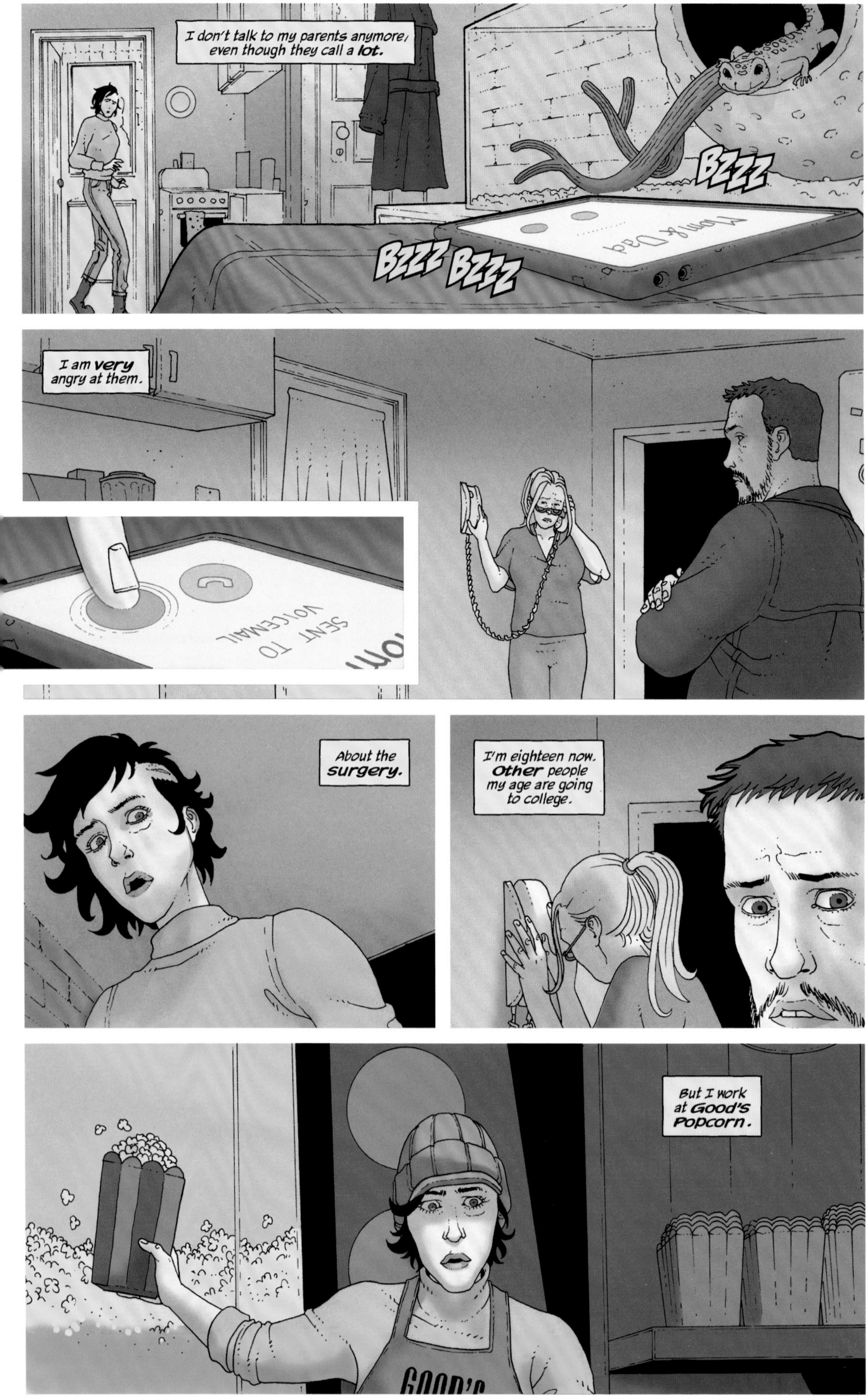
I don't talk to my parents anymore, even though they call a lot.
BZZZ
Mom & Dad
BZZZ BZZZ
I am very angry at them.
SENT TO VOICEMAIL
About the surgery.
I'm eighteen now. Other people my age are going to college.
But I work at Good's Popcorn.

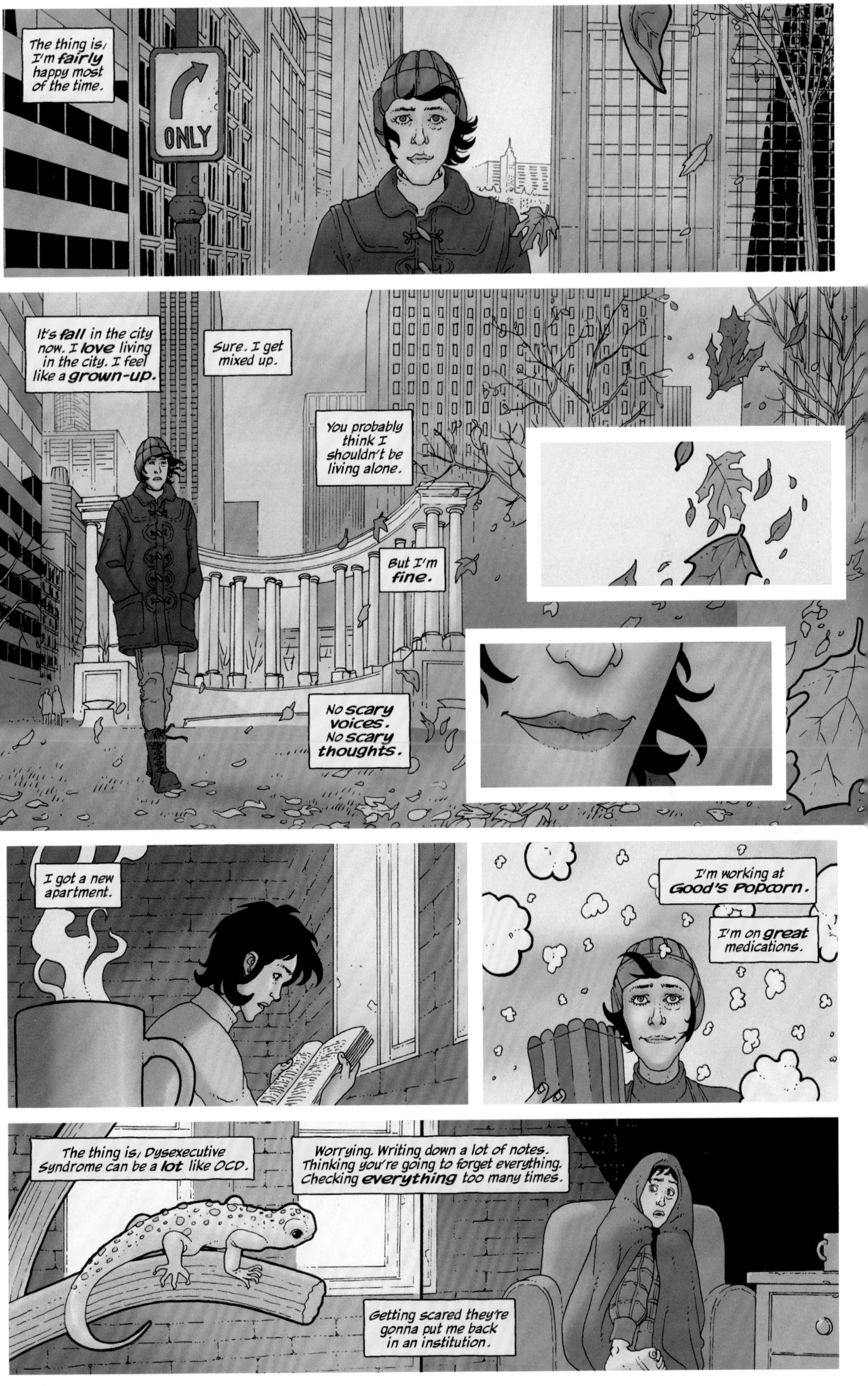
The thing is, I'm fairly happy most of the time.
ONLY
It's fall in the city now. I love living in the city. I feel like a grown-up.
Sure. I get mixed up.
You probably think I shouldn't be living alone.
But I'm fine.
No scary voices. No scary thoughts.
I got a new apartment.
I'm working at Good's Popcorn.
I'm on great medications.
The thing is, Dysexecutive Syndrome can be a lot like OCD.
Worrying. Writing down a lot of notes. Thinking you're going to forget everything. Checking everything too many times.
Getting scared they're gonna put me back in an institution.

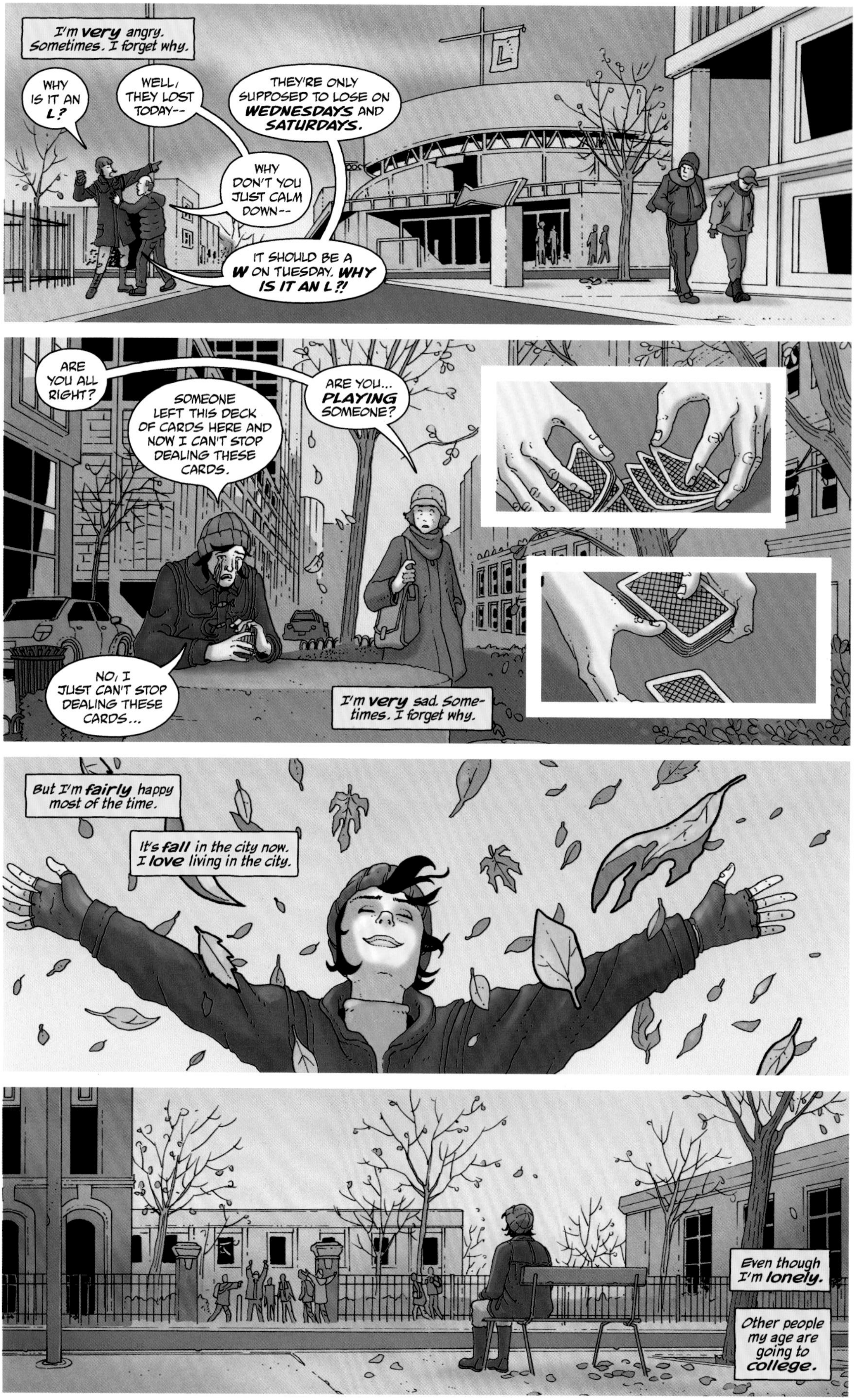
I'm very angry. Sometimes. I forget why.
WHY IS IT AN L?
WELL, THEY LOST TODAY--
THEY'RE ONLY SUPPOSED TO LOSE ON WEDNESDAYS AND SATURDAYS.
WHY DON'T YOU JUST CALM DOWN--
IT SHOULD BE A W ON TUESDAY. WHY IS IT AN L?!
ARE YOU ALL RIGHT?
SOMEONE LEFT THIS DECK OF CARDS HERE AND NOW I CAN'T STOP DEALING THESE CARDS.
ARE YOU... PLAYING SOMEONE?
NO, I JUST CAN'T STOP DEALING THESE CARDS...
I'm very sad. Sometimes. I forget why.
But I'm fairly happy most of the time.
It's fall in the city now. I love living in the city.
Even though I'm lonely.
Other people my age are going to college.

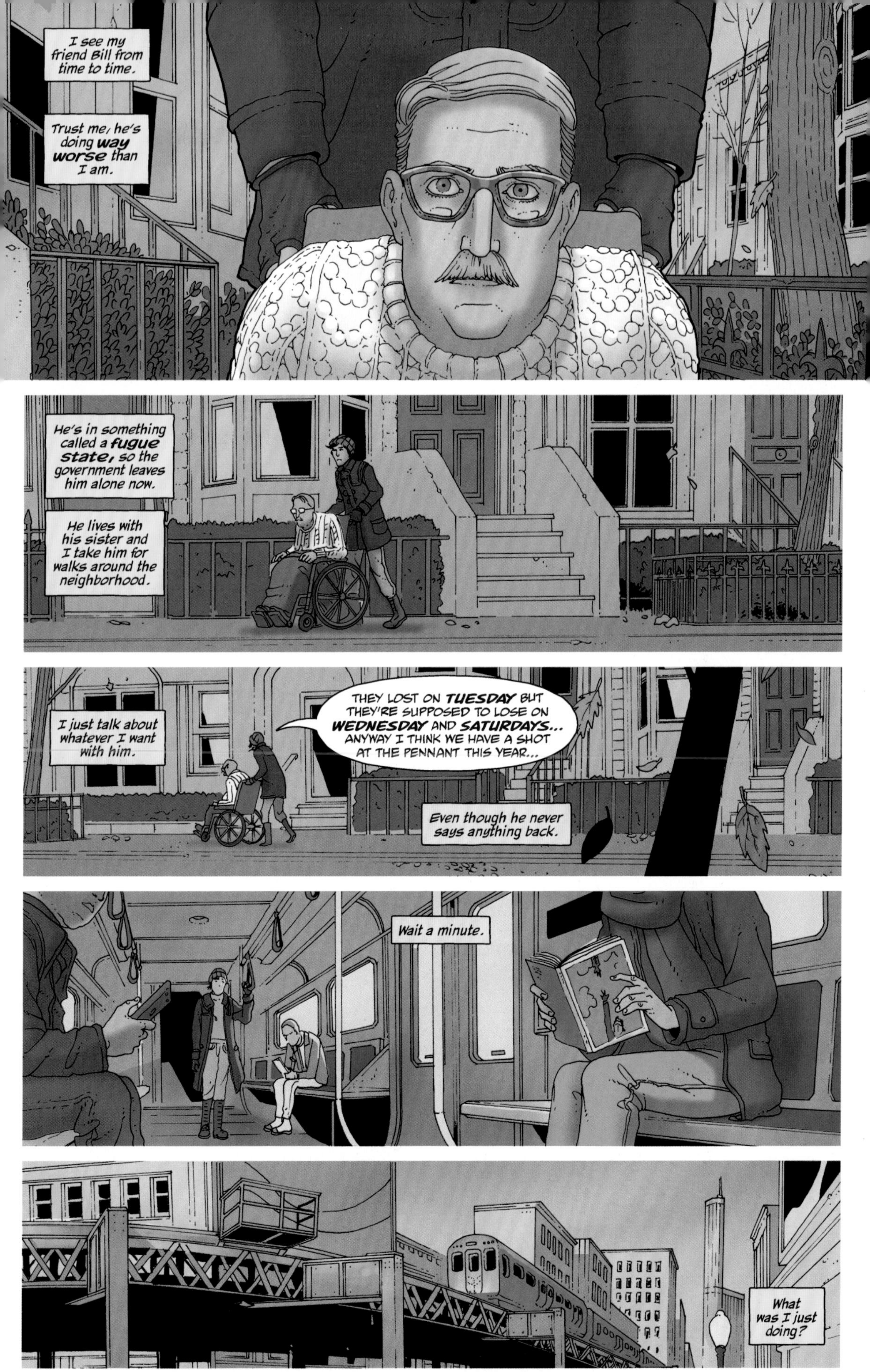
I see my friend Bill from time to time.
Trust me, he's doing **way worse** than I am.
He's in something called a **fugue state,** so the government leaves him alone now.
He lives with his sister and I take him for walks around the neighborhood.
I just talk about whatever I want with him.
THEY LOST ON **TUESDAY** BUT THEY'RE SUPPOSED TO LOSE ON **WEDNESDAY** AND **SATURDAYS...** ANYWAY I THINK WE HAVE A SHOT AT THE PENNANT THIS YEAR...
Even though he never says anything back.
Wait a minute.
What was I just doing?

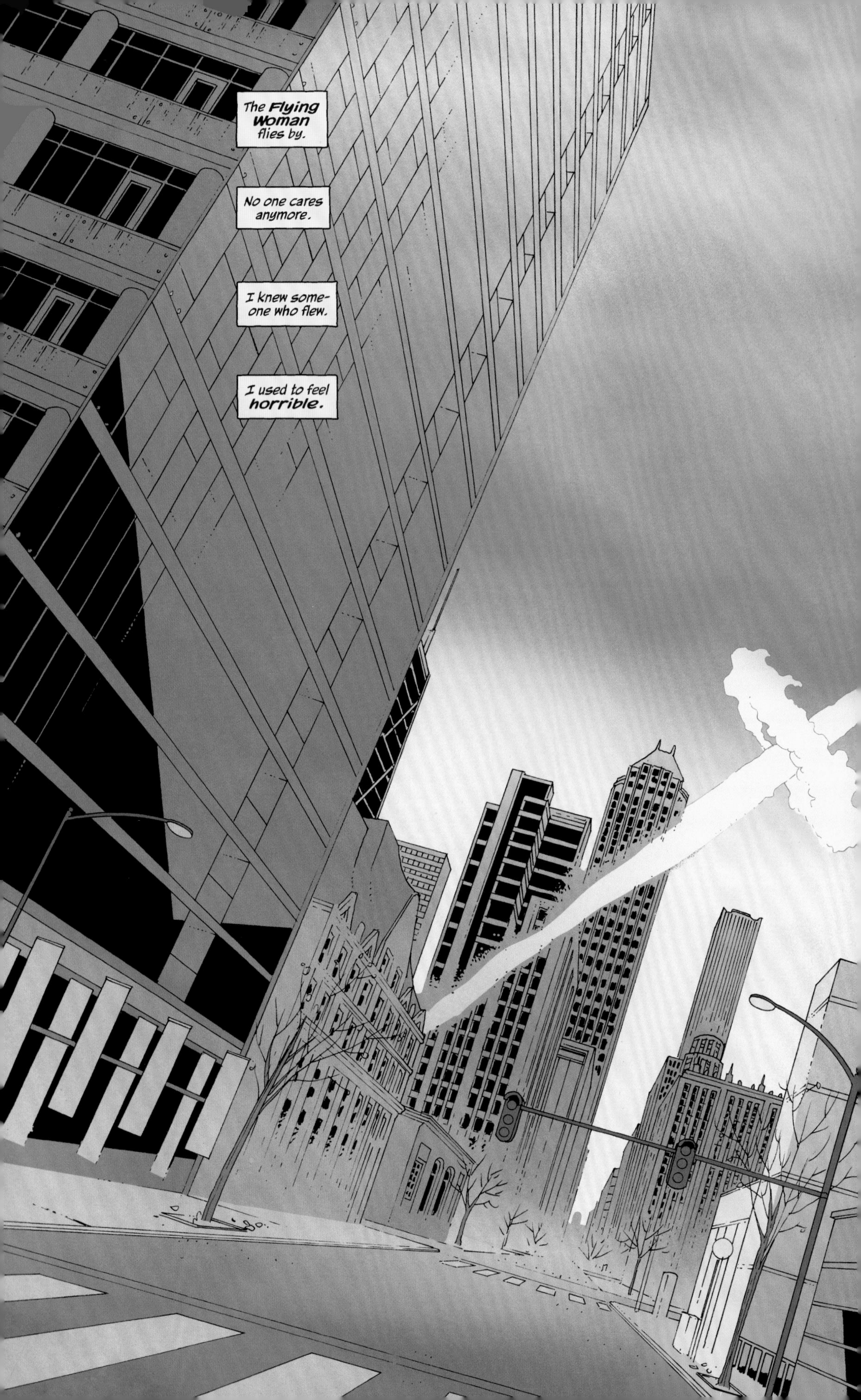
The Flying Woman flies by.
No one cares anymore.
I knew some-one who flew.
I used to feel horrible.

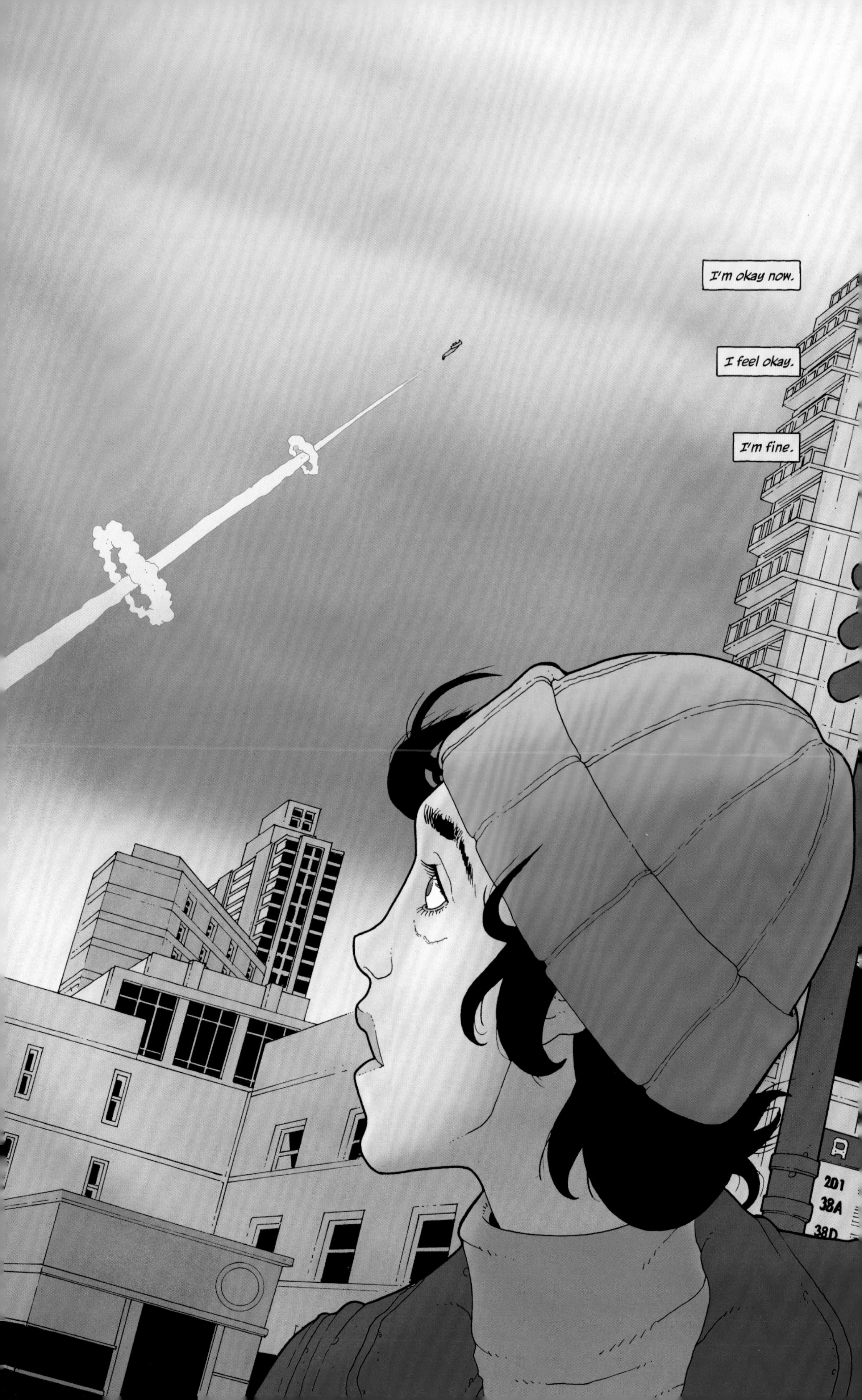
I'm okay now.
I feel okay.
I'm fine.
2D1
38A
38D

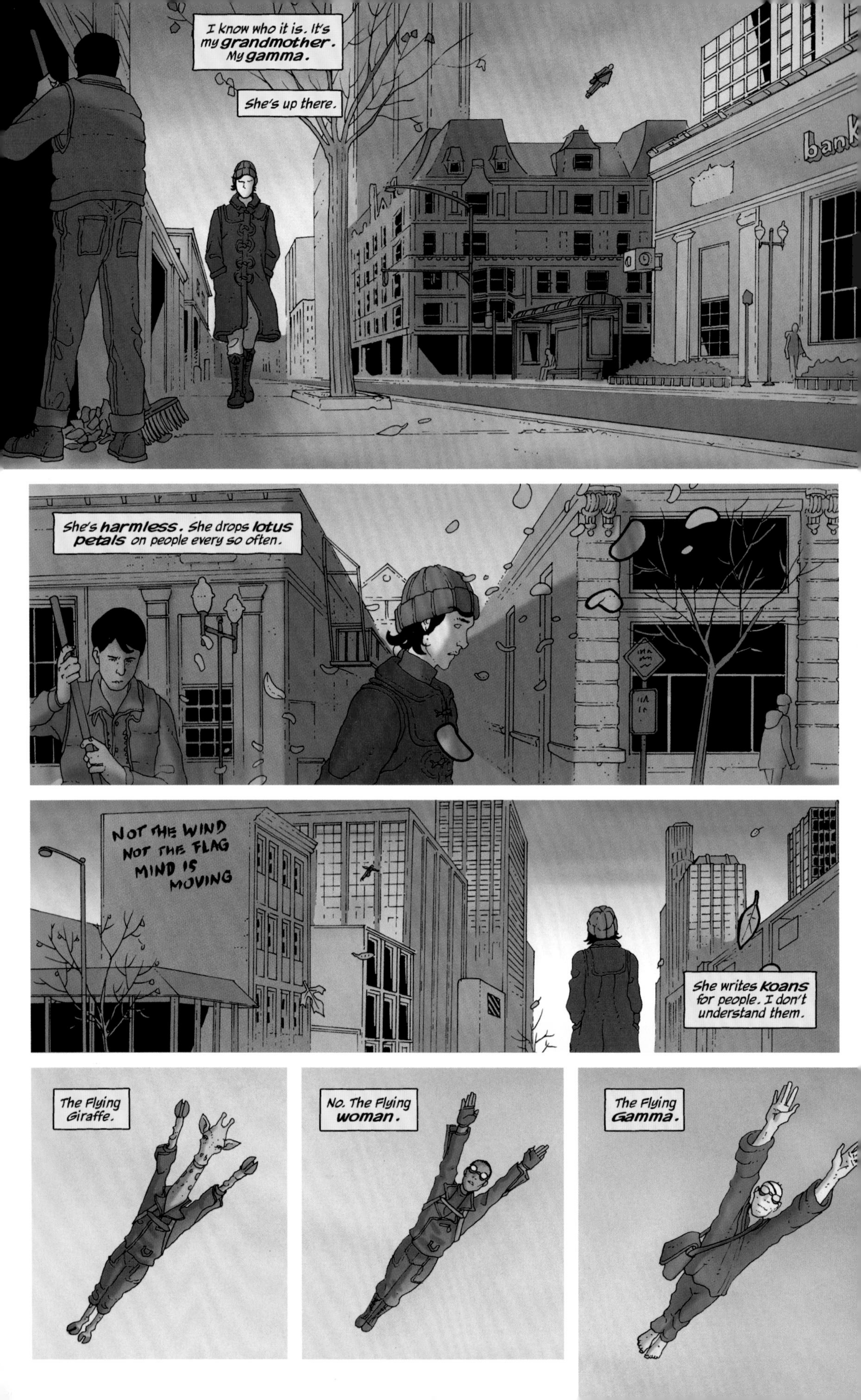
I know who it is. It's my grandmother. My gamma.
She's up there.
bank
She's harmless. She drops lotus petals on people every so often.
NOT THE WIND
NOT THE FLAG
MIND IS
MOVING
She writes koans for people. I don't understand them.
The Flying Giraffe.
No. The Flying woman.
The Flying Gamma.

It's *fall* in the city now.

I *love* living in the city.

Someone is going to *fall*.

I *love* falling.

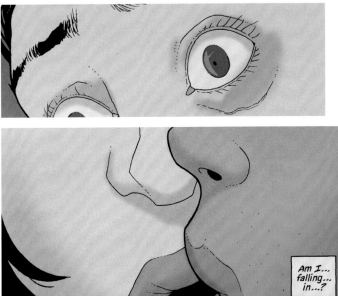

Am I... falling... in...?

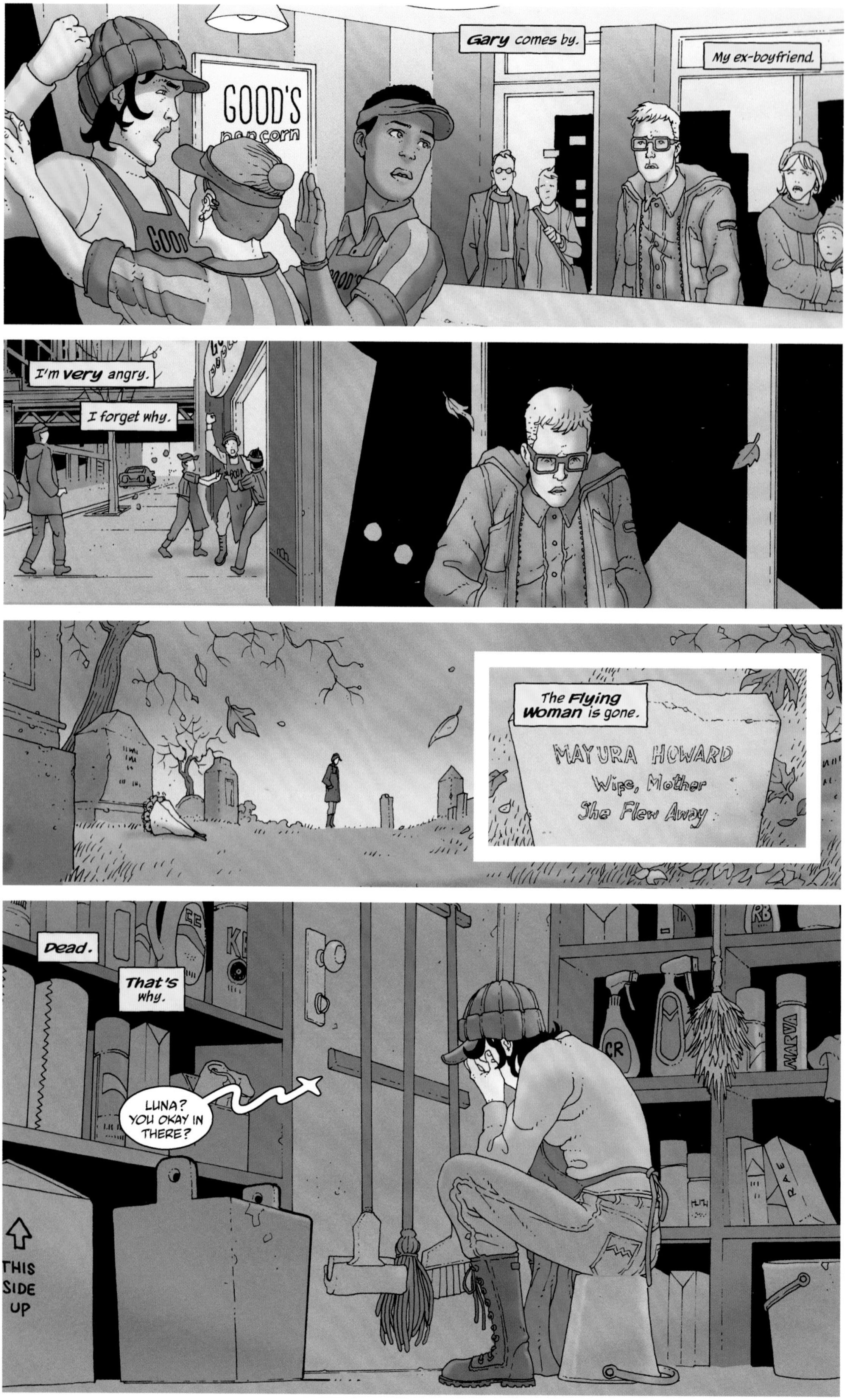
Gary comes by.
My ex-boyfriend.
GOOD'S popcorn
GOOD
GOOD'S
I'm very angry.
I forget why.
The Flying Woman is gone.
MAYURA HOWARD
Wife, Mother
She Flew Away
Dead.
That's why.
LUNA? YOU OKAY IN THERE?
THIS SIDE UP
CR
NARVA
RB
RAE

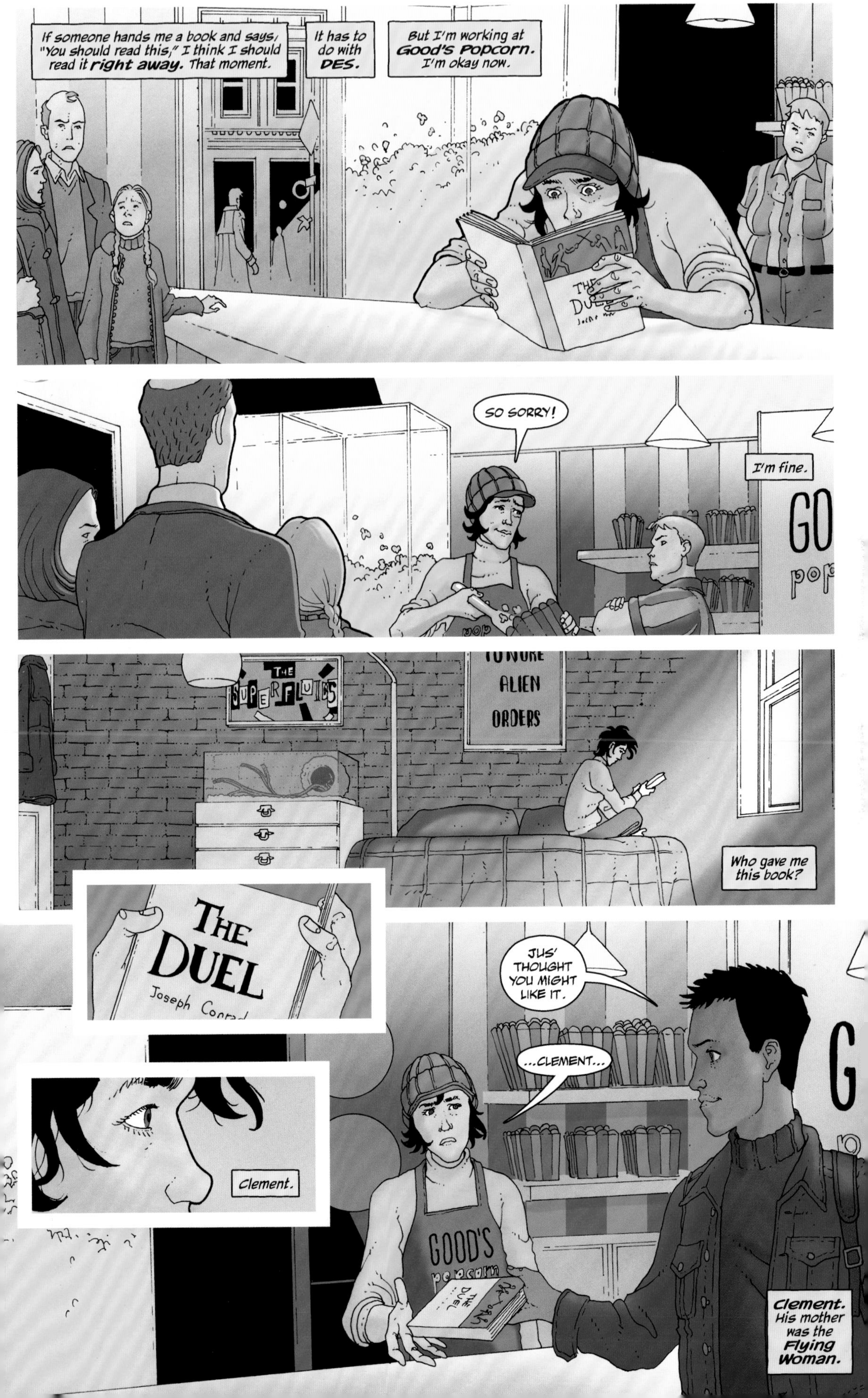
If someone hands me a book and says, "You should read this," I think I should read it right away. That moment.
It has to do with DES.
But I'm working at Good's Popcorn. I'm okay now.
THE DUEL
SO SORRY!
I'm fine.
GOO
pop
THE SUPERFLUIDS
ALIEN ORDERS
Who gave me this book?
THE DUEL
Joseph Conrad
Clement.
JUS' THOUGHT YOU MIGHT LIKE IT.
...CLEMENT...
GOOD'S popcorn
Clement. His mother was the Flying Woman.

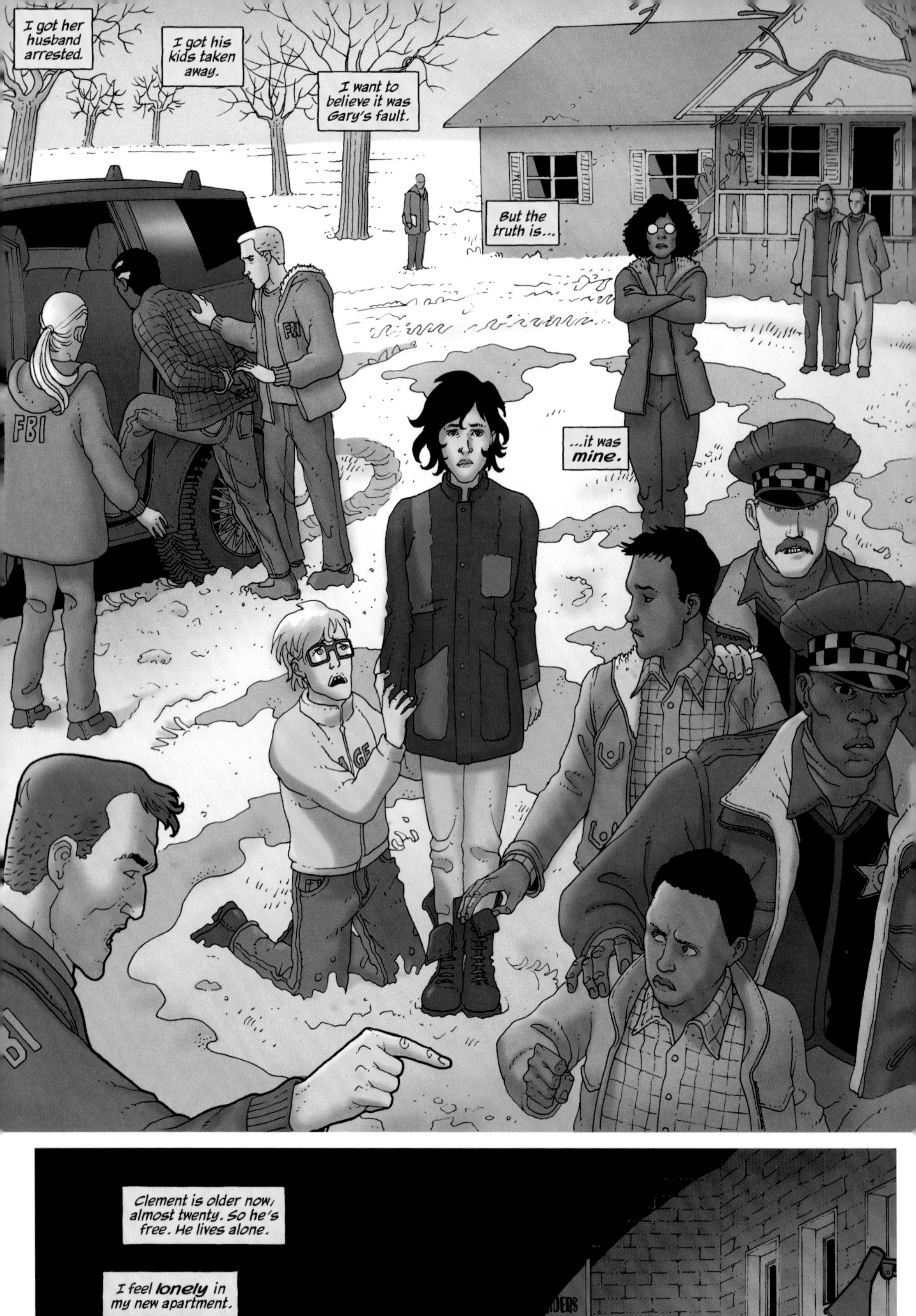

I got her husband arrested.
I got his kids taken away.
I want to believe it was Gary's fault.
But the truth is...
...it was **mine.**
FBI
FBI

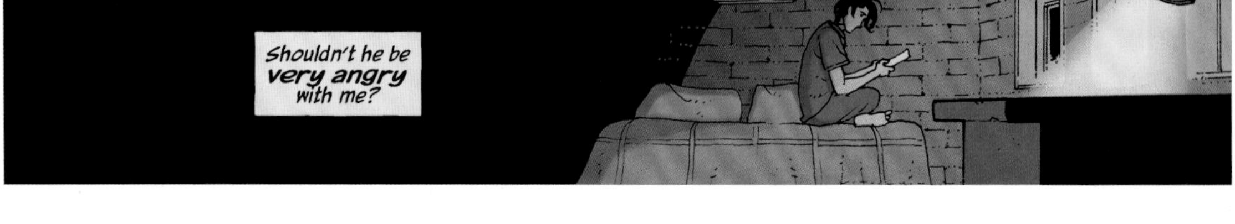

Clement is older now, almost twenty. So he's free. He lives alone.
I feel **lonely** in my new apartment.
Shouldn't he be **very angry** with me?

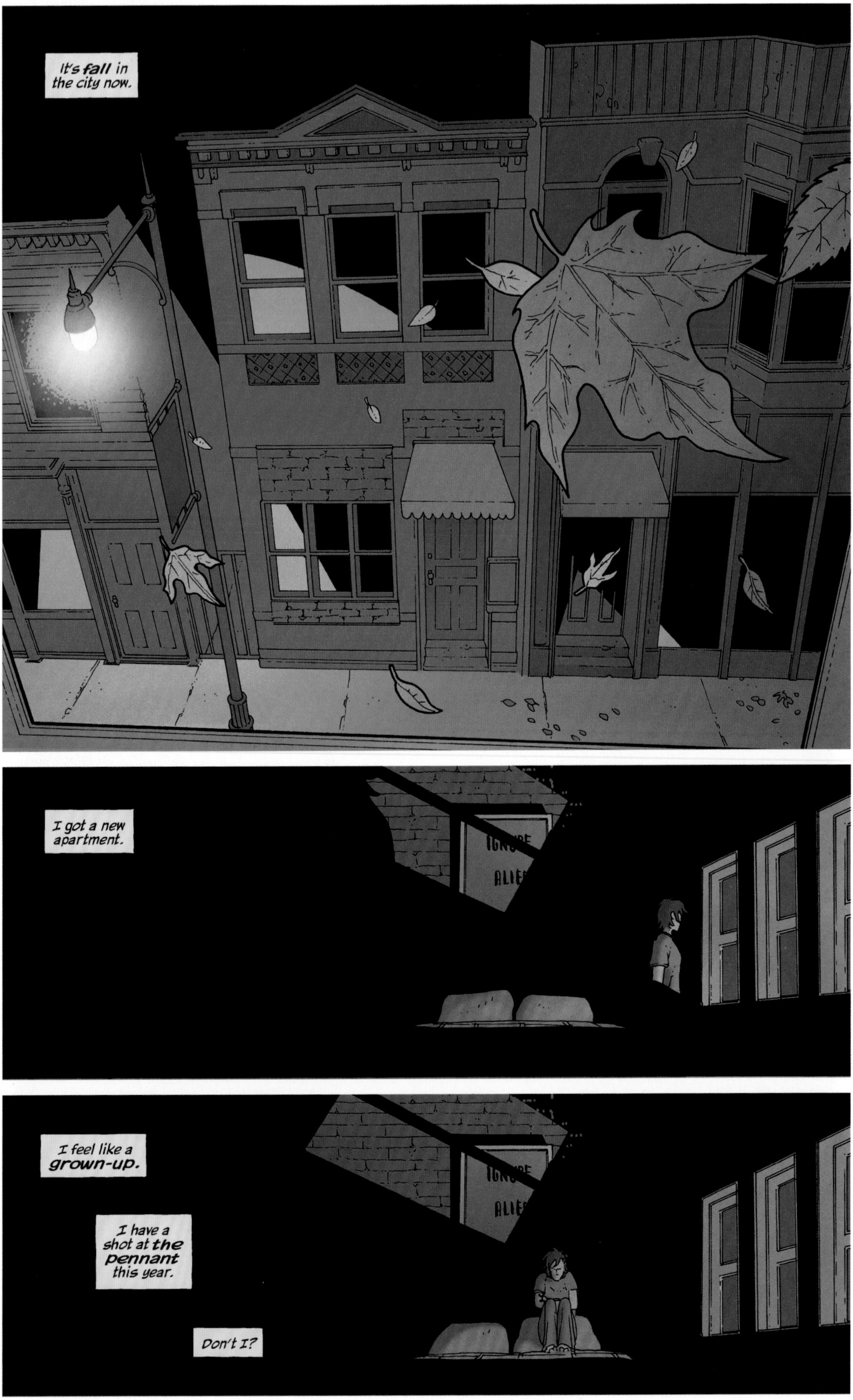
It's fall in the city now.
I got a new apartment.
I feel like a grown-up.
I have a shot at the pennant this year.
Don't I?

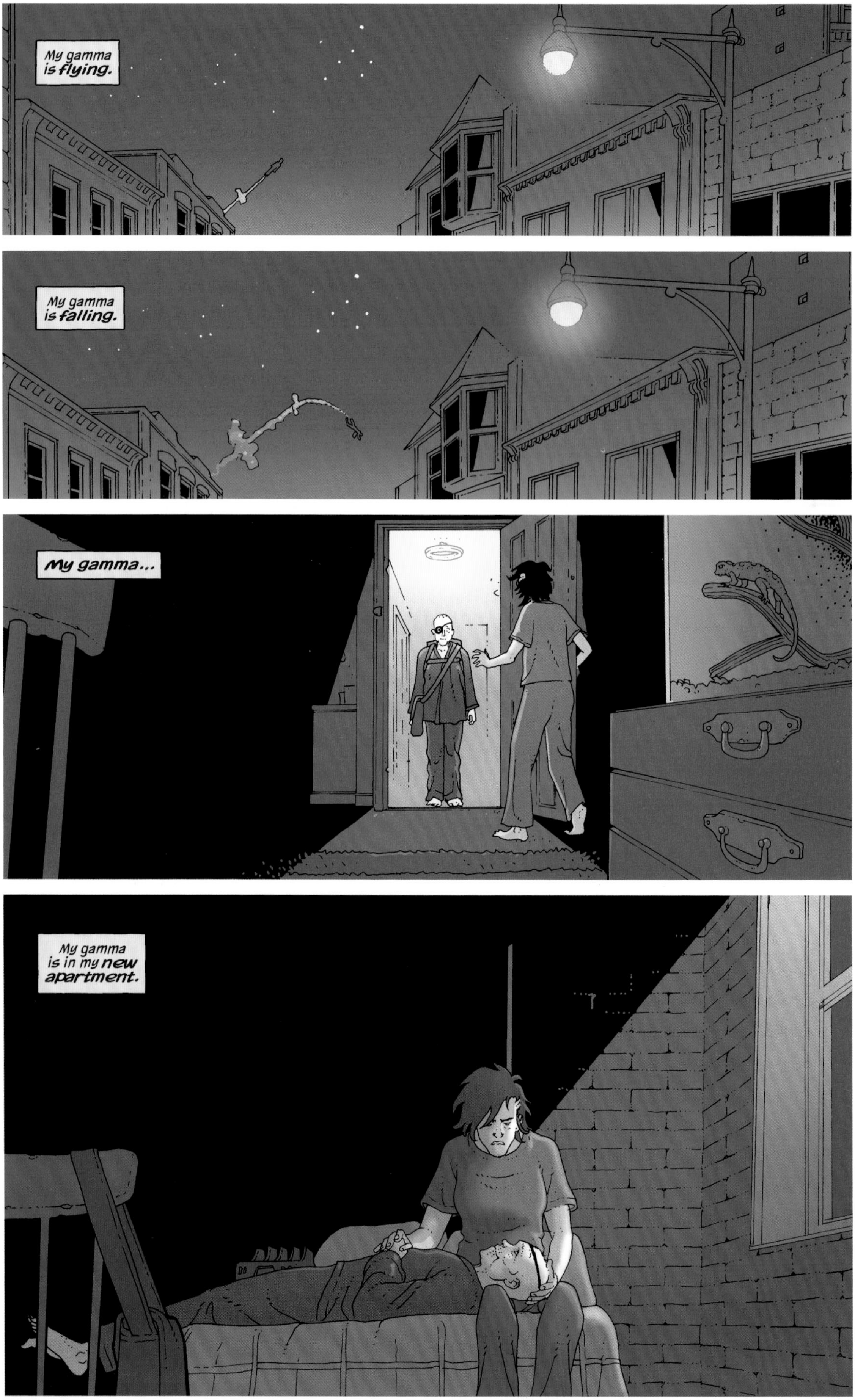
My gamma is flying.
My gamma is falling.
My gamma...
My gamma is in my new apartment.

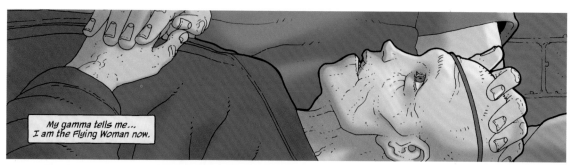

My gamma tells me...
I am the Flying Woman now.

The *Accelerator*.

My friend Bill.

He built this.

I don't talk to **my parents** anymore.

I don't talk to **Gary** anymore.

I don't talk to my gamma anymore.

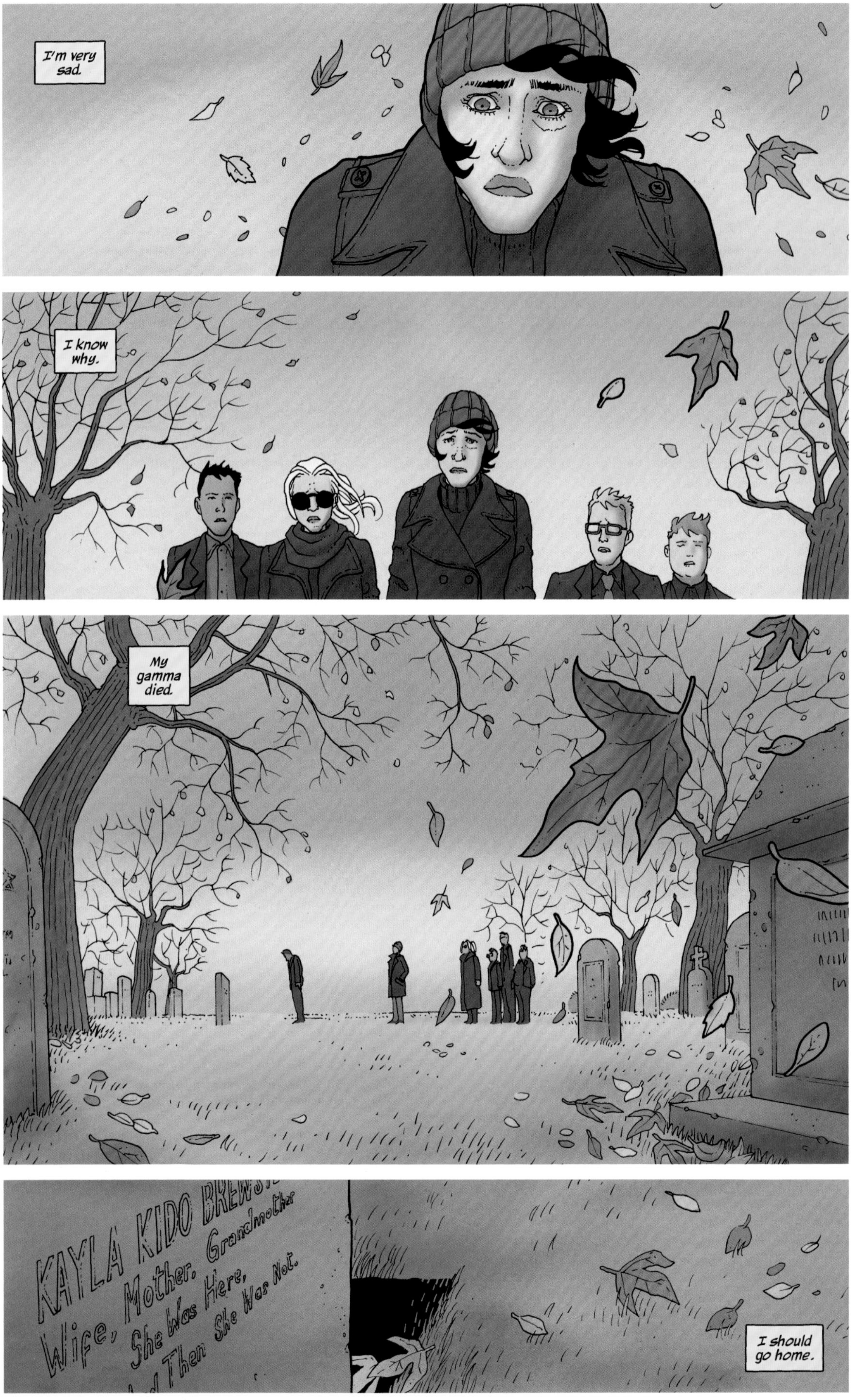
I'm very sad.
I know why.
My gamma died.
KAYLA KIDO BREWST
Wife, Mother, Grandmother
She Was Here,
She Was Not.
I should go home.

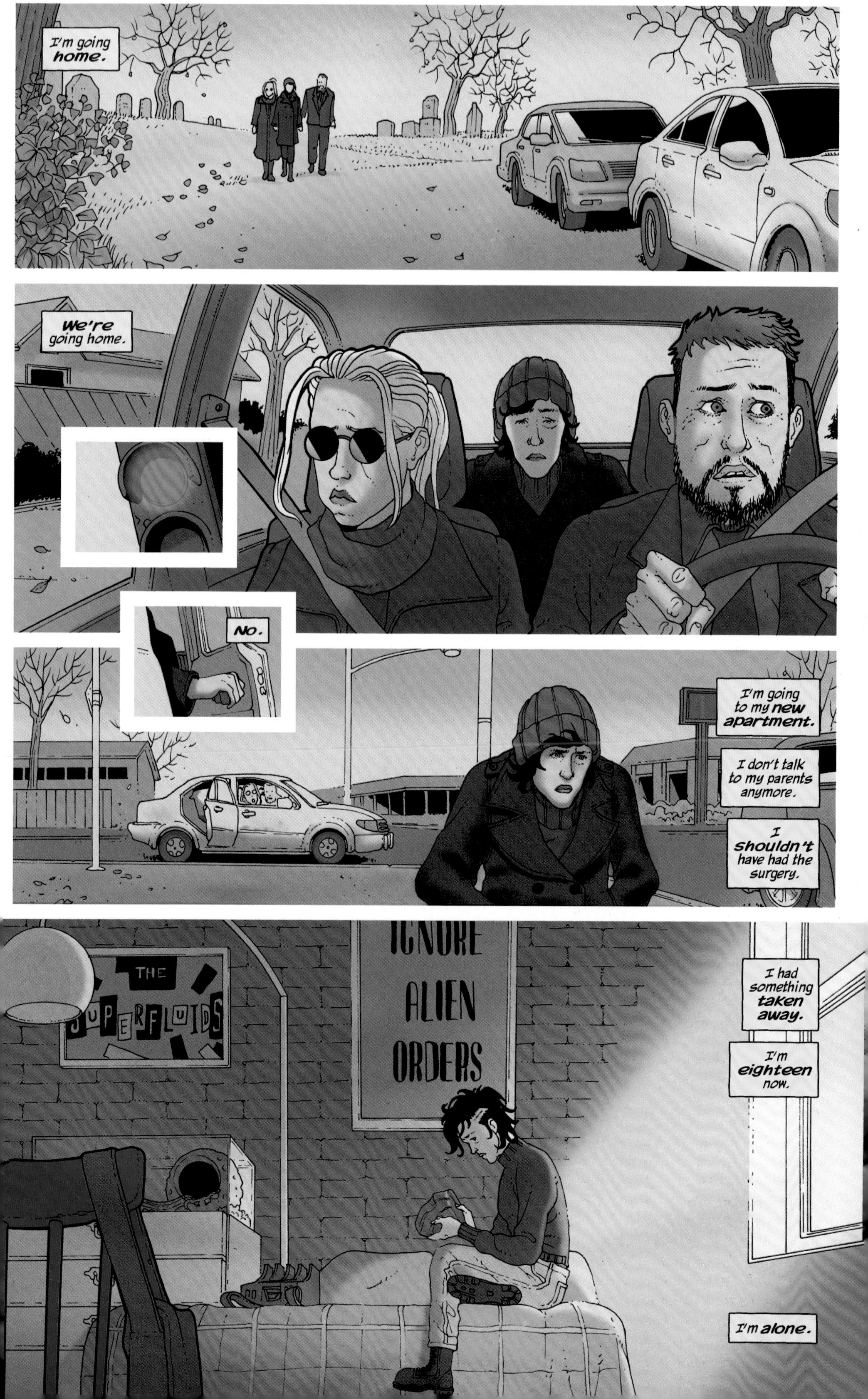
I'm going home.
We're going home.
No.
I'm going to my new apartment.
I don't talk to my parents anymore.
I shouldn't have had the surgery.
THE SUPERFLUIDS
IGNORE ALIEN ORDERS
I had something taken away.
I'm eighteen now.
I'm alone.

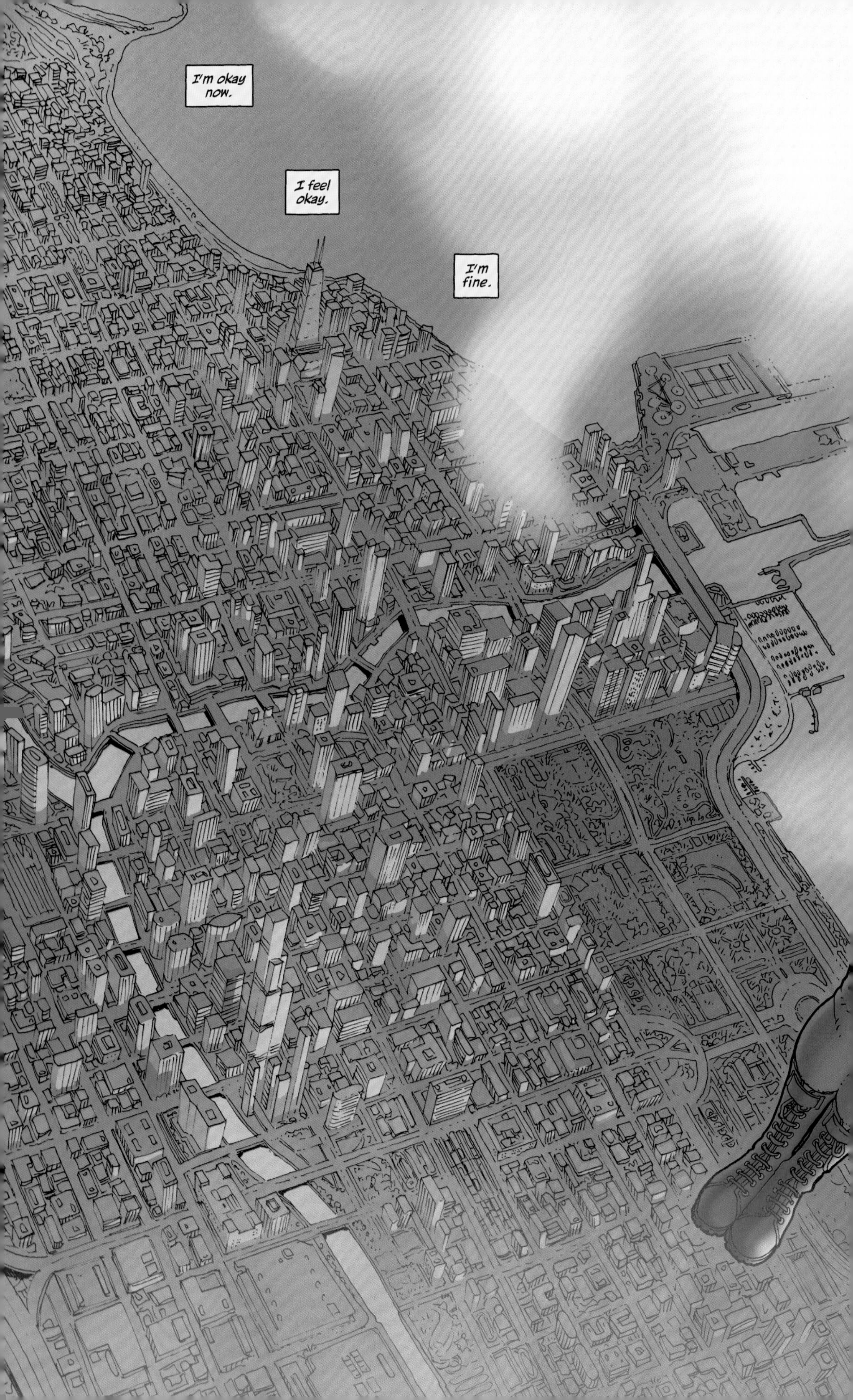
I'm okay now.
I feel okay.
I'm fine.

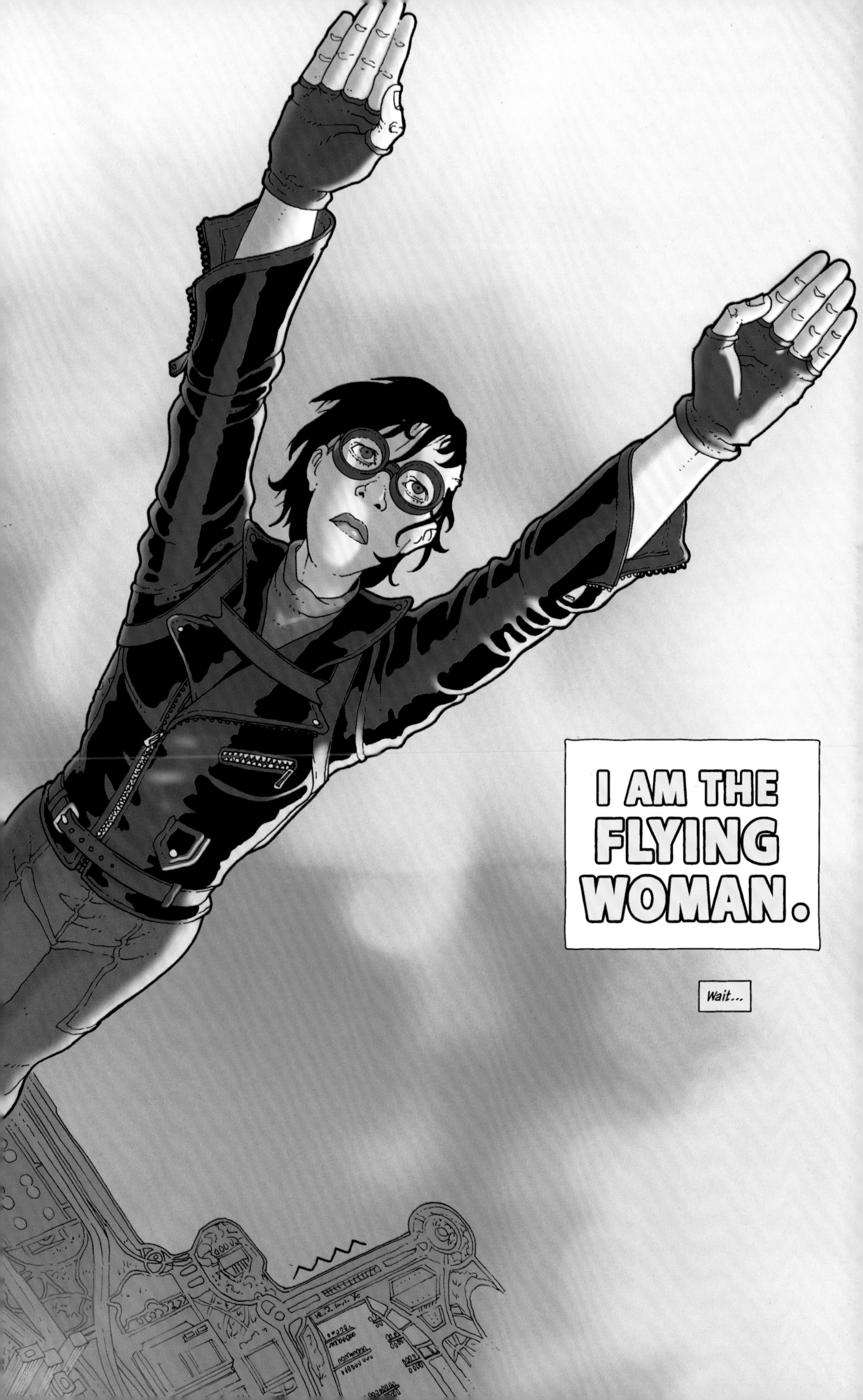
I AM THE FLYING WOMAN.
Wait...

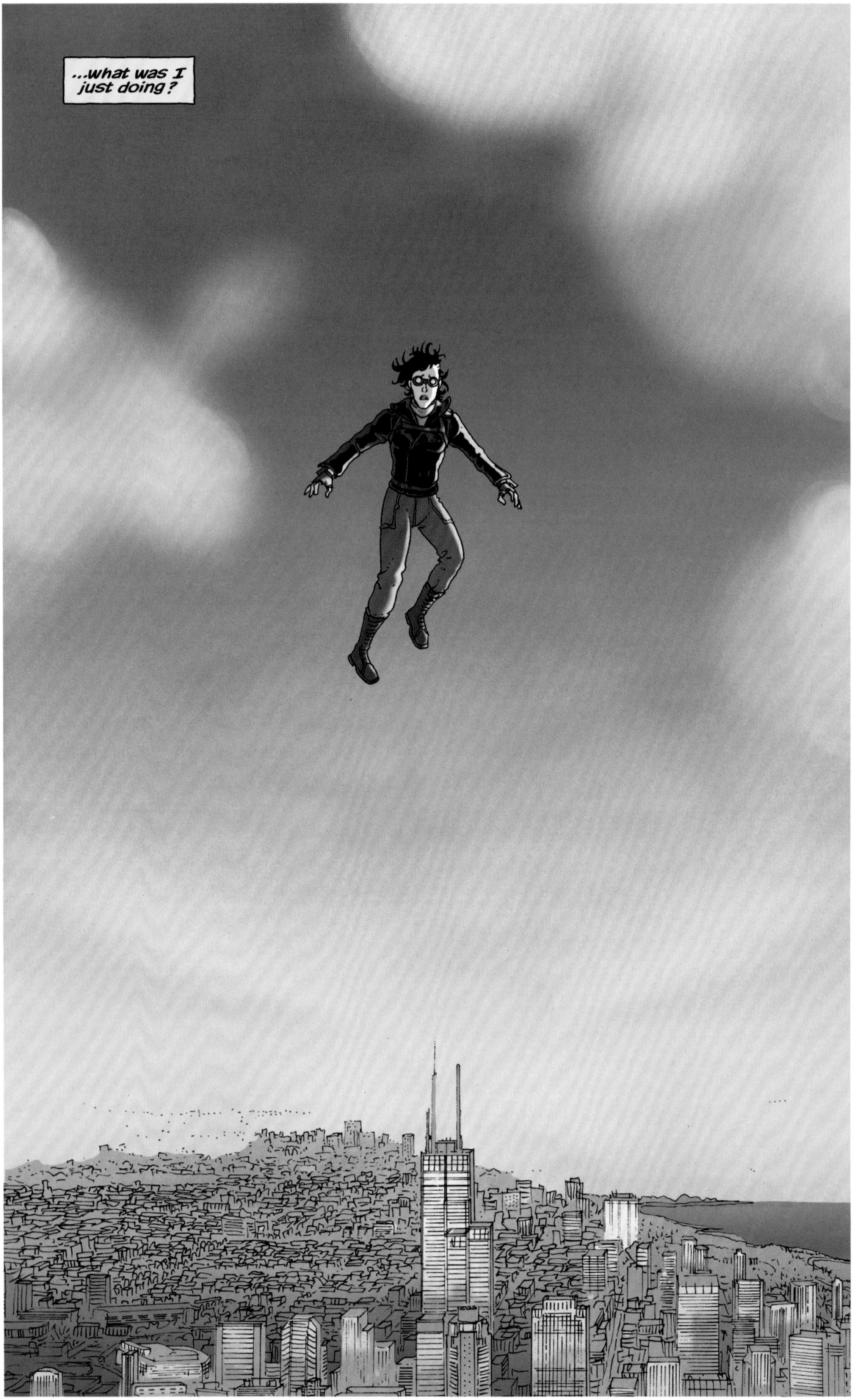
...what was I just doing?

2

This is upsetting but the 9/11 victims and
hijackers
All other air terrorism victims and terrorists
Diego Marin Aguilera
Condorman (right? never saw it)
The man who created the IBM PC and his wife
(died)
Air marshalls
The guy who played Blade but in the movie
Passenger 57
some Vampires
Orko (mnore hovering)
princess leia but that was really fucking weird
man!
Neo and Agent Smith(s)
Kirby from dreamworld but I don't remember if he
was actually from there
Did I say Starscream already?
Green Lantern
The Flyinng Nun
Slim Pickins at the End of Dr. Strangelove
Buzz Liughtyear, momentarily at least
Countless pokemon
falcon
All presidents since Air force One and probably
a few before that
Richard Branson
Marchioness and Countess of Montalembert, the
Countess of Podenas and Miss de Lagarde
Pierre Romain who was the other guy who died
Sophie Blanchard
Rose Isabel spencer
Unnamed boy in glider circa 1853
Leon Delegrange
Thomas Etholen Selfridge
Hubert lAtham

Raymonde De LarRoche
Rene Thomas and Bertram Dickson
Denise Moore
Ricky Nelson
Giullo Givotti
Pyotr Nesterov
Dean Evan lamb and Phil Rader
Eugenie Mikhailovna S?Hakhovskaya
marie Marvingt
Ahmet Ali Celikten
(^^ this was a good run of names here, thanks
library computer!1)
sam 1 Jackson in that snakes movie
the cars in the fast and furious movies, meaning
the drivers of the cars, vin diesel ludacris et
al
batman but only when he glides, common
misconception

nOtE: REEVaLUATING WHETHER FLYING IN SPACE IS
FLYING. Orbital take off qualifies but does space
flying equal flying, or is it something else
(i.e., floating)

M<ail carrier pilots and crew like Fedex and UPS
and the Mail

DB cooper x2 (riding in plane and ljumping out)

NOTE: IS FLYING THE SAME AS
FALLING???

I saw a red balloon flying.

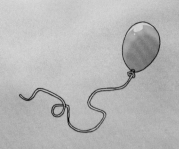

I think a kid let it go because I could hear him crying.

Someone is crying.

Who is it?

It's not *me*, is it?

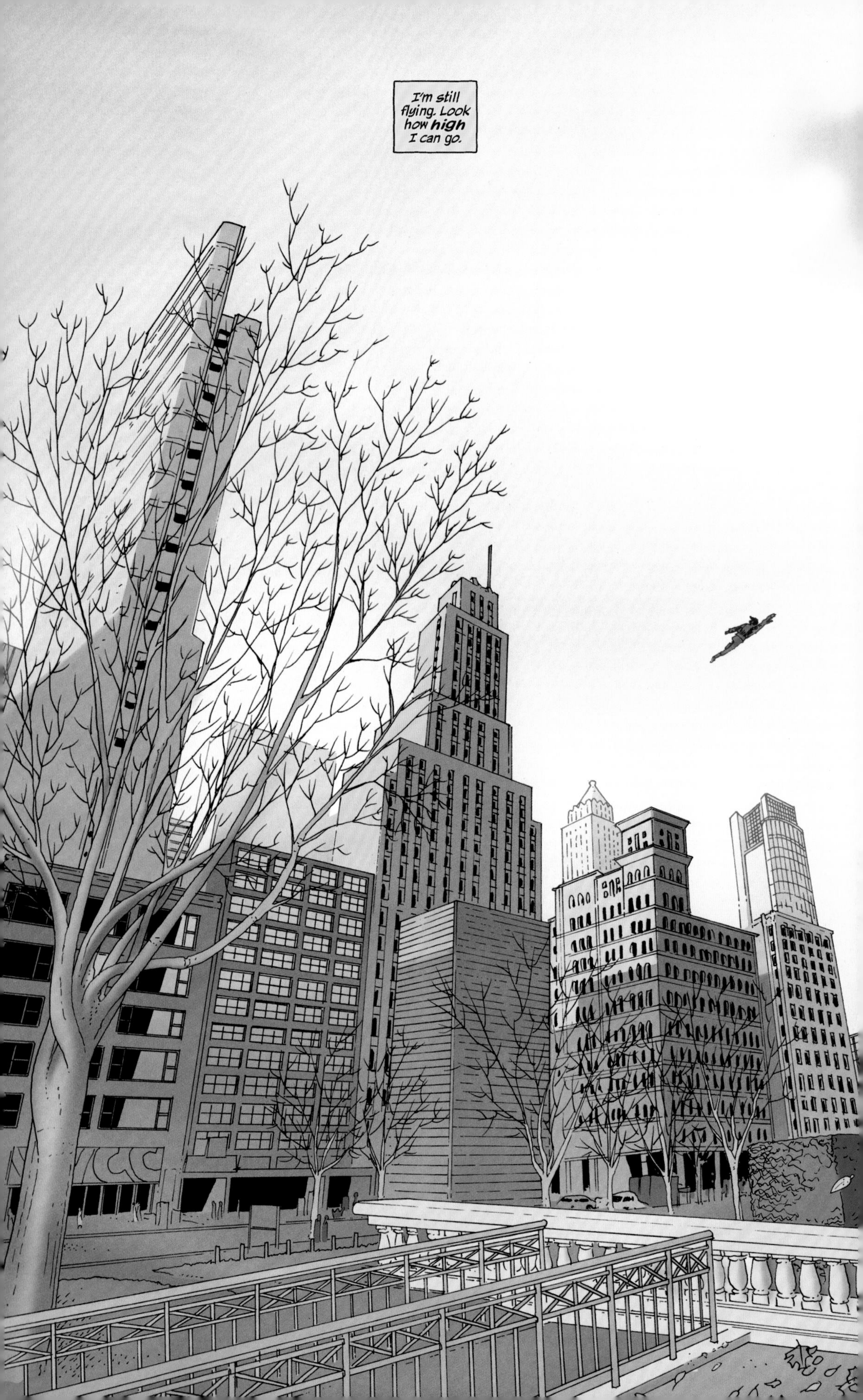
I'm still flying. Look how **high** I can go.

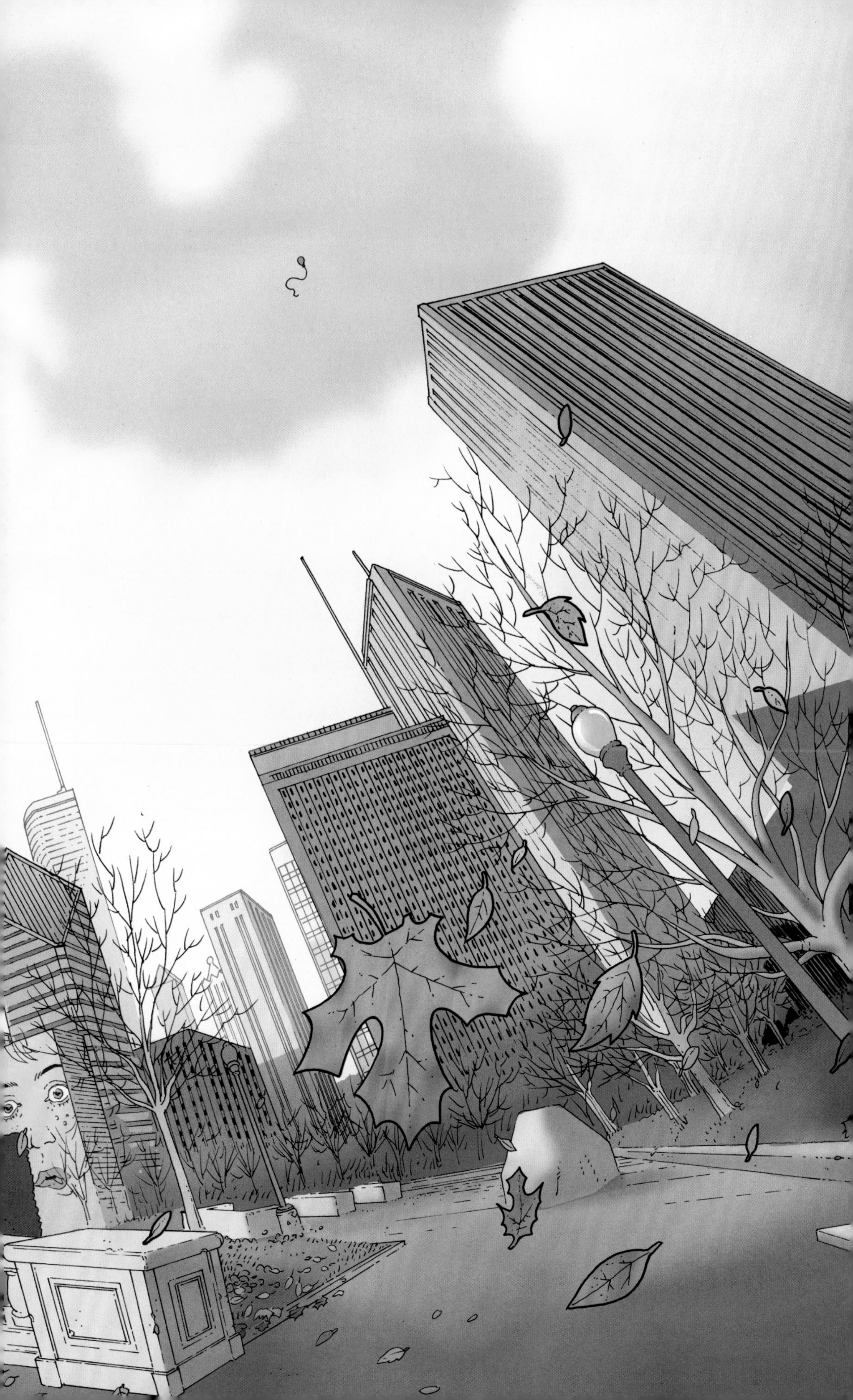

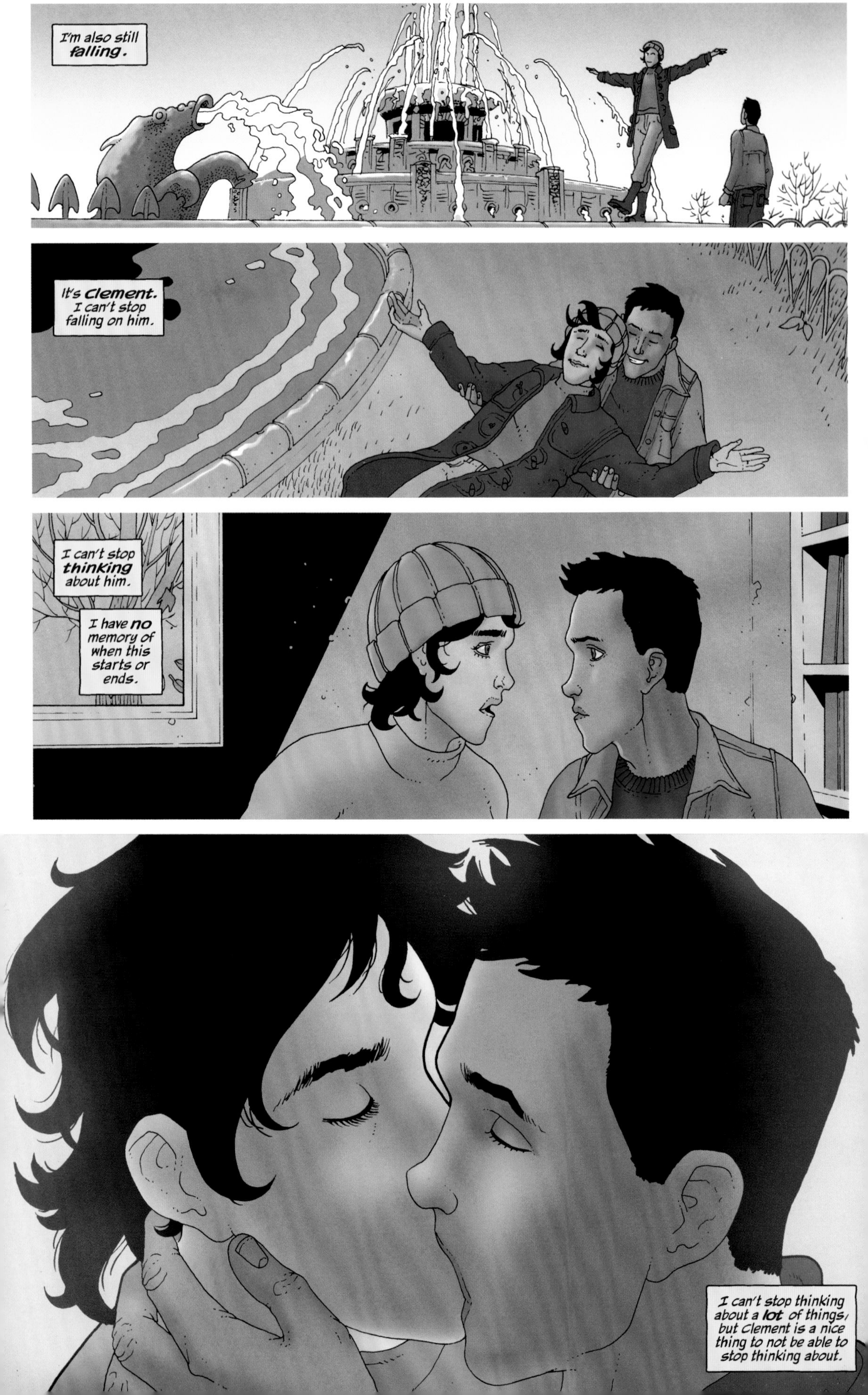
I'm also still **falling**.
It's **Clement**. I can't stop falling on him.
I can't stop **thinking** about him.
I have **no** memory of when this starts or ends.
I can't stop thinking about a **lot** of things, but Clement is a nice thing to not be able to stop thinking about.

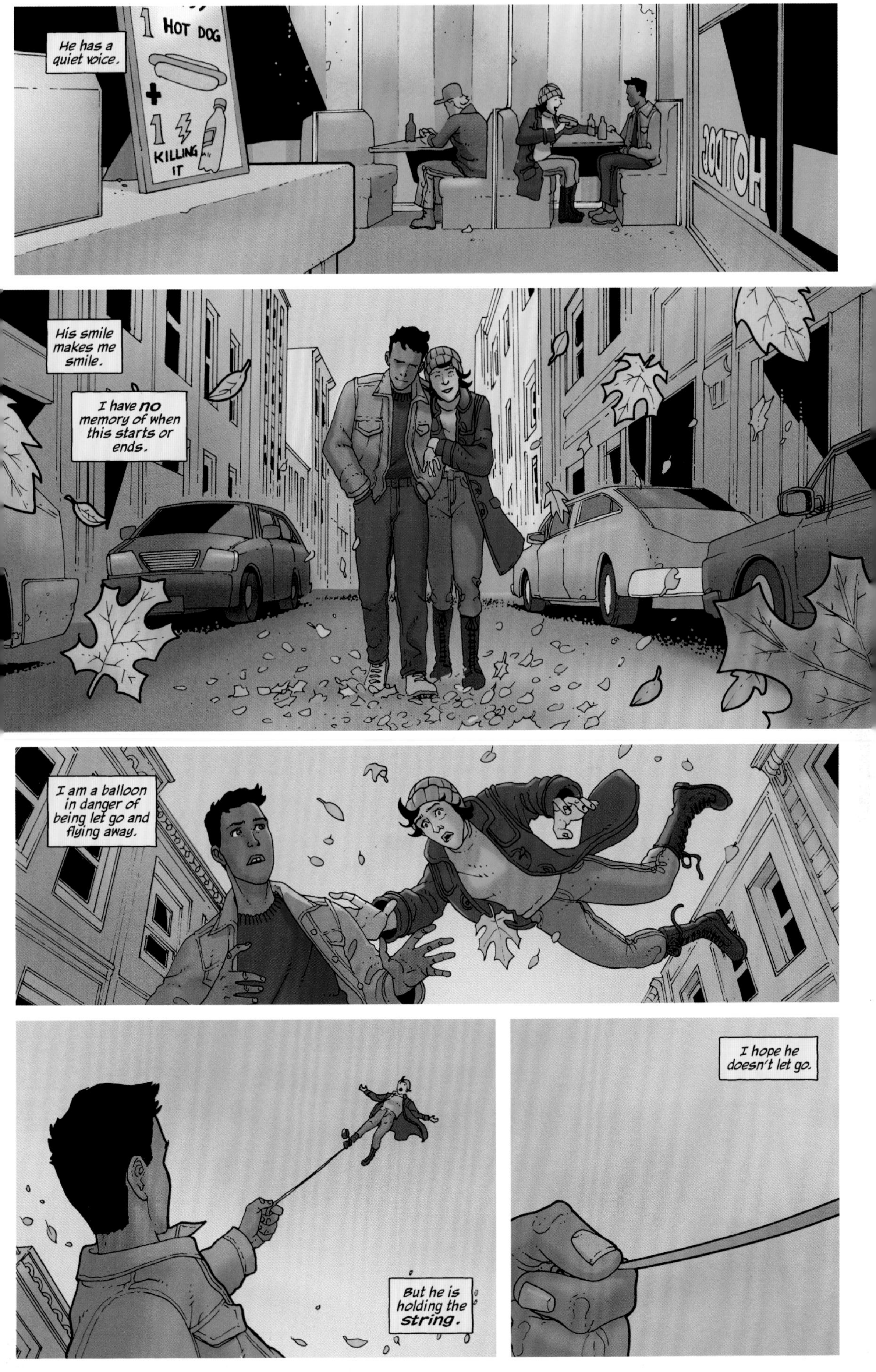
1 HOT DOG
+
1
KILLING IT
He has a quiet voice.
HOTDOG
His smile makes me smile.
I have **no** memory of when this starts or ends.
I am a balloon in danger of being let go and flying away.
But he is holding the **string**.
I hope he doesn't let go.

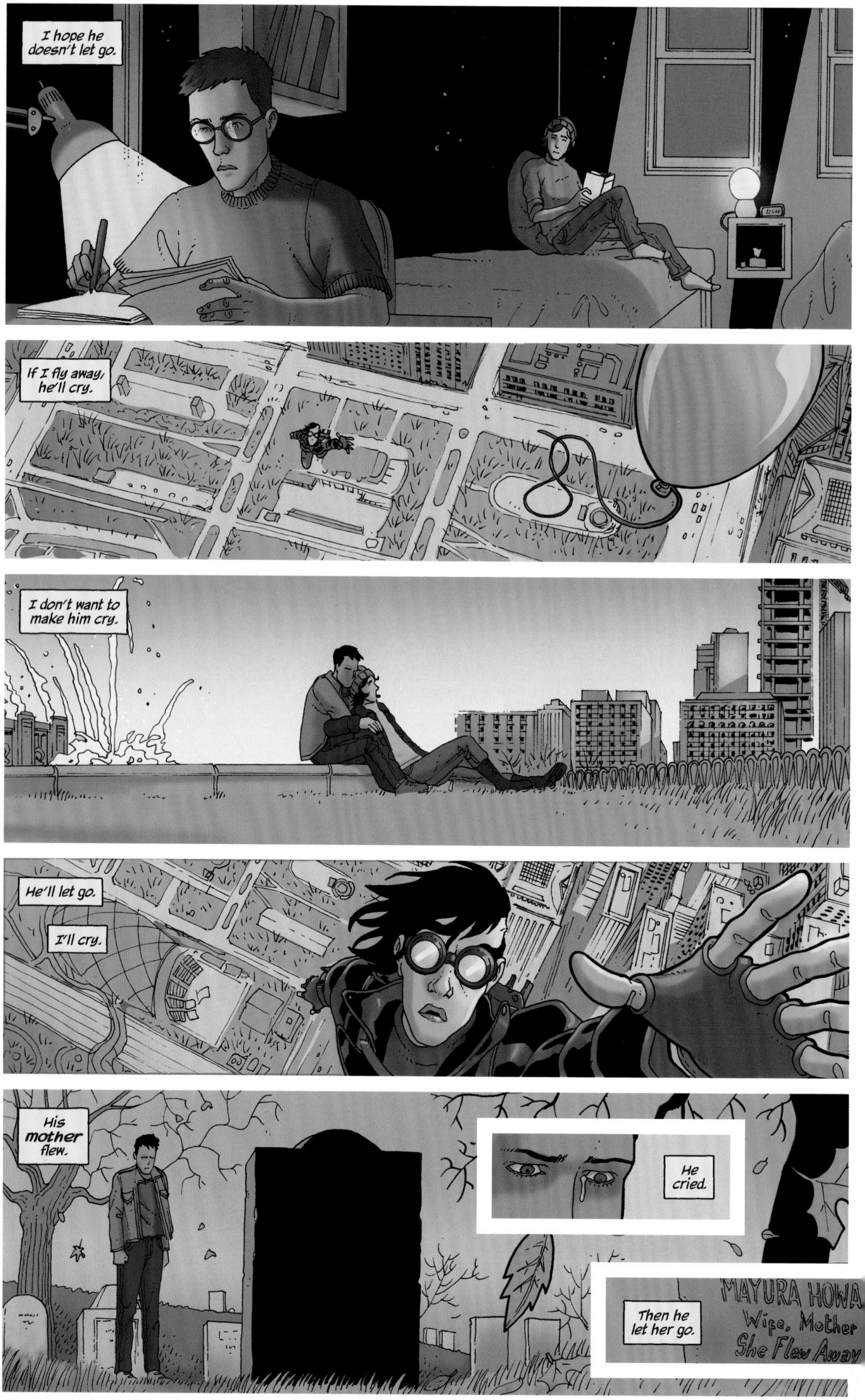
I hope he doesn't let go.
If I fly away, he'll cry.
I don't want to make him cry.
He'll let go.
I'll cry.
His mother flew.
He cried.
Then he let her go.
MAYURA HOWA
Wife, Mother
She Flew Away

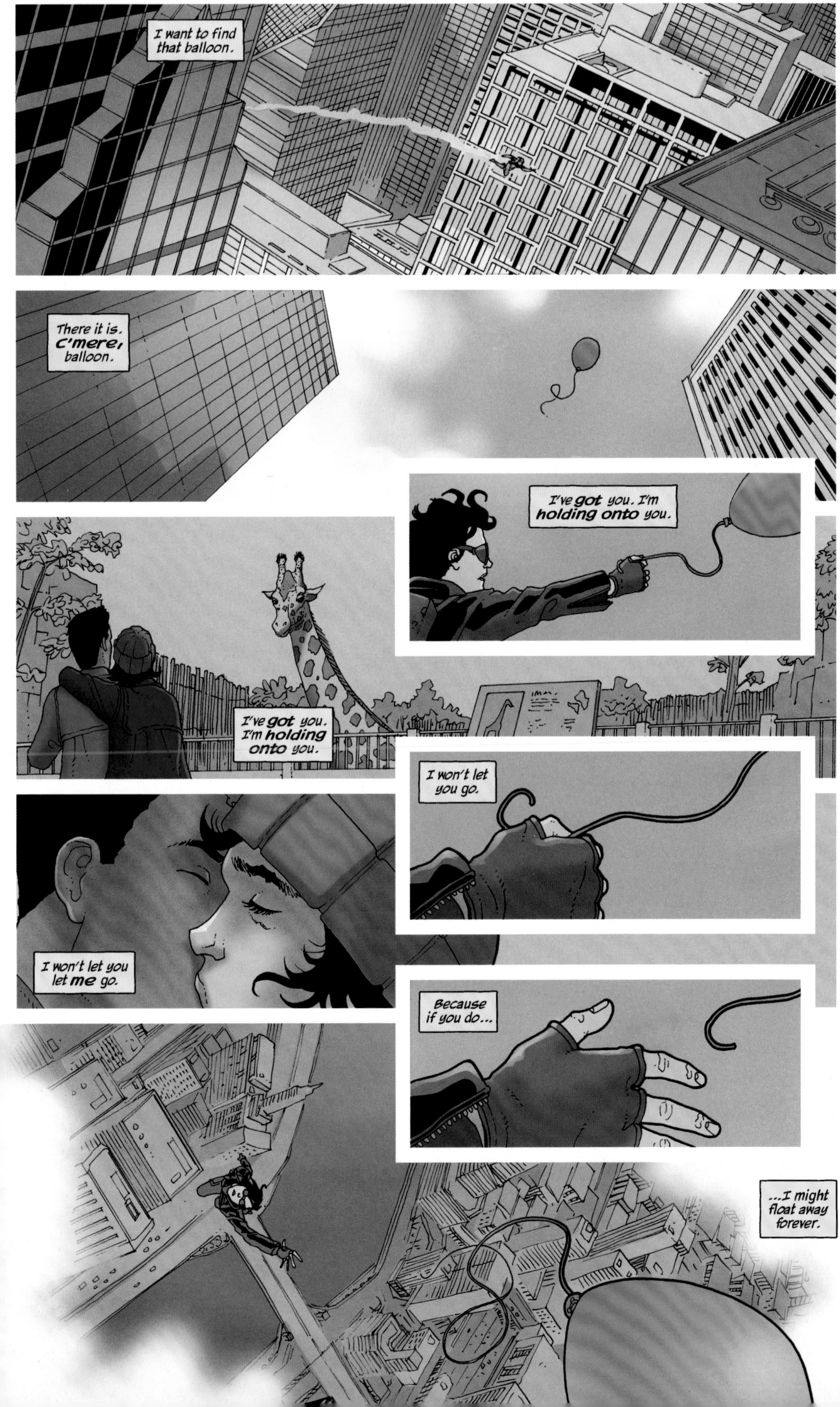
I want to find that balloon.
There it is. C'mere, balloon.
I've got you. I'm holding onto you.
I've got you. I'm holding onto you.
I won't let you go.
I won't let you let me go.
Because if you do...
...I might float away forever.

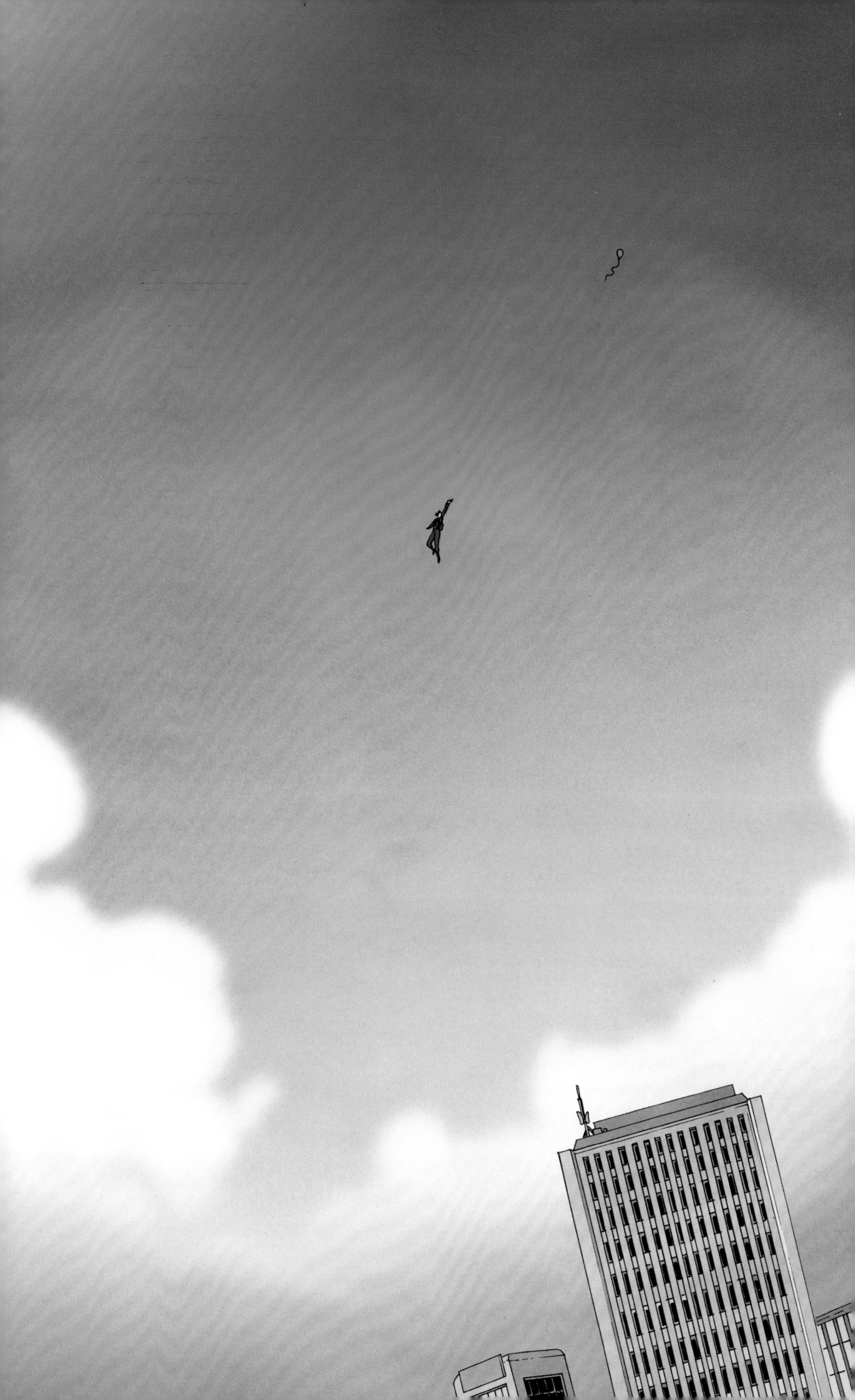

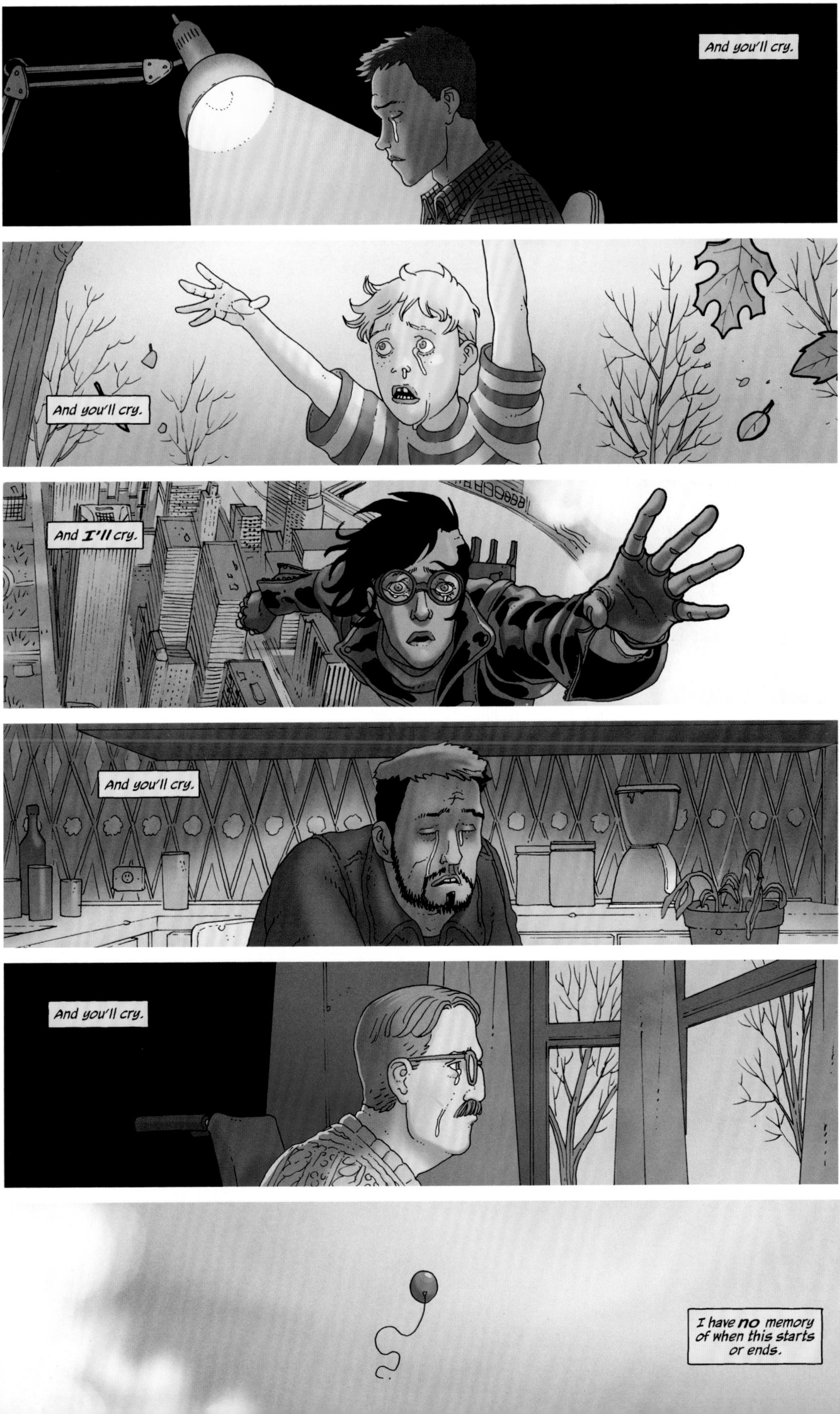
And you'll cry.
And you'll cry.
And I'll cry.
And you'll cry.
And you'll cry.
I have no memory of when this starts or ends.

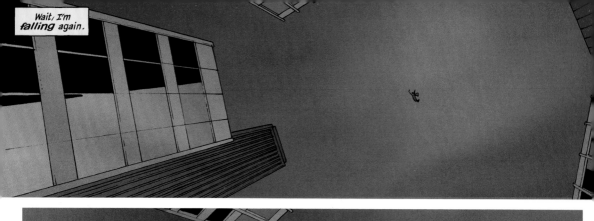

Wait, I'm *falling* again.

No...it isn't me.

Some are saying it's a SUICIDE.

But **where** did she jump from?

How did she land there?

When she was falling did she mistake any of it for **flying?**

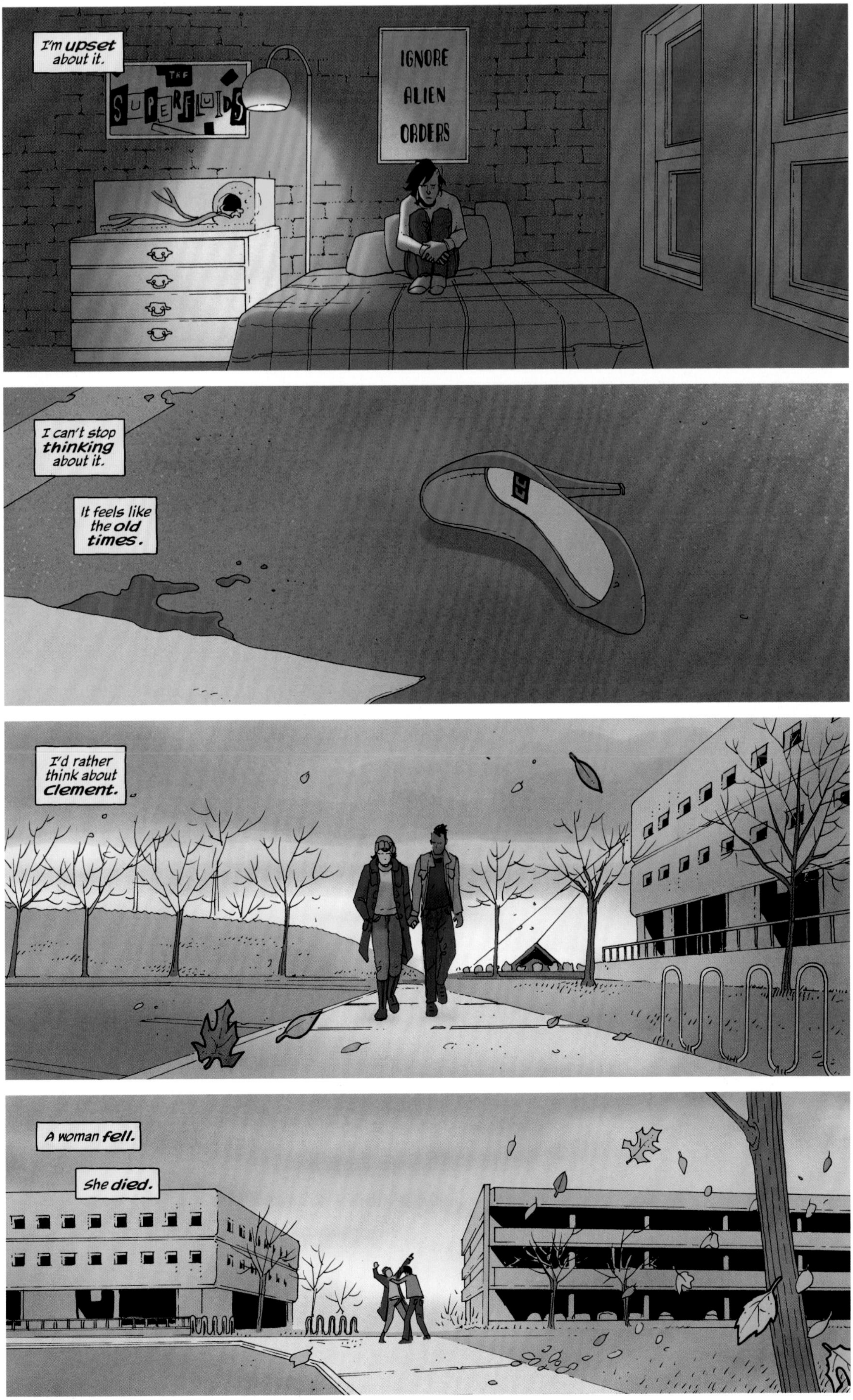

I'm upset about it.
THE SUPERFLUIDS
IGNORE ALIEN ORDERS
I can't stop thinking about it.
It feels like the old times.
I'd rather think about Clement.
A woman fell.
She died.

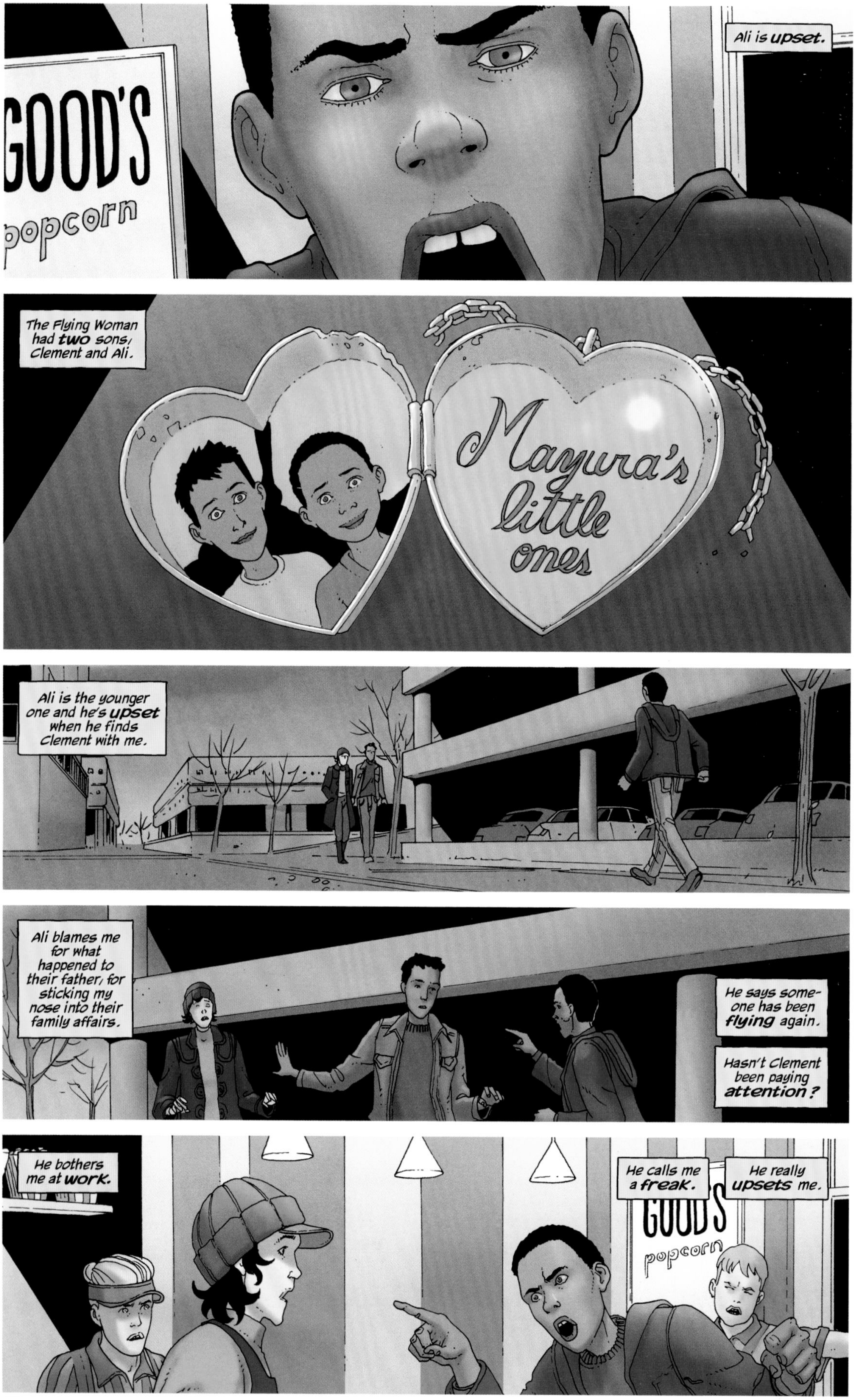

GOOD'S
popcorn
Ali is upset.
The Flying Woman had two sons, Clement and Ali.
Mayura's little ones
Ali is the younger one and he's upset when he finds Clement with me.
Ali blames me for what happened to their father, for sticking my nose into their family affairs.
He says someone has been flying again.
Hasn't Clement been paying attention?
He bothers me at work.
He calls me a freak.
He really upsets me.
GOOD'S
popcorn

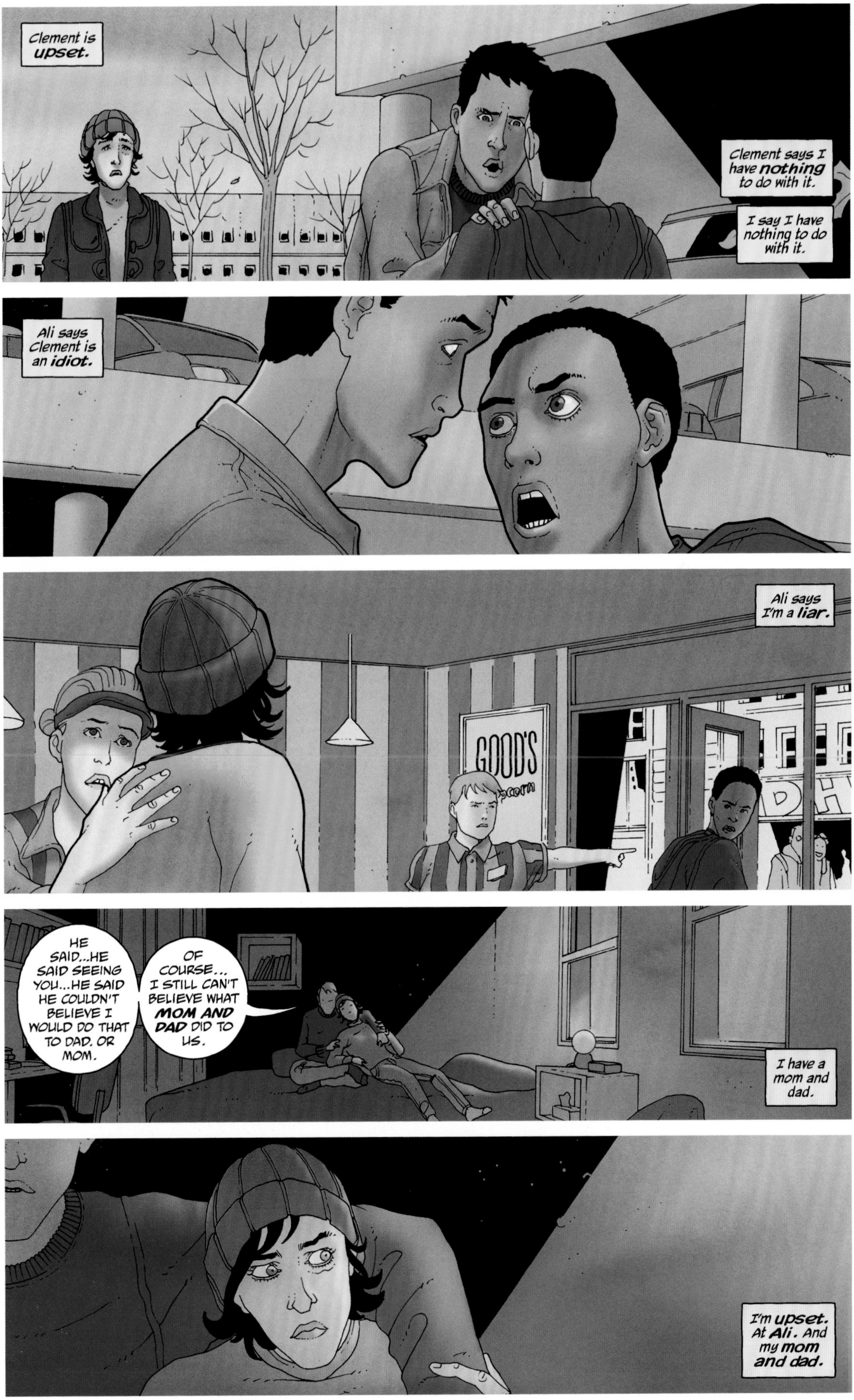
Clement is upset.
Clement says I have nothing to do with it.
I say I have nothing to do with it.
Ali says Clement is an idiot.
Ali says I'm a liar.
GOOD'S
HE SAID...HE SAID SEEING YOU...HE SAID HE COULDN'T BELIEVE I WOULD DO THAT TO DAD. OR MOM.
OF COURSE... I STILL CAN'T BELIEVE WHAT MOM AND DAD DID TO US.
I have a mom and dad.
I'm upset. At Ali. And my mom and dad.

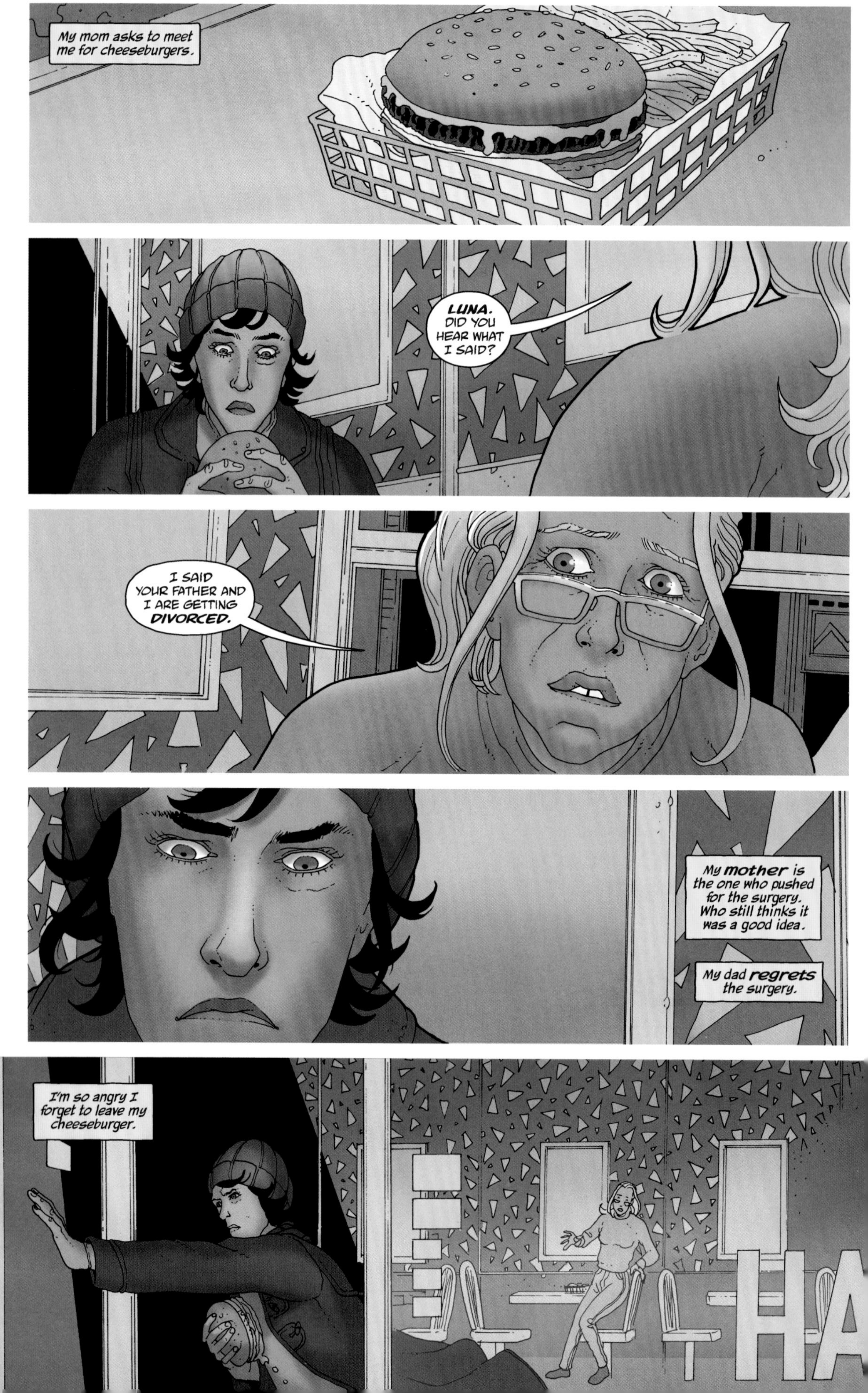
My mom asks to meet me for cheeseburgers.
LUNA. DID YOU HEAR WHAT I SAID?
I SAID YOUR FATHER AND I ARE GETTING DIVORCED.
My mother is the one who pushed for the surgery. Who still thinks it was a good idea.
My dad regrets the surgery.
I'm so angry I forget to leave my cheeseburger.
HA

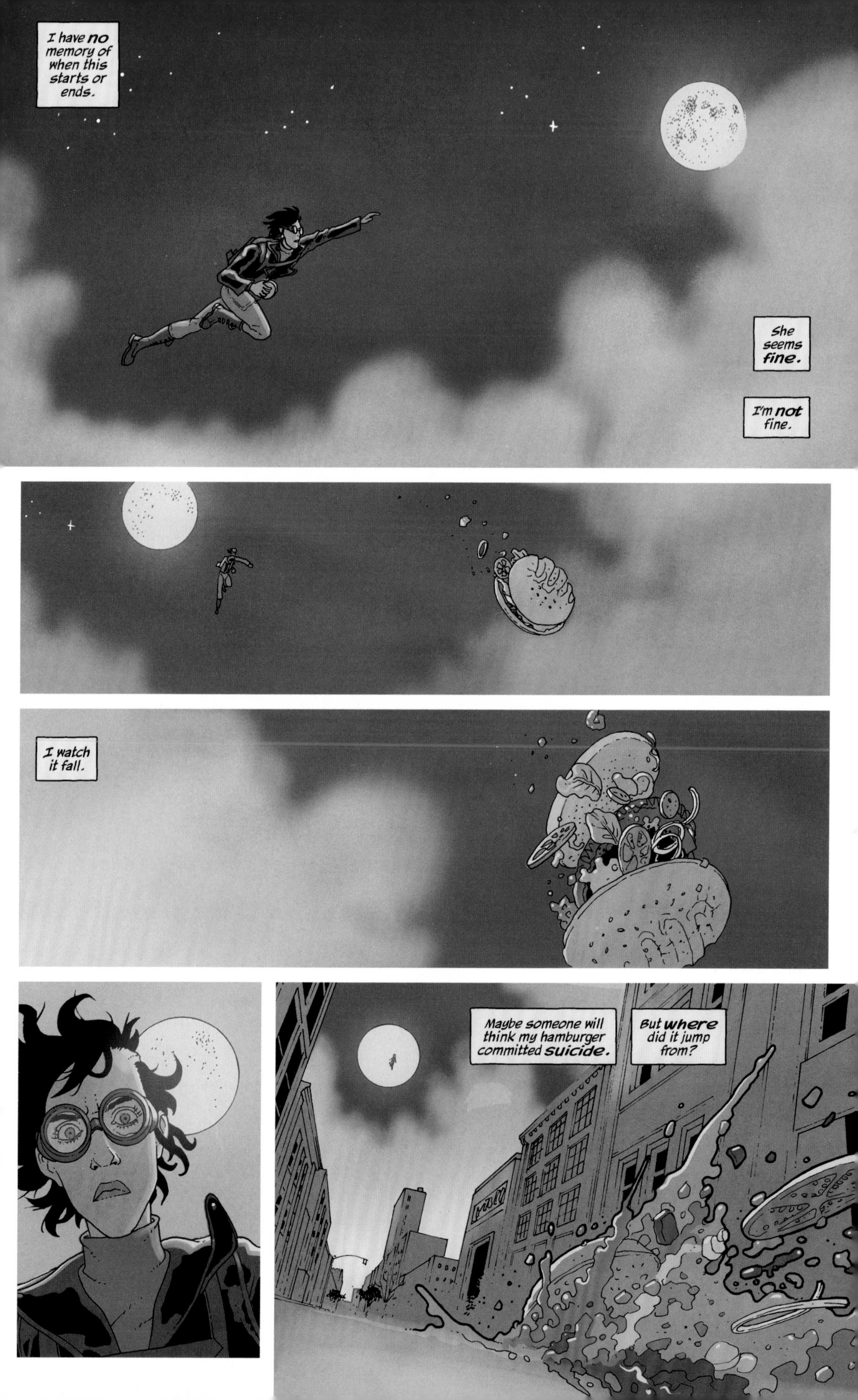

I have **no** memory of when this starts or ends.
She seems **fine.**
I'm **not** fine.
I watch it fall.
Maybe someone will think my hamburger committed **suicide.**
But **where** did it jump from?

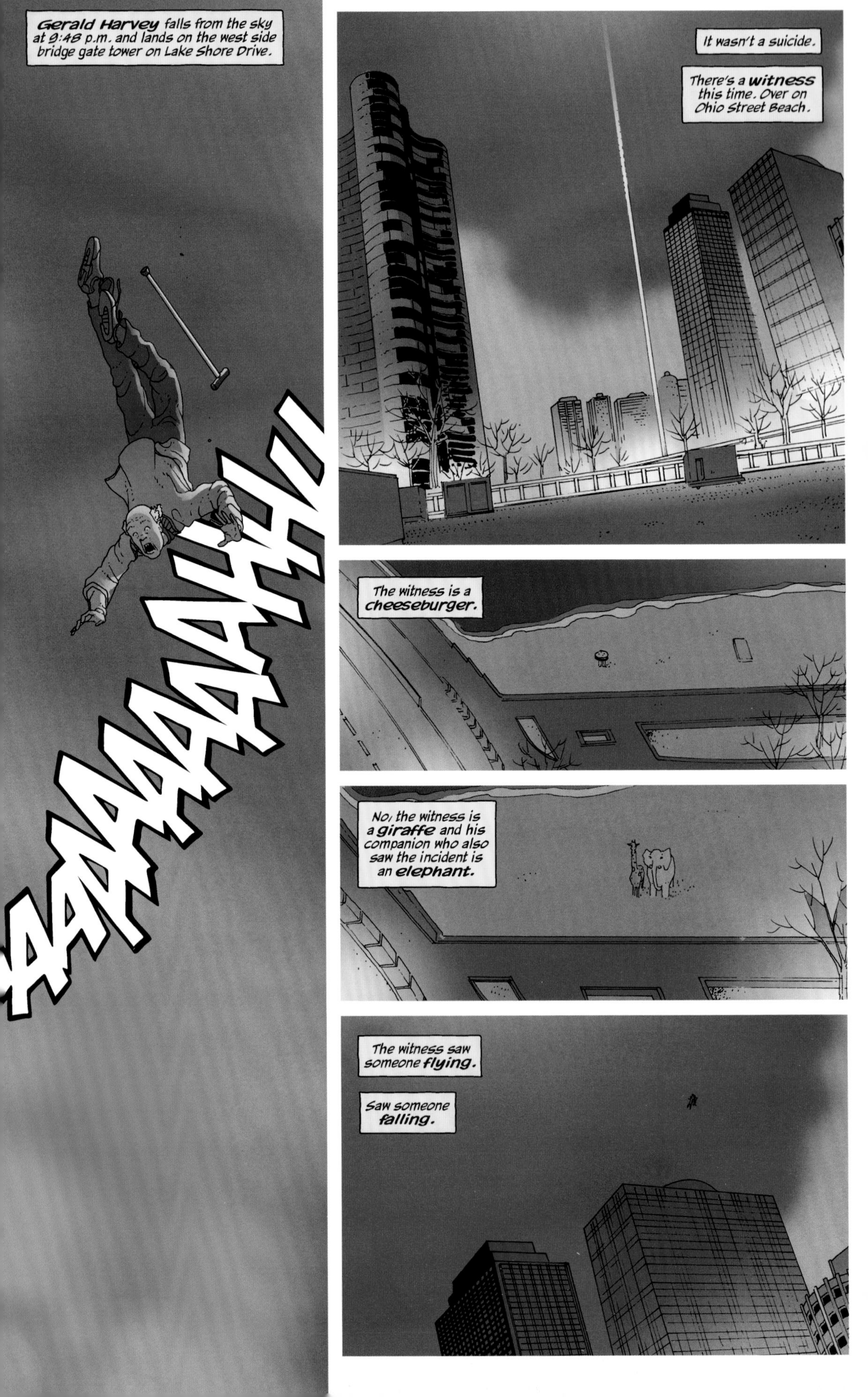

Gerald Harvey falls from the sky at 9:48 p.m. and lands on the west side bridge gate tower on Lake Shore Drive.
It wasn't a suicide.
There's a witness this time. Over on Ohio Street Beach.
The witness is a cheeseburger.
No, the witness is a giraffe and his companion who also saw the incident is an elephant.
The witness saw someone flying.
Saw someone falling.

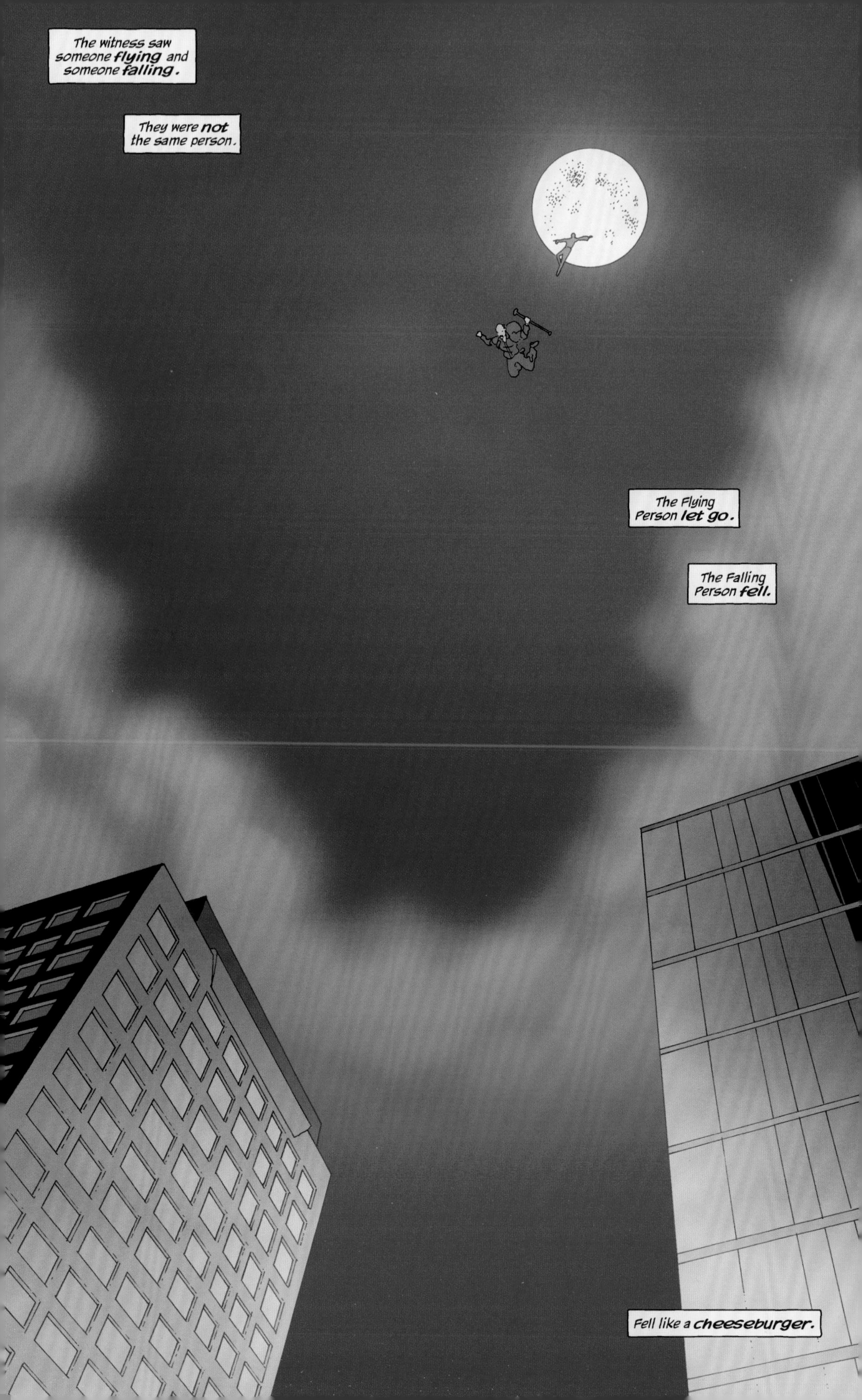
The witness saw someone flying and someone falling.
They were not the same person.
The Flying Person let go.
The Falling Person fell.
Fell like a cheeseburger.

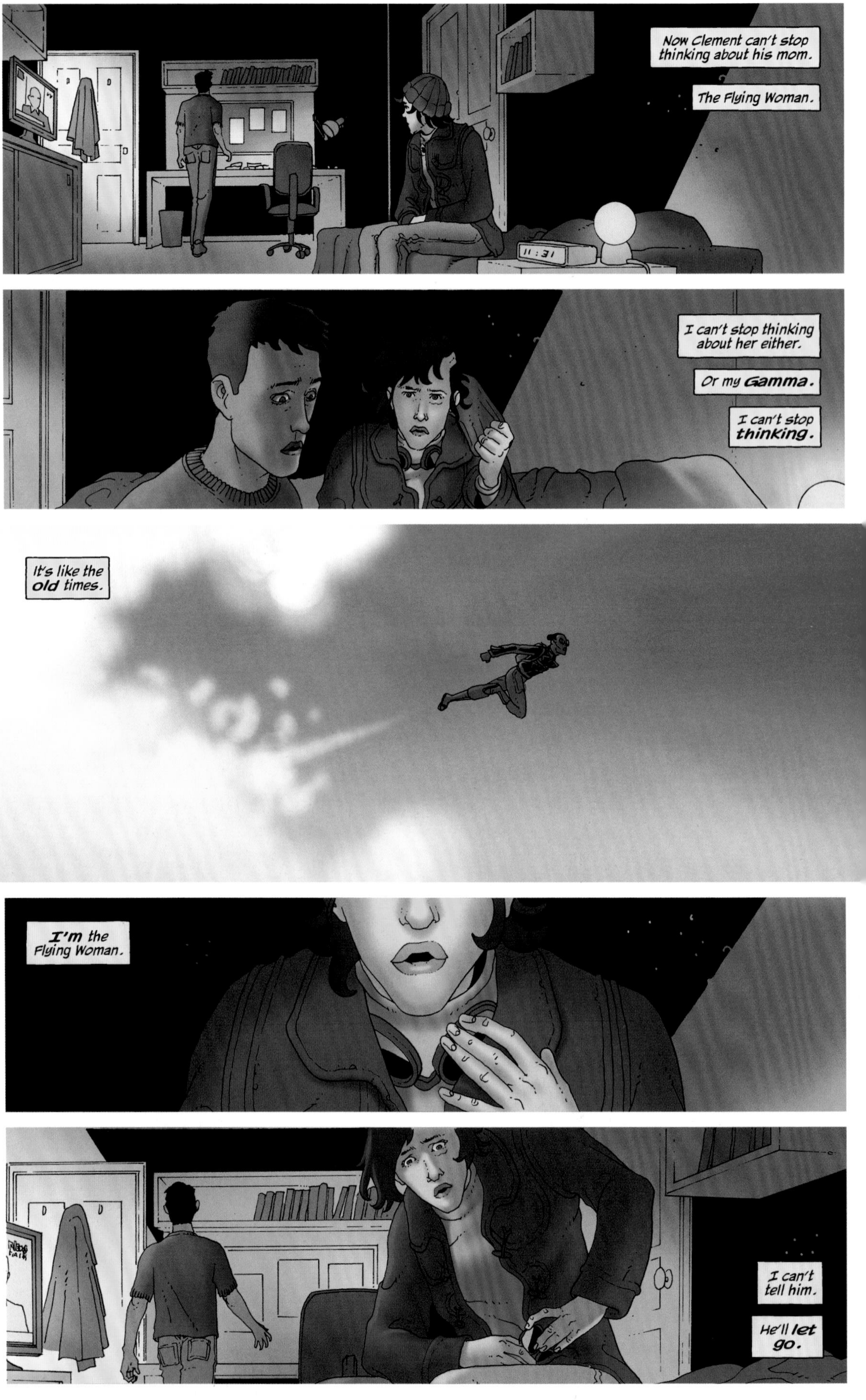
Now Clement can't stop thinking about his mom.
The Flying Woman.
11:31
I can't stop thinking about her either.
Or my **Gamma**.
I can't stop **thinking**.
It's like the **old** times.
I'm the Flying Woman.
I can't tell him.
He'll **let go**.

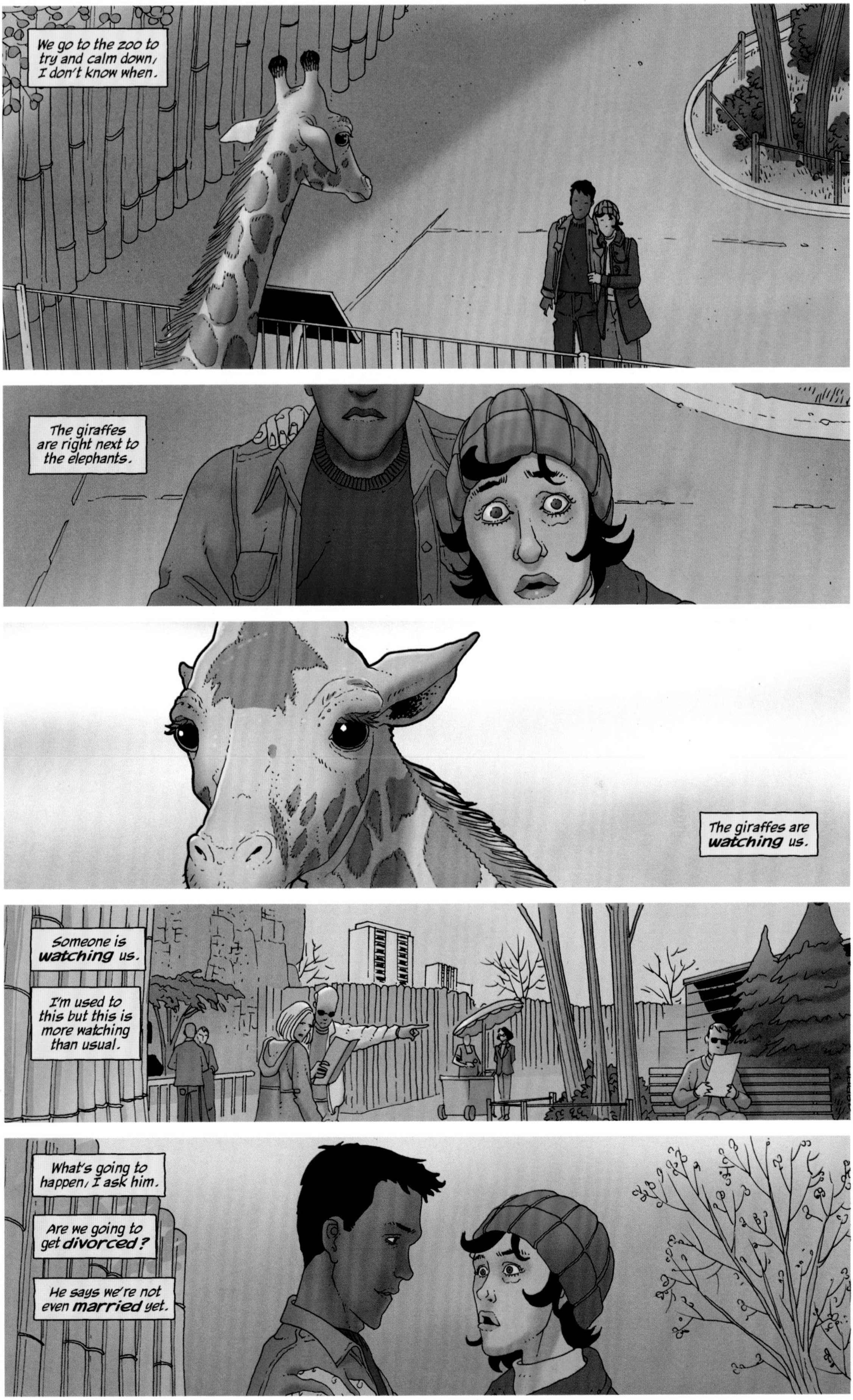
We go to the zoo to try and calm down, I don't know when.
The giraffes are right next to the elephants.
The giraffes are *watching* us.
Someone is *watching* us.
I'm used to this but this is more watching than usual.
What's going to happen, I ask him.
Are we going to get *divorced?*
He says we're not even *married* yet.

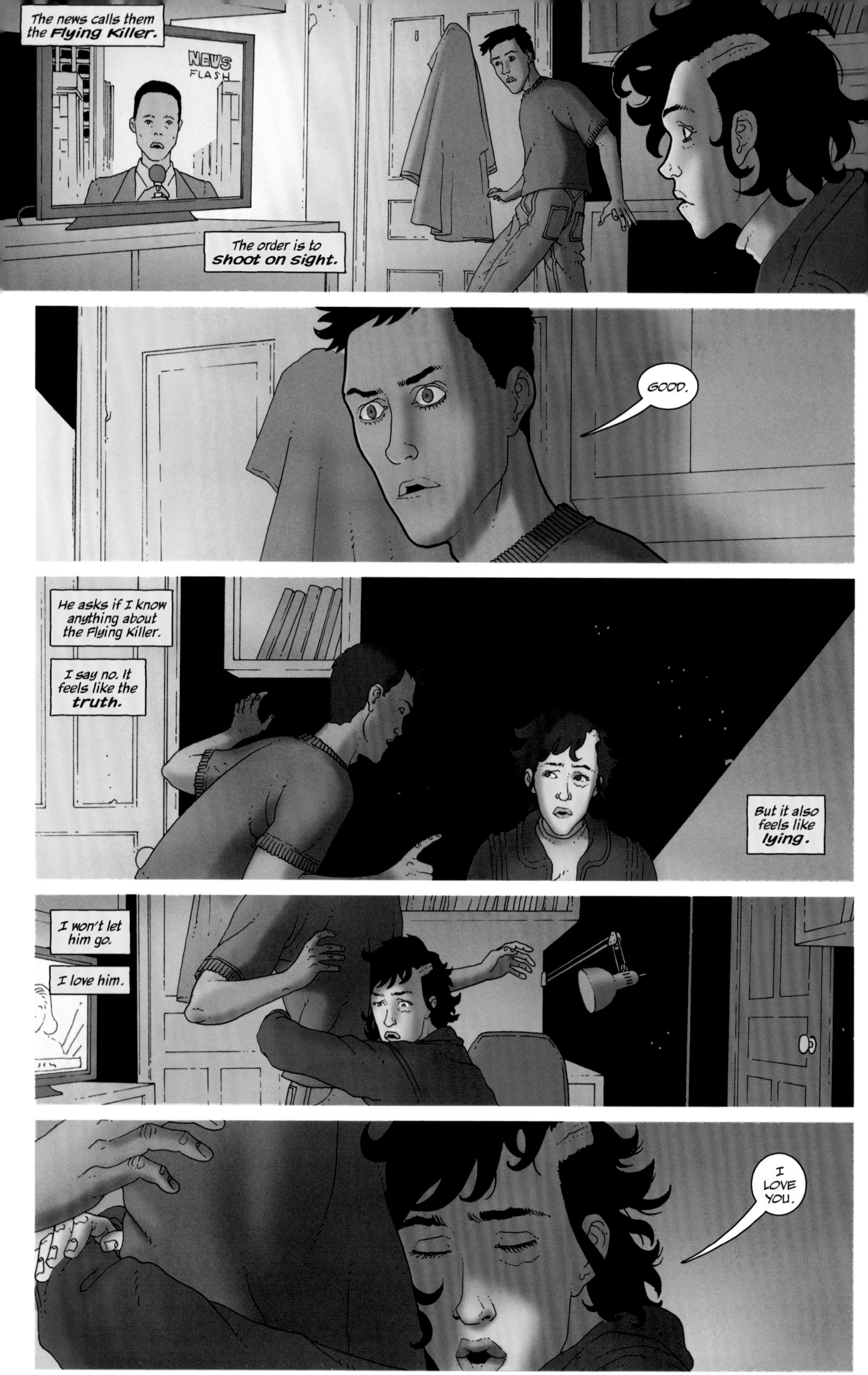
The news calls them the Flying Killer.
NEWS FLASH
The order is to shoot on sight.
GOOD.
He asks if I know anything about the Flying Killer.
I say no. It feels like the truth.
But it also feels like lying.
I won't let him go.
I love him.
I LOVE YOU.

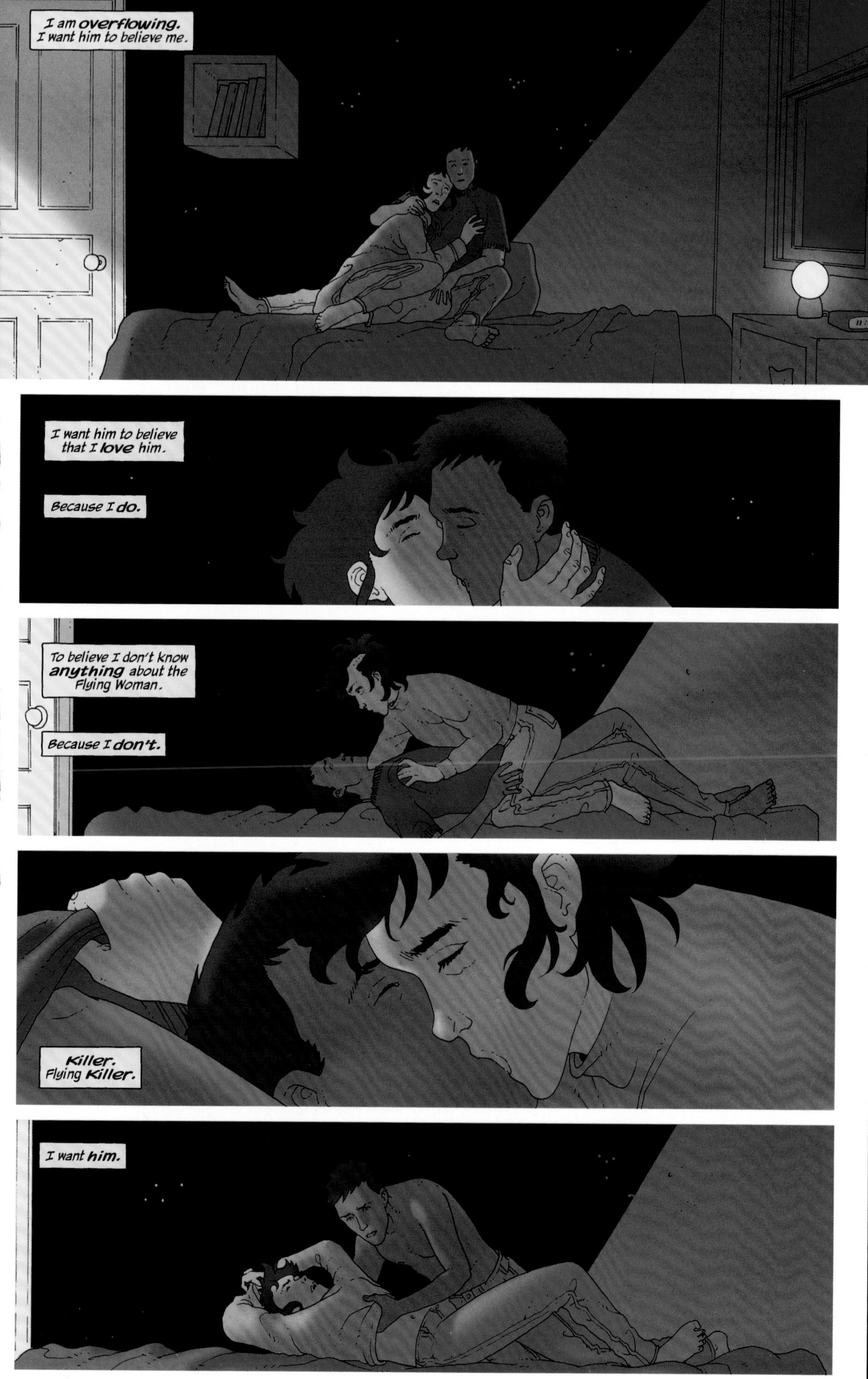
I am overflowing.
I want him to believe me.
I want him to believe that I love him.
Because I do.
To believe I don't know anything about the Flying Woman.
Because I don't.
Killer. Flying Killer.
I want him.

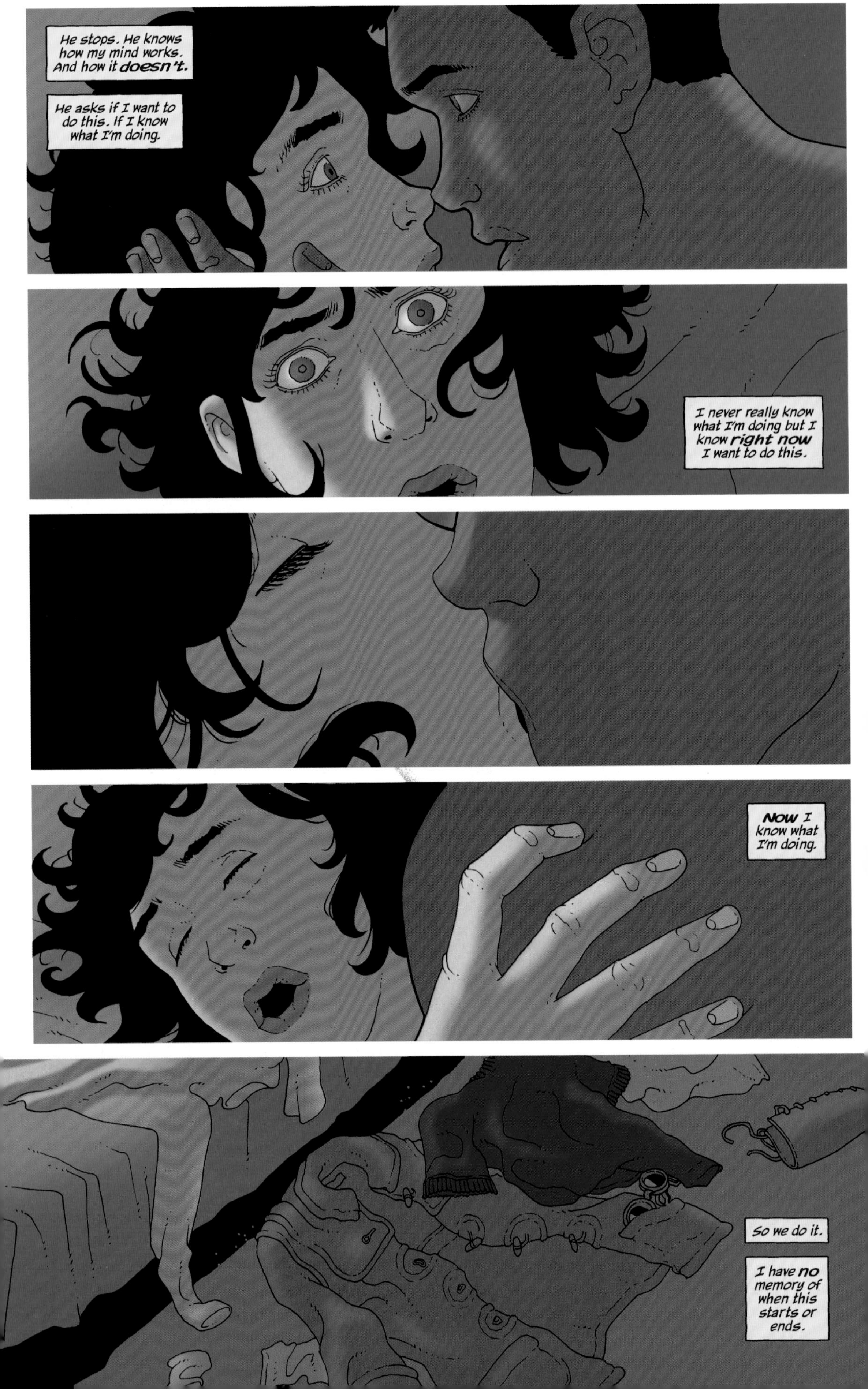
He stops. He knows how my mind works. And how it **doesn't.**
He asks if I want to do this. If I know what I'm doing.
I never really know what I'm doing but I know **right now** I want to do this.
NOW I know what I'm doing.
So we do it.
I have **no** memory of when this starts or ends.

3.

FALLIG IS NOT THE SAME AS FLYING.
FLYING = SUSTAINED DURATION AND CONTROL IN THE
AIR FOR A DURATION OF TIME

that disqualifies the following;
parachutists
suicide jumps
falling accidents
foolish leapers
EArLY SUPERMAN when he JUST LEAPED PLACES
THE HULK JUST LEAPS TOO.
The Red Bull guy thart fell to Earth

I AM NOT FEELIG SPACE FLIGHT RIGHT NOW EITHER
No Star Wars
No Star Trek

ALSO I BELIEVE FLIGHT MUST BE AT LEAST FROM
A HEIGHT WHERE FALLING COULD LEAD TO SERIOUS
IMNJURY OR DEATH, SO COMMONLY I WOULD SAY ABOVE
50 FEET

Albdrt Cushing Read
John Macready
Lowell H Smith
Margo von Etzdorf
Alexei Cheremunnkhin (helicopter)
Eric Warsitz
Chuck Yeager
H ROSS PEROT Jr
(^^ another library visit)
Icarus
The othr roman and Greek gods but not all of them
The whole Marvel and DC roster of flying people
I don't find interest in listing anymore of them
individually

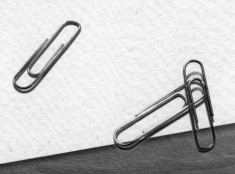

All helicopter tourists and tourist pilots in
Hawaii
The wounded in MASH
Sometimes the doctors in MASH
Certainlty the pilots in MASH though a lot of
them aren't ever characters and were proibably
actually pilots from real life just in costume

I WILL GIVE A PASS TO HANG GLIDERS I STILL THINK
THIS QUALIFIES

The Blue angels
Coast Guard pilots and crew
The Red Bull CAN DOES FLY BECAUSE IT HAS WINGS
The character represented by any action figure or
toy that is tied to a balloon or put into a paper
plane that can sail at least twenty feet or put
into an RC copter or drone or plane and flone
so in the right circumstances the love boat crew
could technically qualify
Sports teams that travel by plane,
All other space shuttle astroaunts
the people from the story ALIVE where they
crashed and had to eat some of the dead
My Mom

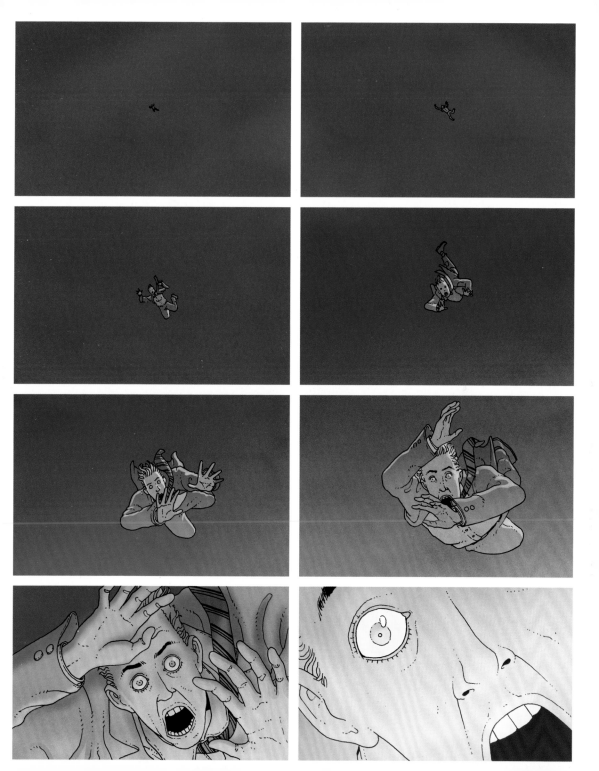

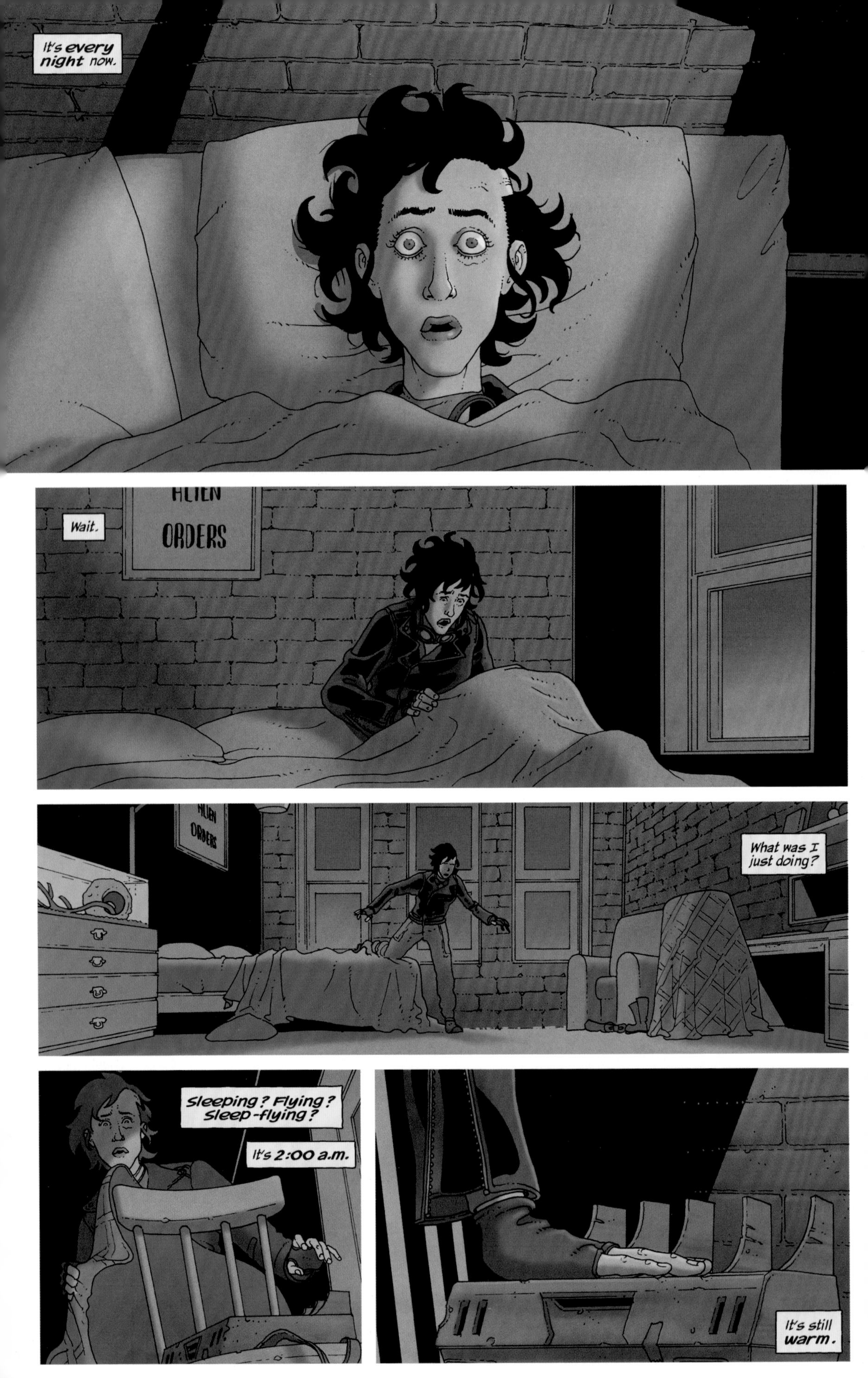
It's every night now.
ALIEN ORDERS
Wait.
ALIEN ORDERS
What was I just doing?
Sleeping? Flying? Sleep-flying?
It's 2:00 a.m.
It's still warm.

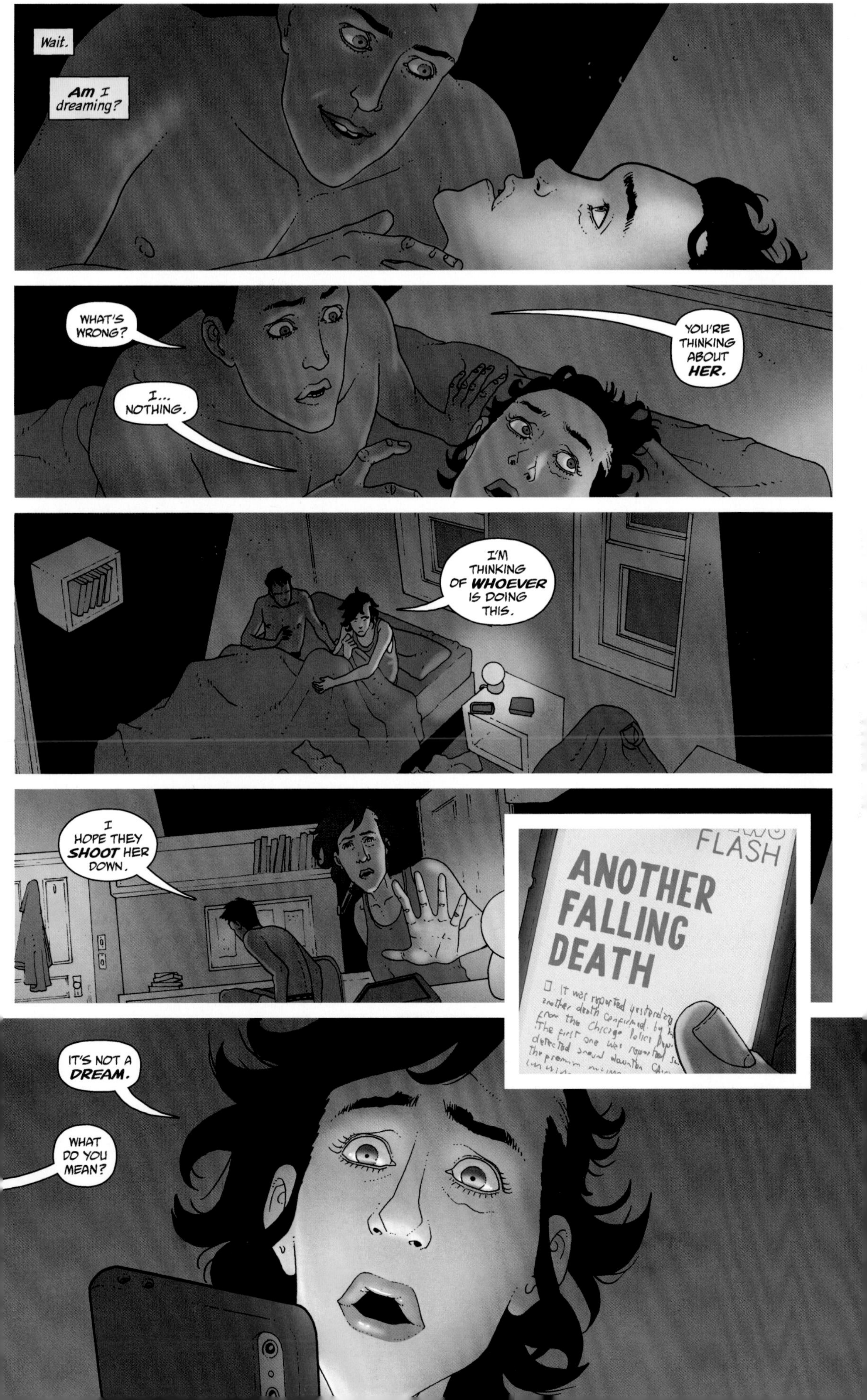
Wait.
Am I dreaming?
WHAT'S WRONG?
YOU'RE THINKING ABOUT HER.
I... NOTHING.
I'M THINKING OF WHOEVER IS DOING THIS.
I HOPE THEY SHOOT HER DOWN.
FLASH
ANOTHER FALLING DEATH
IT'S NOT A DREAM.
WHAT DO YOU MEAN?

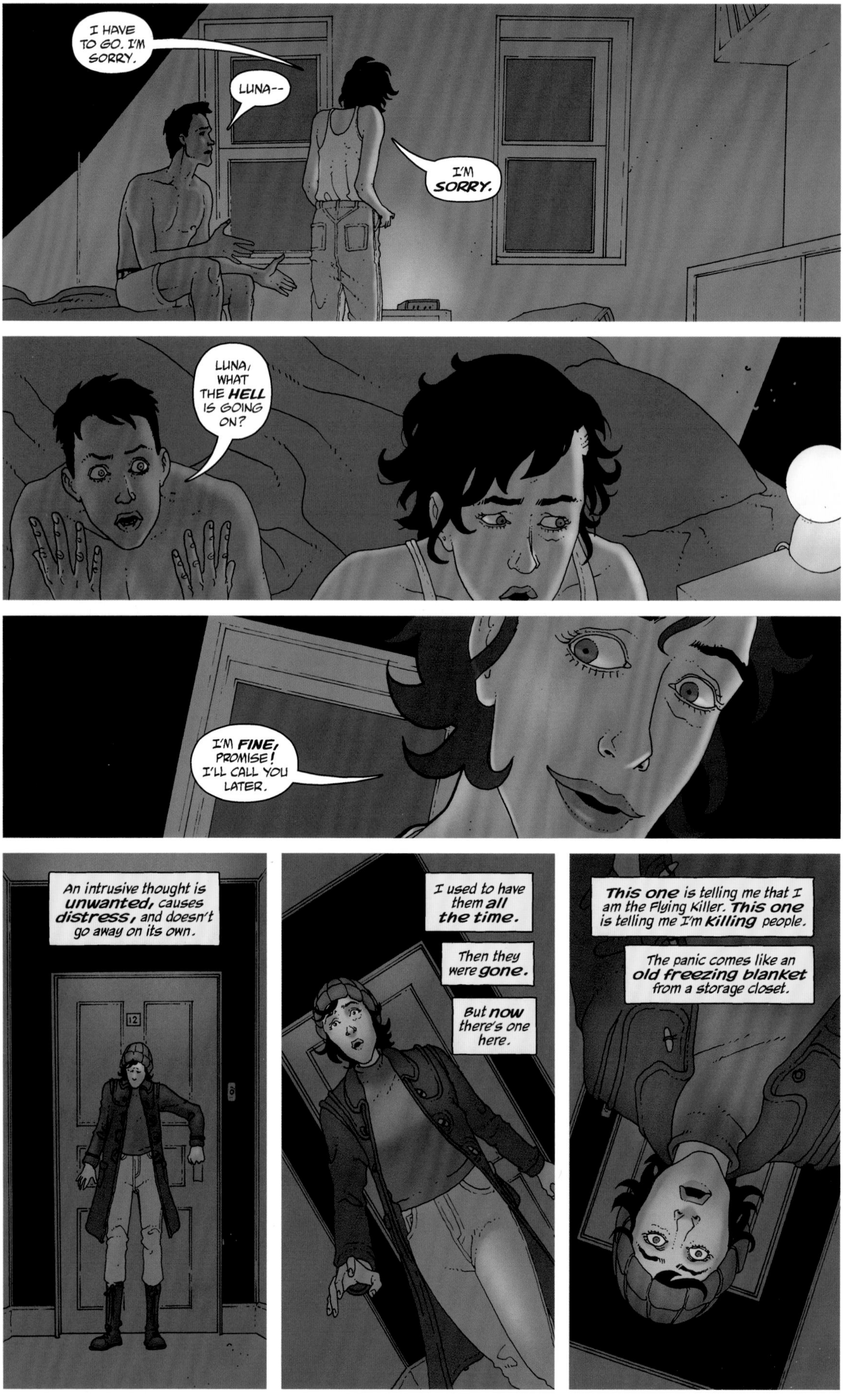
I HAVE TO GO. I'M SORRY.
LUNA--
I'M SORRY.
LUNA, WHAT THE HELL IS GOING ON?
I'M FINE, PROMISE! I'LL CALL YOU LATER.
An intrusive thought is unwanted, causes distress, and doesn't go away on its own.
12
I used to have them all the time.
Then they were gone.
But now there's one here.
This one is telling me that I am the Flying Killer. This one is telling me I'm killing people.
The panic comes like an old freezing blanket from a storage closet.

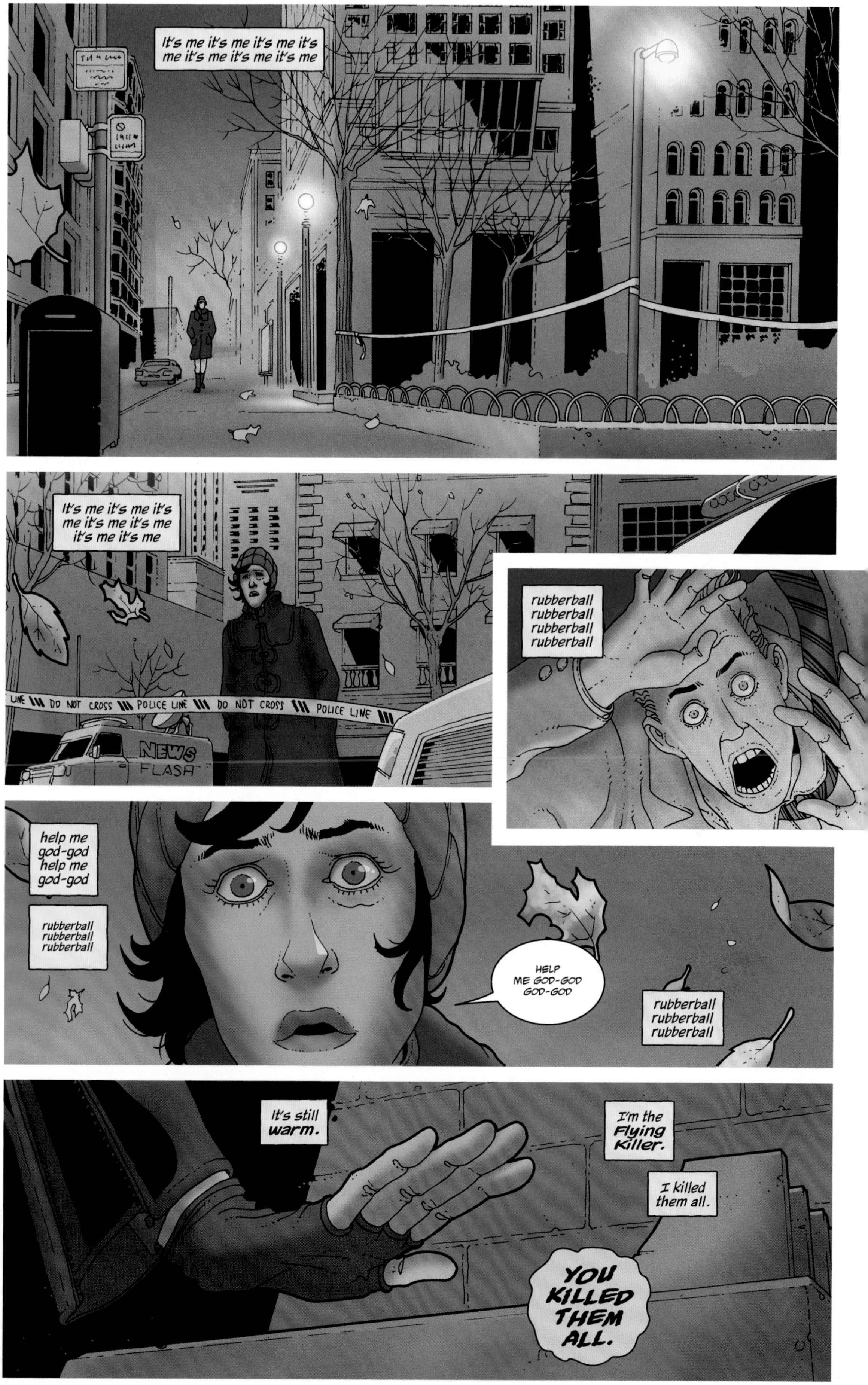
It's me it's me it's me it's me it's me it's me it's me
It's me it's me it's me it's me it's me it's me it's me
LINE DO NOT CROSS POLICE LINE DO NOT CROSS POLICE LINE
NEWS FLASH
rubberball rubberball rubberball rubberball
help me god-god help me god-god
rubberball rubberball rubberball
HELP ME GOD-GOD GOD-GOD
rubberball rubberball rubberball
It's still warm.
I'm the Flying Killer.
I killed them all.
YOU KILLED THEM ALL.

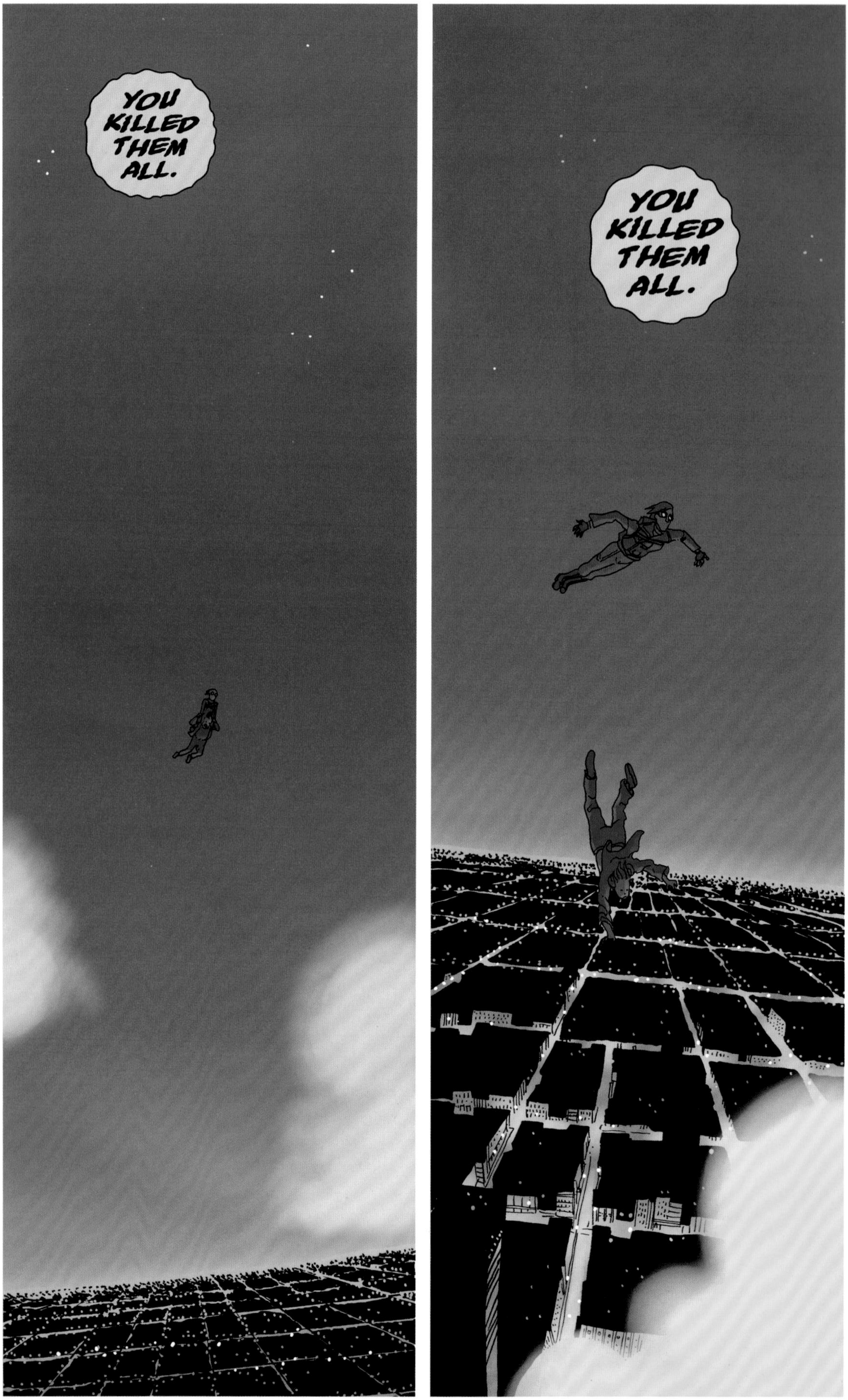
YOU KILLED THEM ALL.
YOU KILLED THEM ALL.

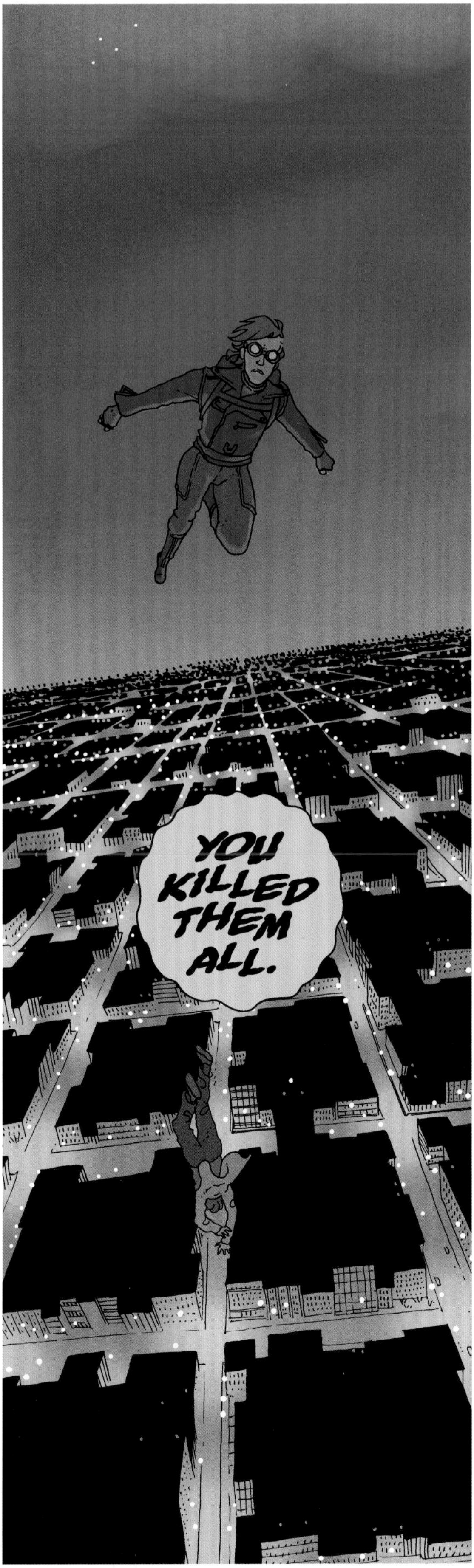
YOU KILLED THEM ALL.

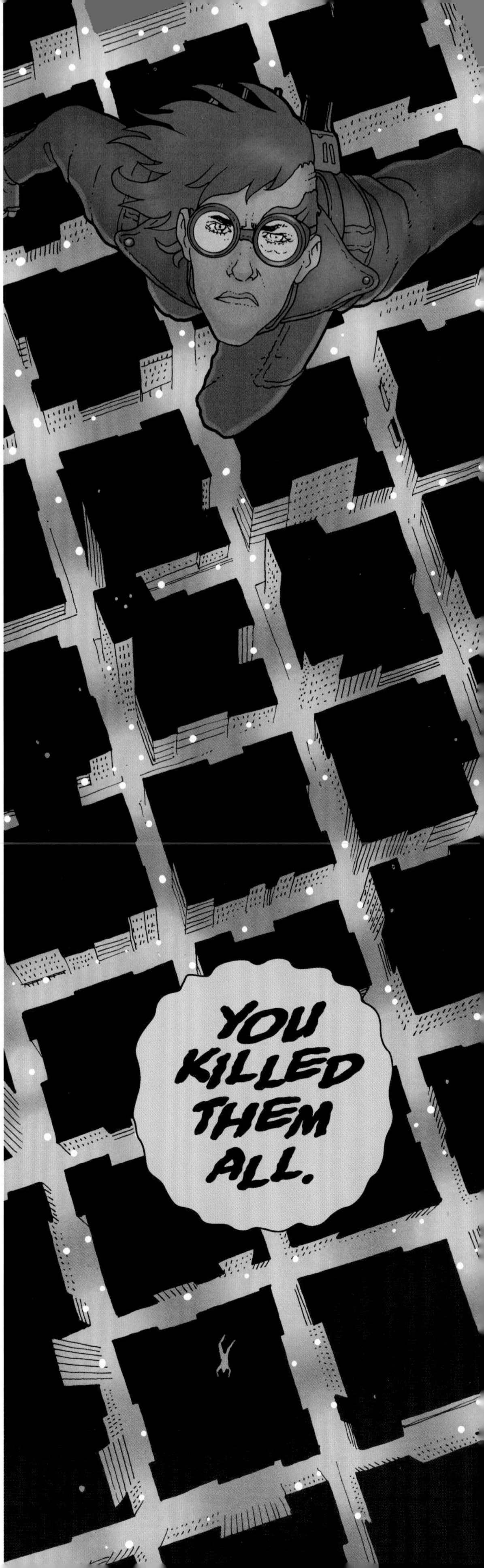
YOU KILLED THEM ALL.

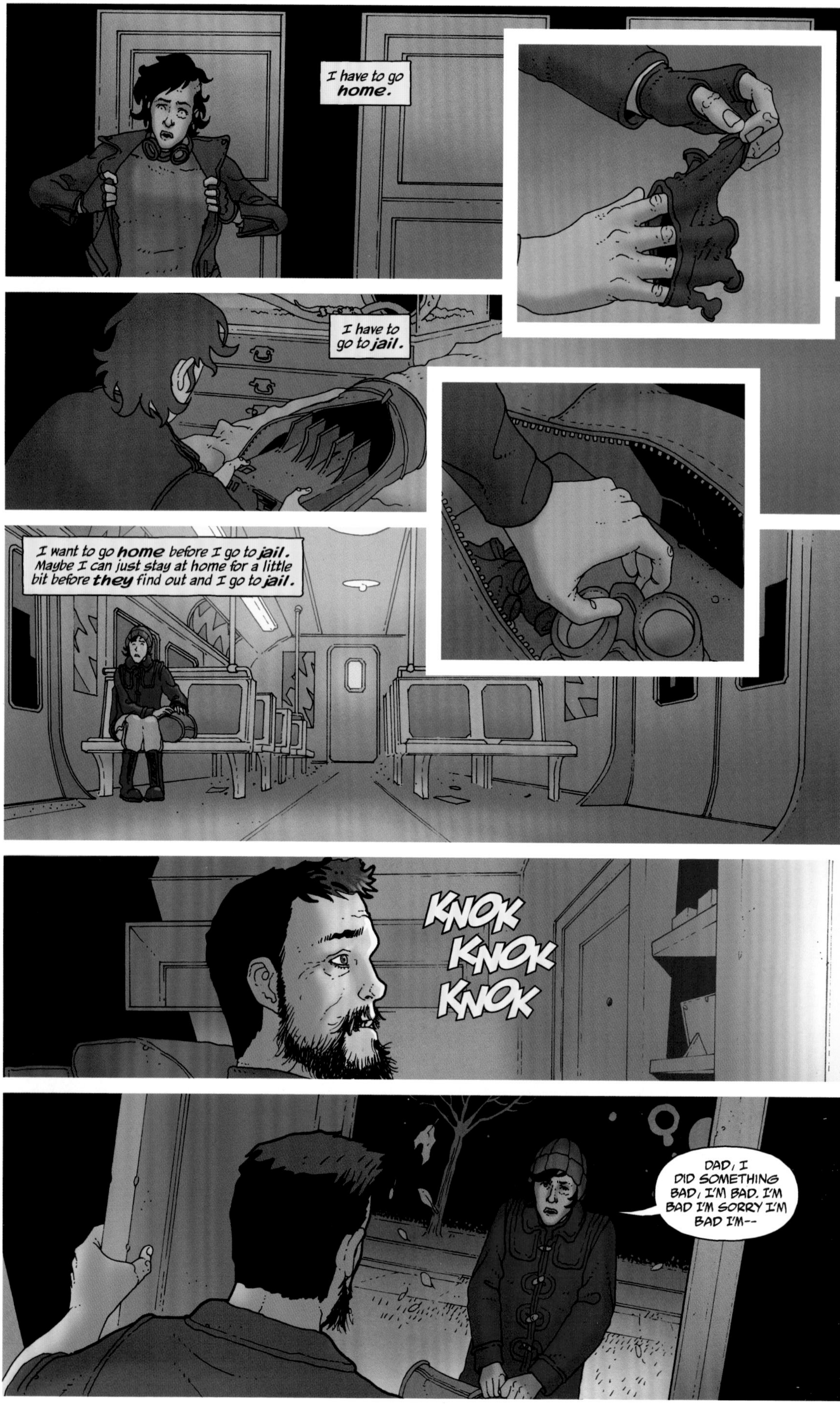
I have to go home.
I have to go to jail.
I want to go home before I go to jail. Maybe I can just stay at home for a little bit before they find out and I go to jail.
KNOK KNOK KNOK
DAD, I DID SOMETHING BAD, I'M BAD. I'M BAD I'M SORRY I'M BAD I'M--

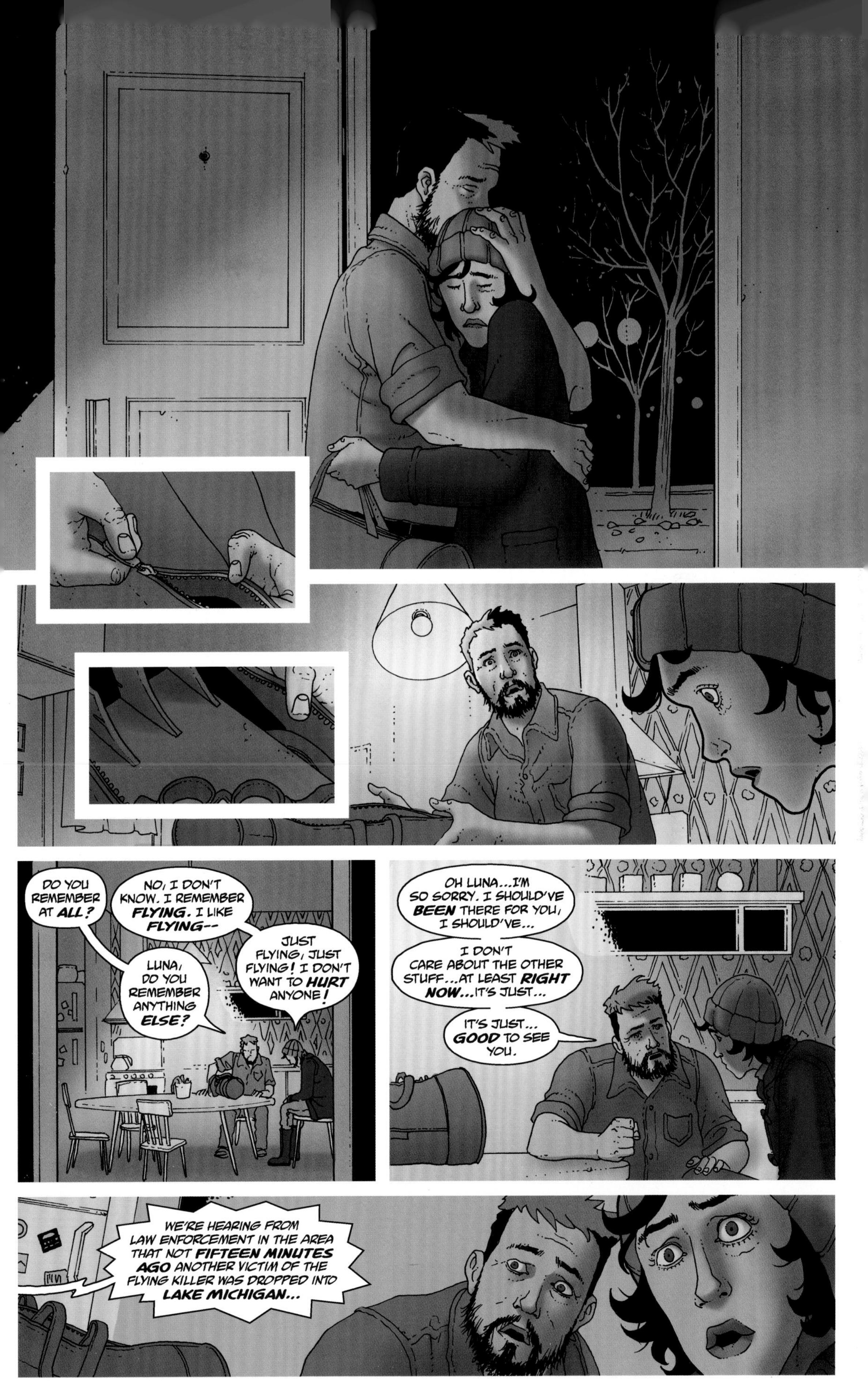
DO YOU REMEMBER AT ALL?
NO, I DON'T KNOW. I REMEMBER FLYING. I LIKE FLYING--
LUNA, DO YOU REMEMBER ANYTHING ELSE?
JUST FLYING, JUST FLYING! I DON'T WANT TO HURT ANYONE!
OH LUNA...I'M SO SORRY. I SHOULD'VE BEEN THERE FOR YOU, I SHOULD'VE...
I DON'T CARE ABOUT THE OTHER STUFF...AT LEAST RIGHT NOW...IT'S JUST...
IT'S JUST... GOOD TO SEE YOU.
WE'RE HEARING FROM LAW ENFORCEMENT IN THE AREA THAT NOT FIFTEEN MINUTES AGO ANOTHER VICTIM OF THE FLYING KILLER WAS DROPPED INTO LAKE MICHIGAN...

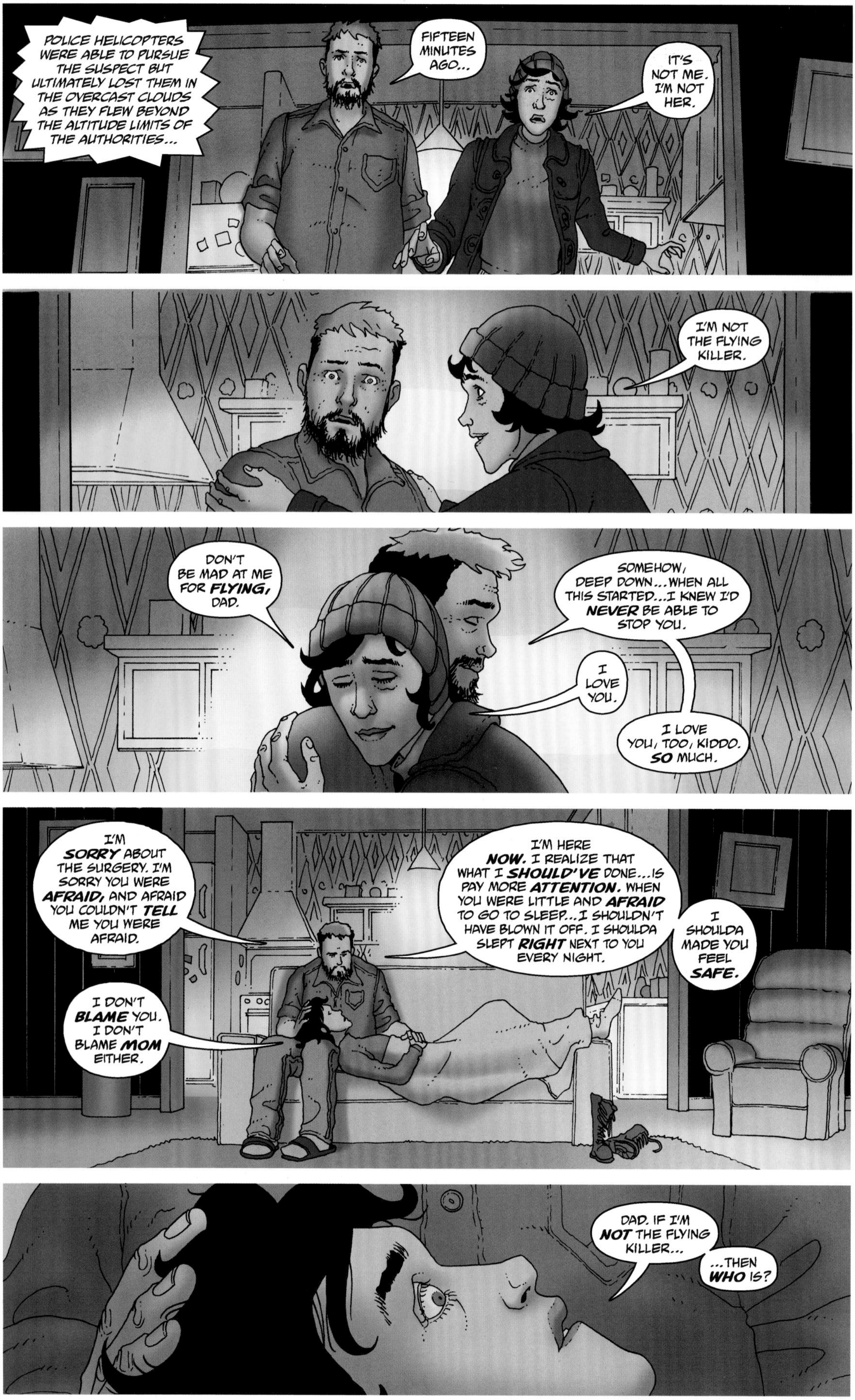
POLICE HELICOPTERS WERE ABLE TO PURSUE THE SUSPECT BUT ULTIMATELY LOST THEM IN THE OVERCAST CLOUDS AS THEY FLEW BEYOND THE ALTITUDE LIMITS OF THE AUTHORITIES...
FIFTEEN MINUTES AGO...
IT'S NOT ME. I'M NOT HER.
I'M NOT THE FLYING KILLER.
DON'T BE MAD AT ME FOR FLYING, DAD.
SOMEHOW, DEEP DOWN... WHEN ALL THIS STARTED... I KNEW I'D NEVER BE ABLE TO STOP YOU.
I LOVE YOU.
I LOVE YOU, TOO, KIDDO. SO MUCH.
I'M SORRY ABOUT THE SURGERY. I'M SORRY YOU WERE AFRAID, AND AFRAID YOU COULDN'T TELL ME YOU WERE AFRAID.
I'M HERE NOW. I REALIZE THAT WHAT I SHOULD'VE DONE... IS PAY MORE ATTENTION. WHEN YOU WERE LITTLE AND AFRAID TO GO TO SLEEP... I SHOULDN'T HAVE BLOWN IT OFF. I SHOULDA SLEPT RIGHT NEXT TO YOU EVERY NIGHT.
I SHOULDA MADE YOU FEEL SAFE.
I DON'T BLAME YOU. I DON'T BLAME MOM EITHER.
DAD. IF I'M NOT THE FLYING KILLER...
...THEN WHO IS?

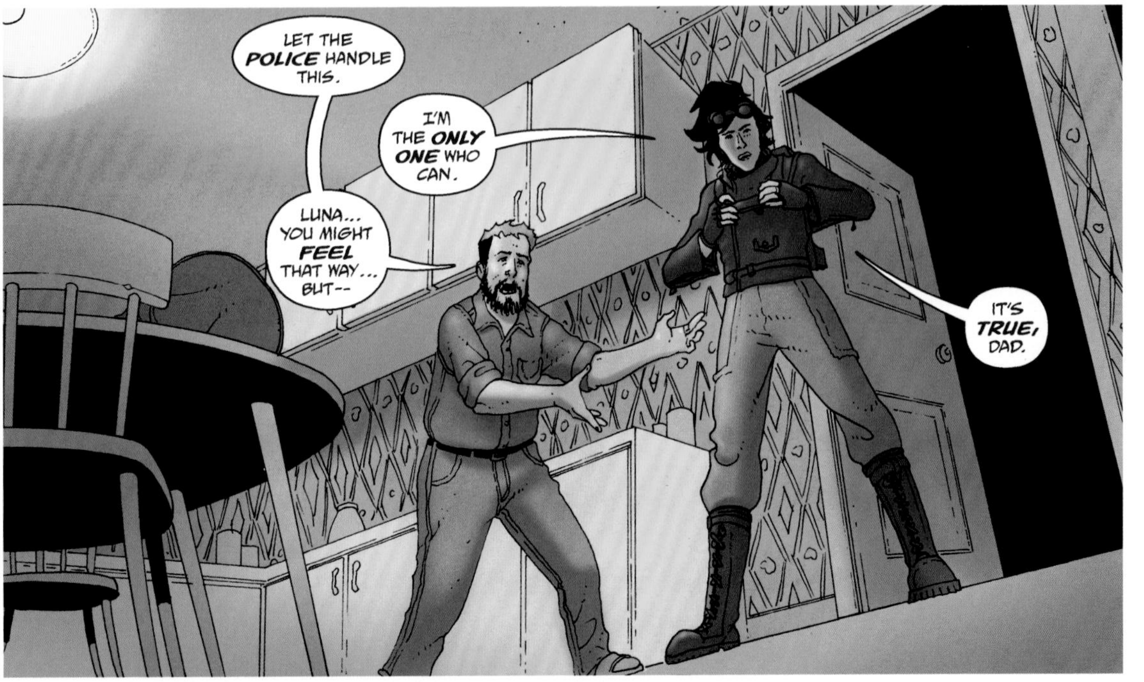
LET THE POLICE HANDLE THIS.
I'M THE ONLY ONE WHO CAN.
LUNA... YOU MIGHT FEEL THAT WAY... BUT--
IT'S TRUE, DAD.

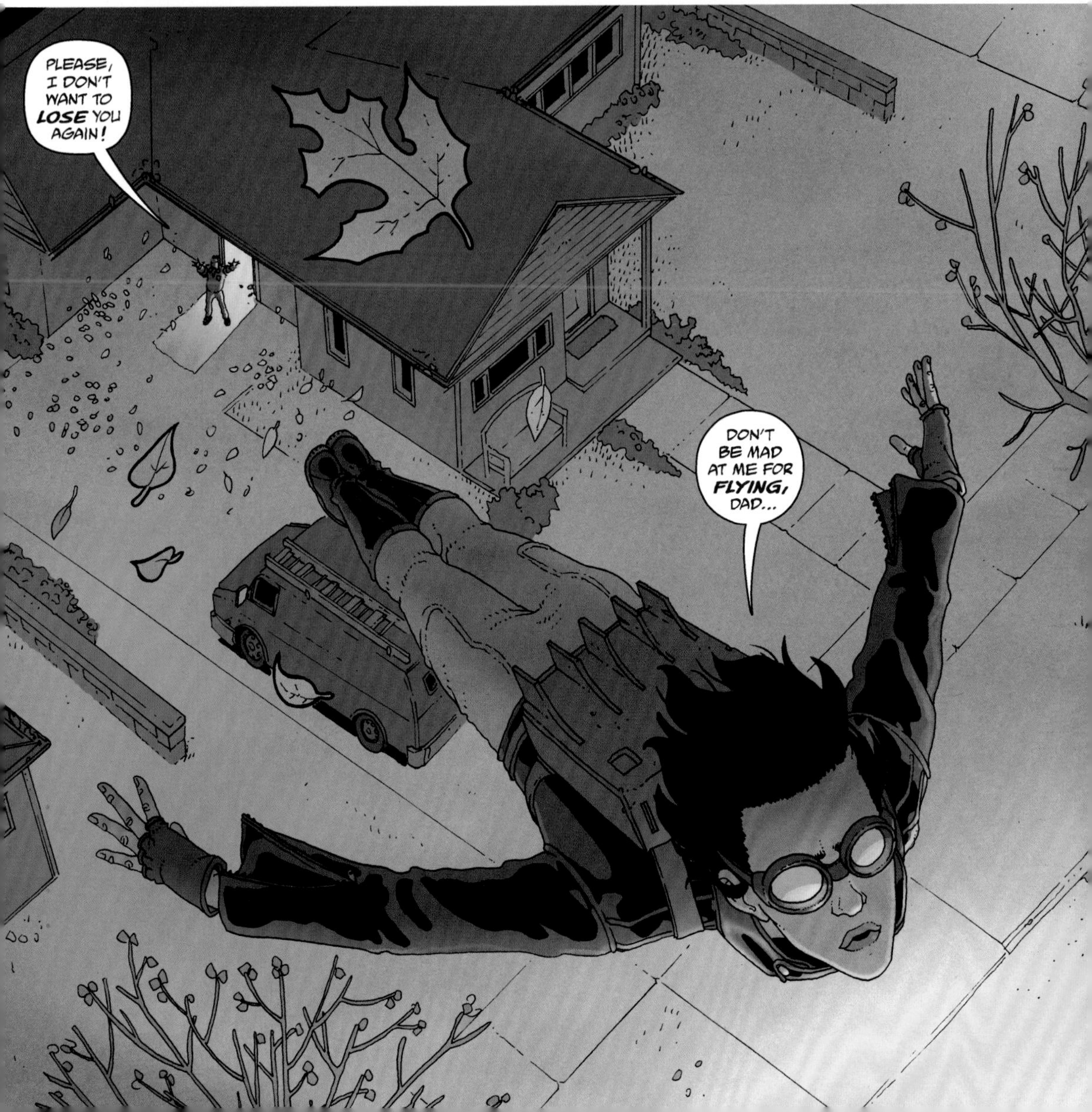
PLEASE, I DON'T WANT TO LOSE YOU AGAIN!
DON'T BE MAD AT ME FOR FLYING, DAD...

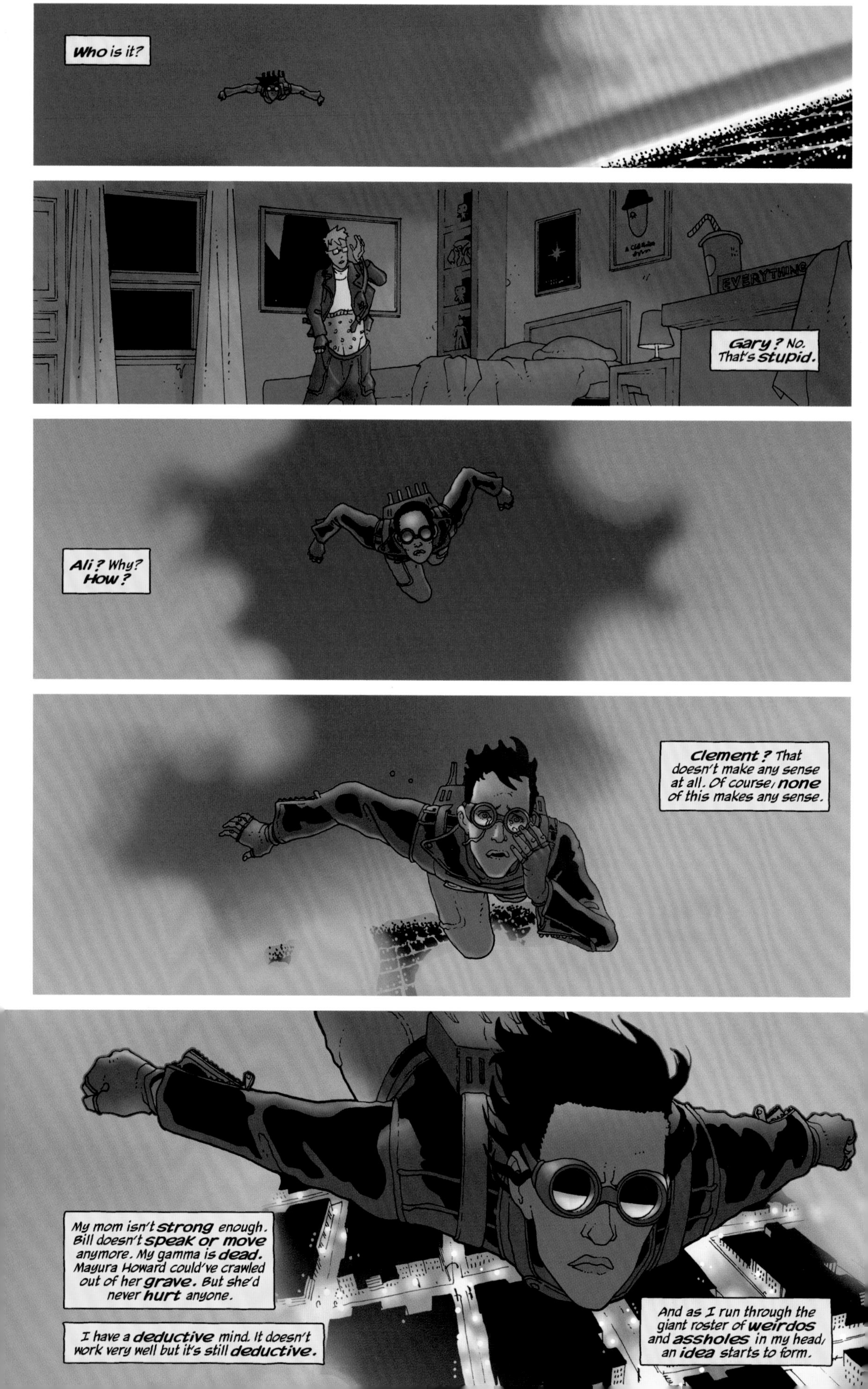
Who is it?
Gary? No. That's stupid.
Ali? Why? How?
Clement? That doesn't make any sense at all. Of course, none of this makes any sense.
My mom isn't strong enough. Bill doesn't speak or move anymore. My gamma is dead. Mayura Howard could've crawled out of her grave. But she'd never hurt anyone.
I have a deductive mind. It doesn't work very well but it's still deductive.
And as I run through the giant roster of weirdos and assholes in my head, an idea starts to form.
EVERYTHING

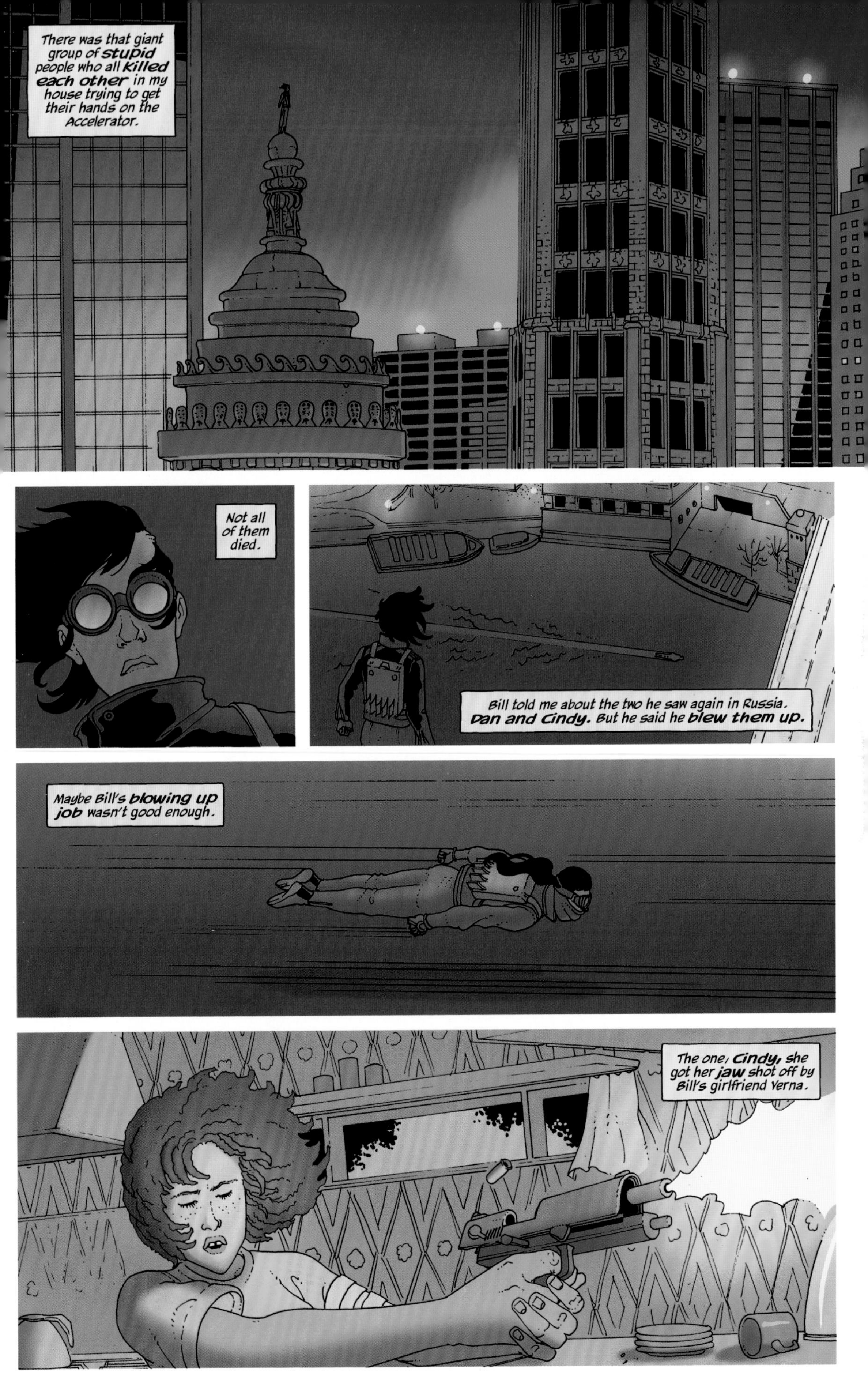
There was that giant group of stupid people who all killed each other in my house trying to get their hands on the Accelerator.
Not all of them died.
Bill told me about the two he saw again in Russia. Dan and Cindy. But he said he blew them up.
Maybe Bill's blowing up job wasn't good enough.
The one, Cindy, she got her jaw shot off by Bill's girlfriend Verna.

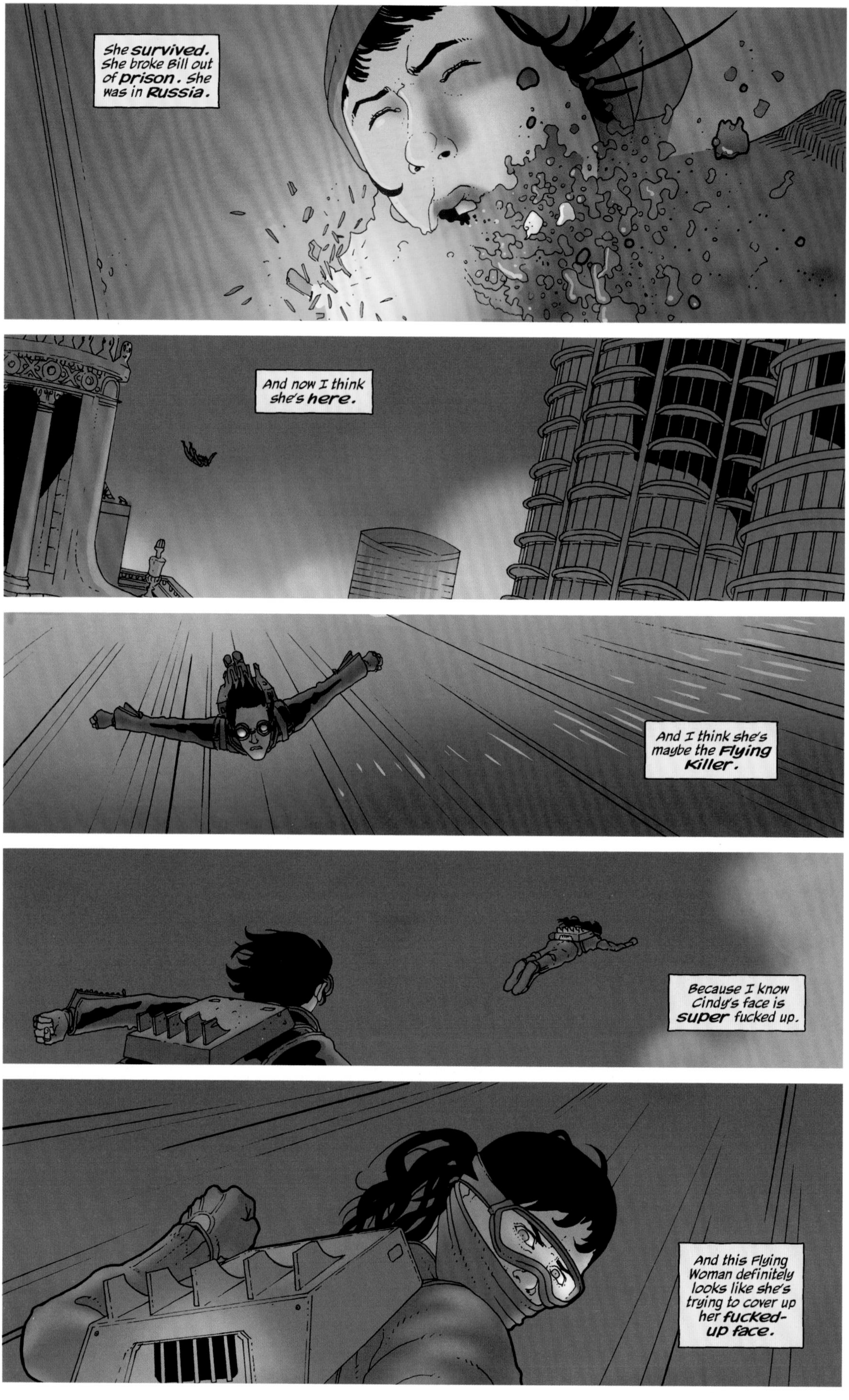
She survived. She broke Bill out of prison. She was in Russia.
And now I think she's here.
And I think she's maybe the Flying Killer.
Because I know Cindy's face is super fucked up.
And this Flying Woman definitely looks like she's trying to cover up her fucked-up face.

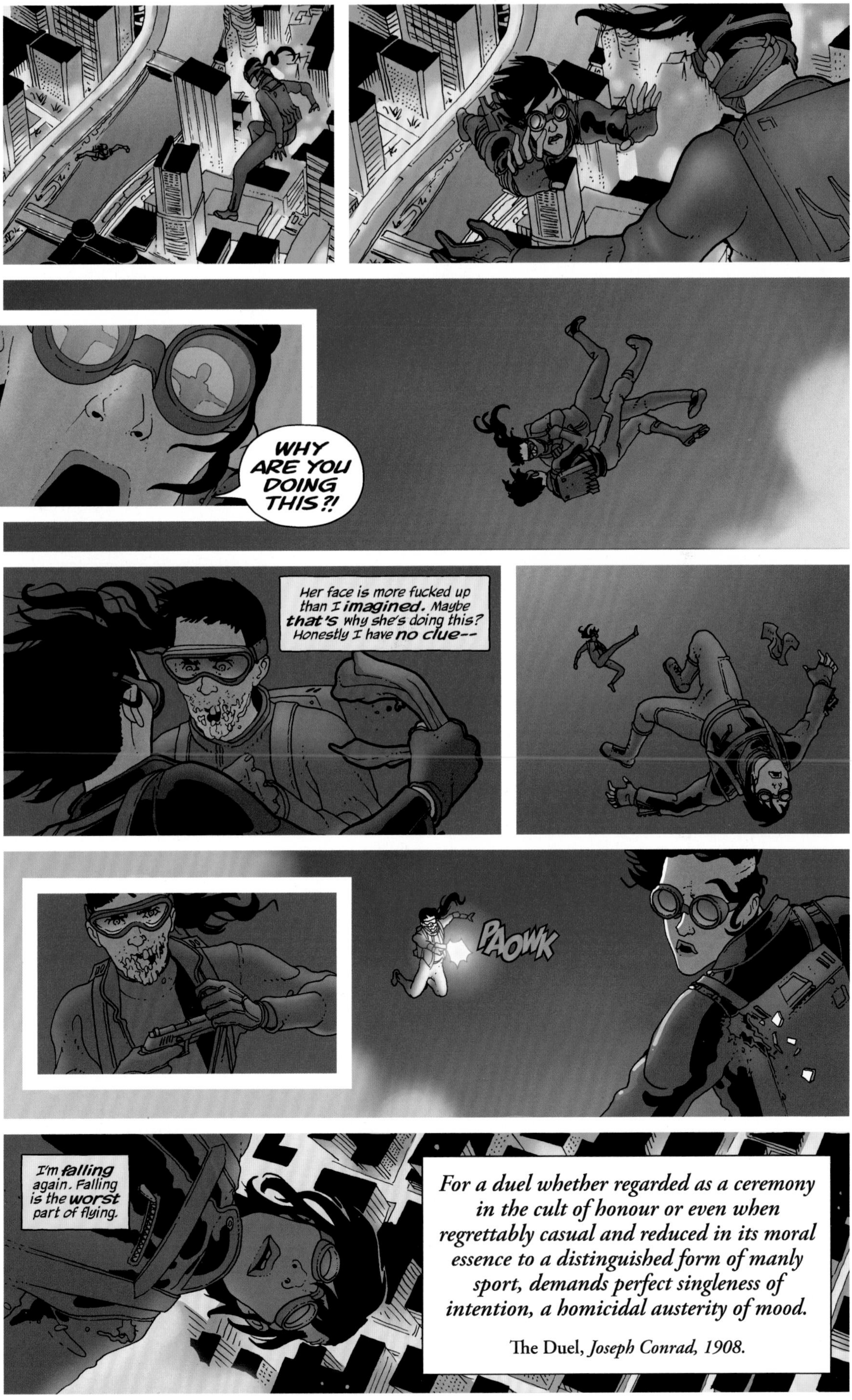
WHY ARE YOU DOING THIS?!
Her face is more fucked up than I imagined. Maybe that's why she's doing this? Honestly I have no clue--
PAOWK
I'm falling again. Falling is the worst part of flying.
For a duel whether regarded as a ceremony in the cult of honour or even when regrettably casual and reduced in its moral essence to a distinguished form of manly sport, demands perfect singleness of intention, a homicidal austerity of mood.
The Duel, Joseph Conrad, 1908.

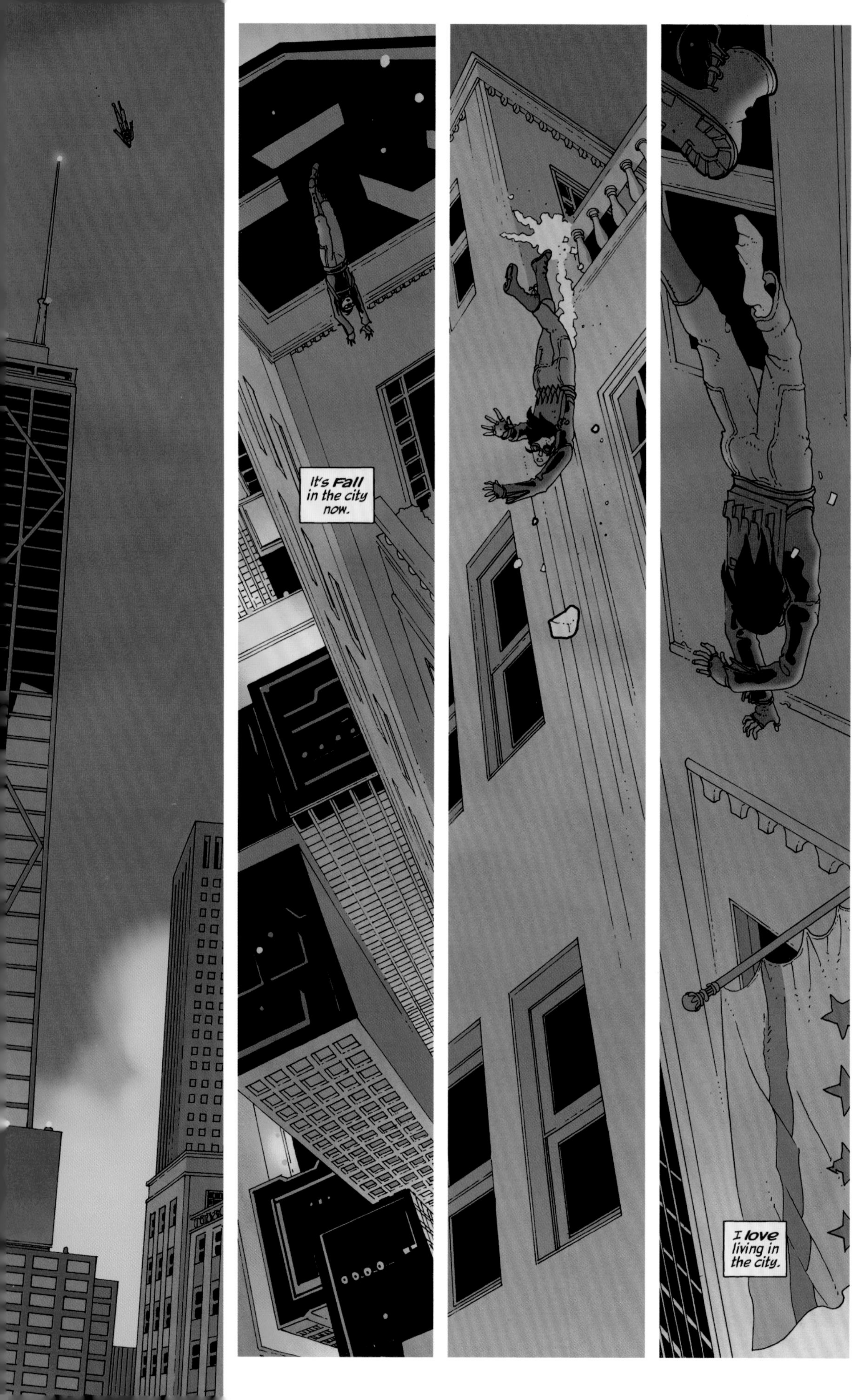

It's **Fall** in the city now.
I **love** living in the city.

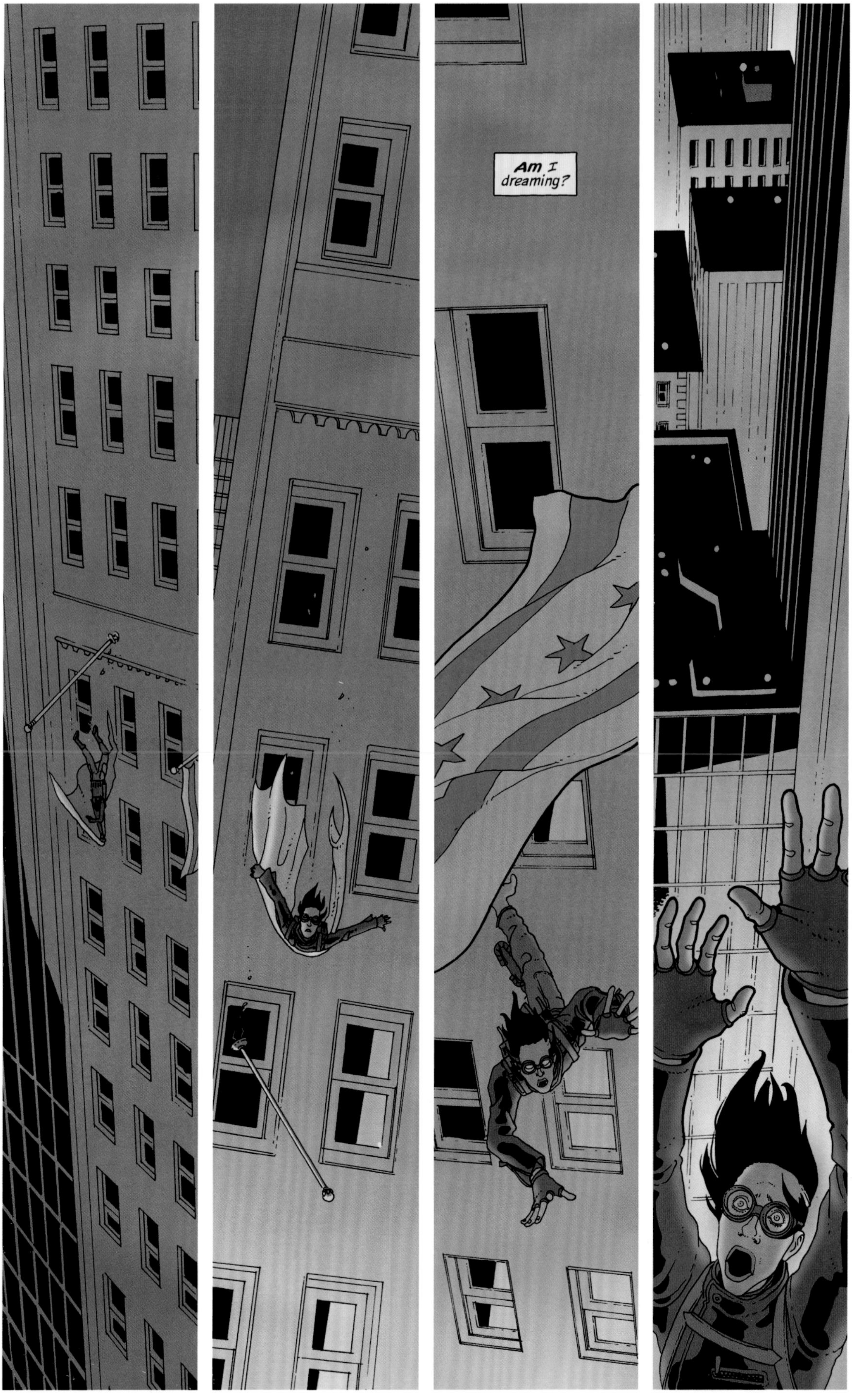
Am I dreaming?

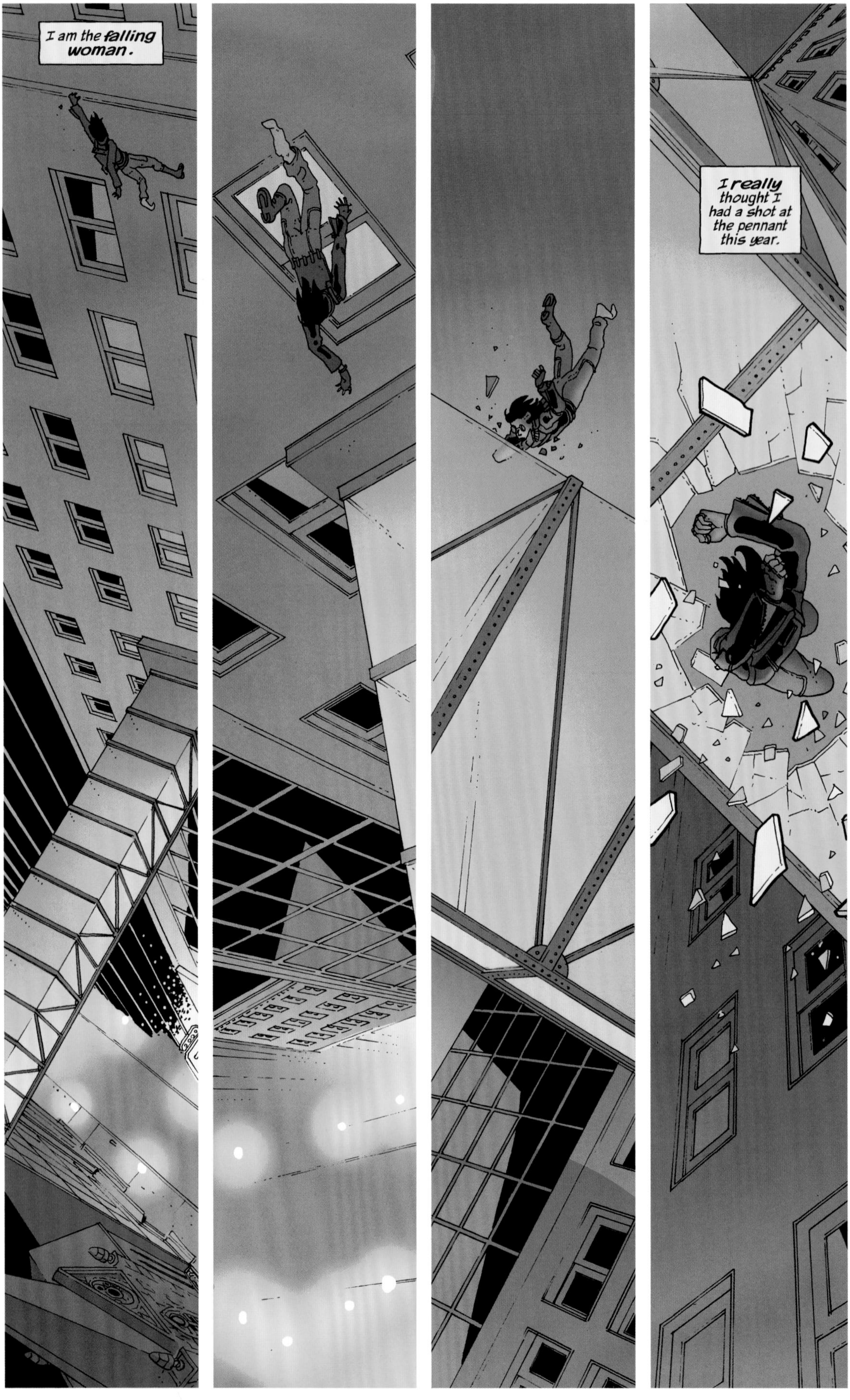
I am the falling woman.
I really thought I had a shot at the pennant this year.

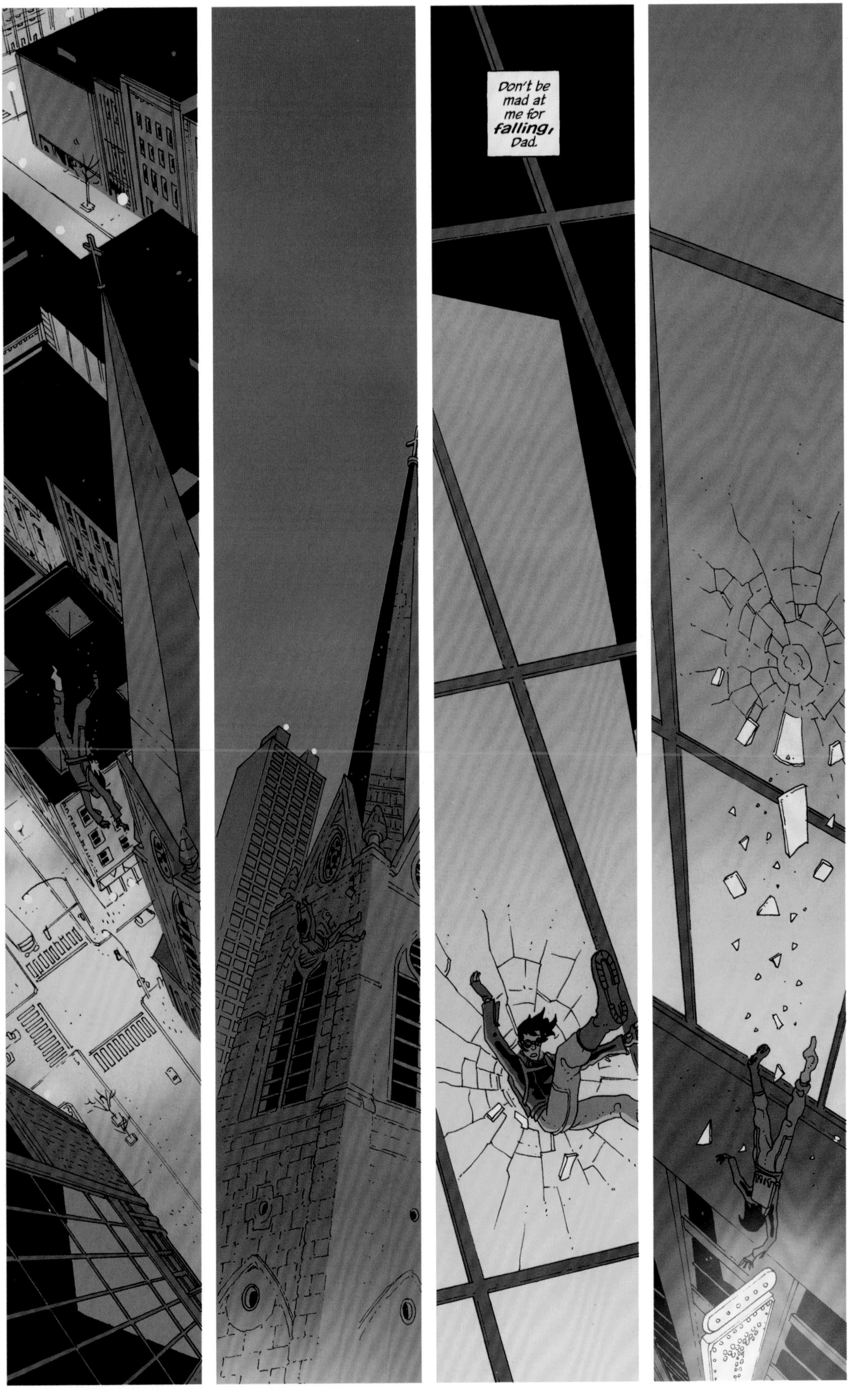

Don't be mad at me for falling, Dad.

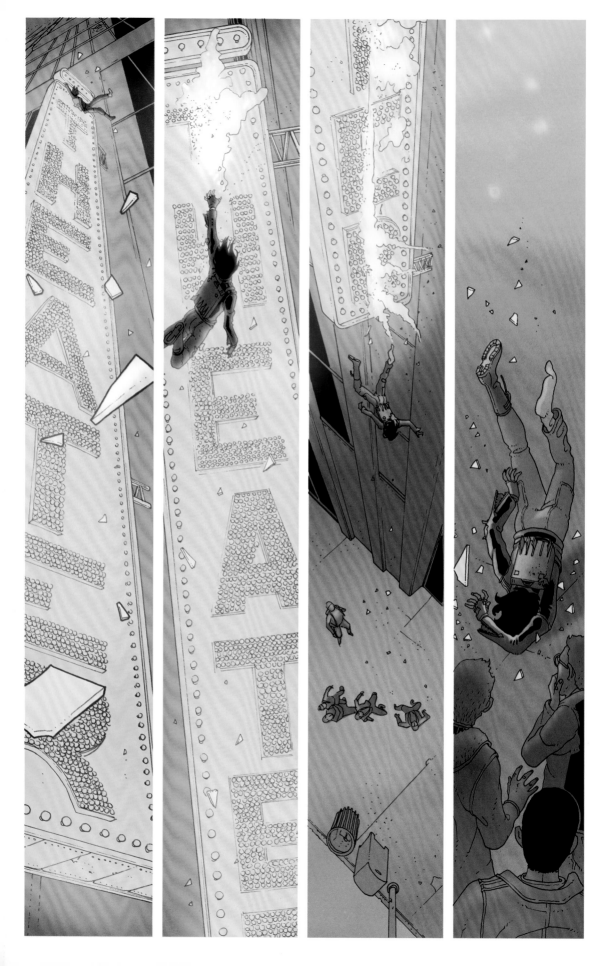

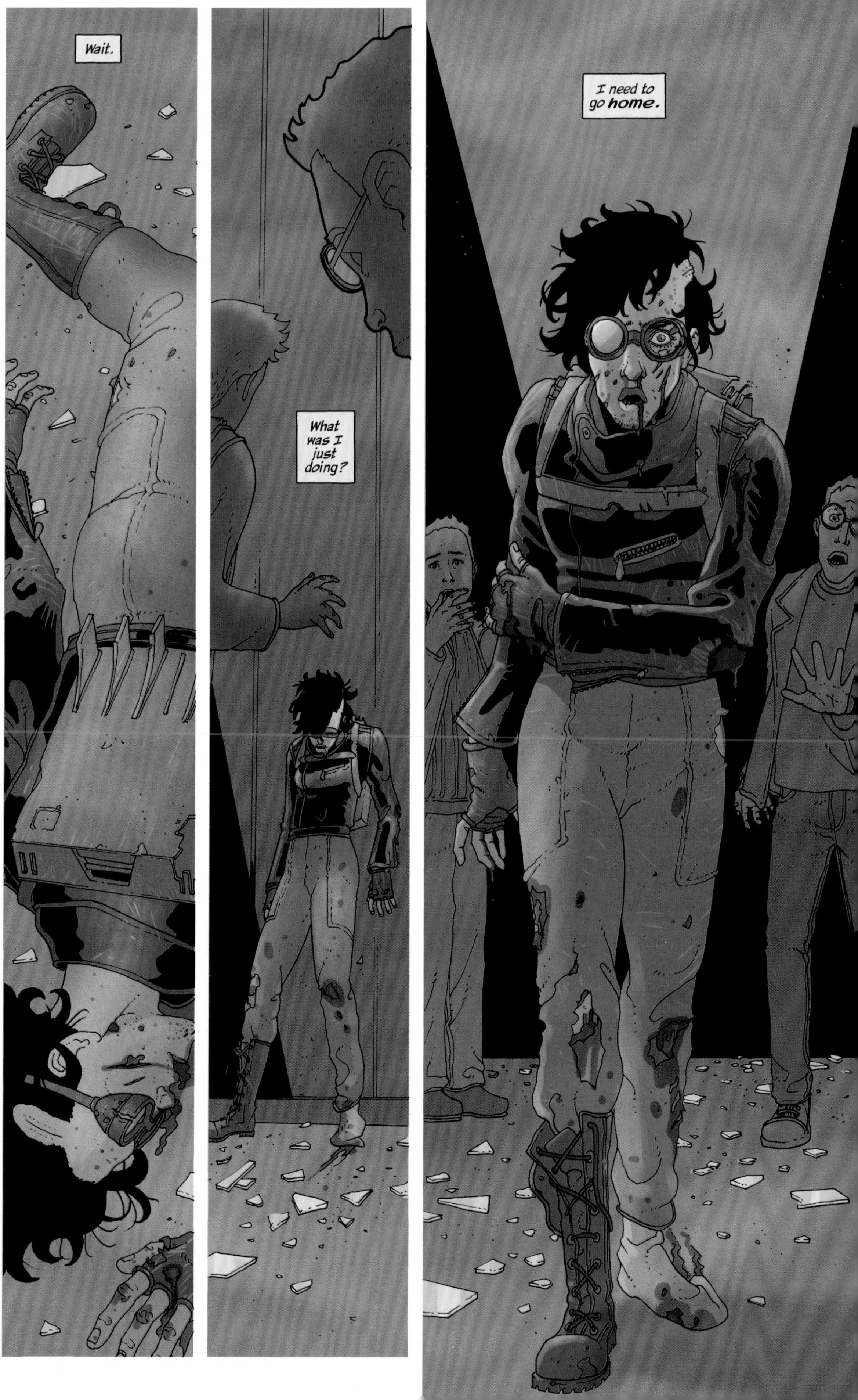
Wait.
What was I just doing?
I need to go **home.**

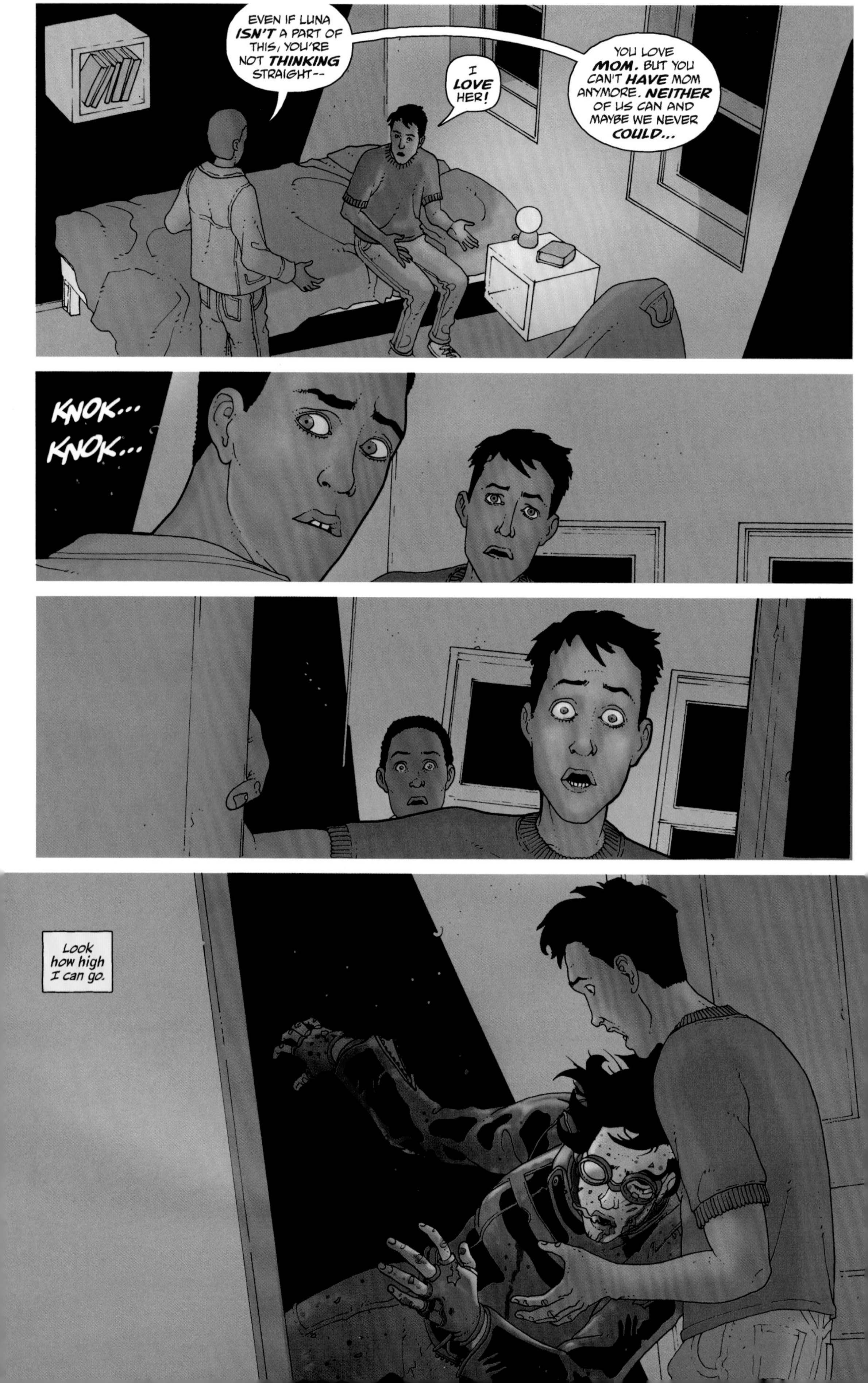
EVEN IF LUNA ISN'T A PART OF THIS, YOU'RE NOT THINKING STRAIGHT--
I LOVE HER!
YOU LOVE MOM. BUT YOU CAN'T HAVE MOM ANYMORE. NEITHER OF US CAN AND MAYBE WE NEVER COULD...
KNOK... KNOK...
Look how high I can go.

4.

Mr. Flying Man
mr. and Mrs Flying People
The Flying Kid
Fly Baby Alpha
Fly Man
Fly guy
^^ I just made these up because I'm bored.
my Dad but only five times which is weird,
mostly trips to Michigan and once to salt Like
City for a wedding
The Flying Graysons (just kidding they didn't
fly they just fell and died)
The people who dropped atomic bombs on
hiroshima and Nagasaki
The people who dropped atomic bombs for tests
Firebombers in Vietnam laos and Cambodia
All of the people onboard the Malaysia Flight
that disappeared
Members of Leonard Skynyrd
The Air Force Officer in Twin Peaks who was
part of Project Blue Book
Anyonne in a movie or tv show who gets on a
plane
Maverick and goose (included in the above but
felt worth mentioning)
Iceman
merlin
Viper
jester
Hollywood
Wolfman
sundown

slider
I already said tom Cruise
The iron eagle Kid who goes to get his dad
~~The Last Starfighter~~ SPACE, DISQUALIFIED
~~Flight of the Navigator kid~~ SPACE, DISQUALIFIED
~~space Camp kids~~ SPACE DISQUALIFIED
~~The Explorers kids including ethan hawke~~ SPACE,
DISQUALIFIED
Unnammed spirits or entitiies in paintings that
are depicted in the air
I forgot Maverick's dad, who didn't bug out

I don't want to do this anymore.

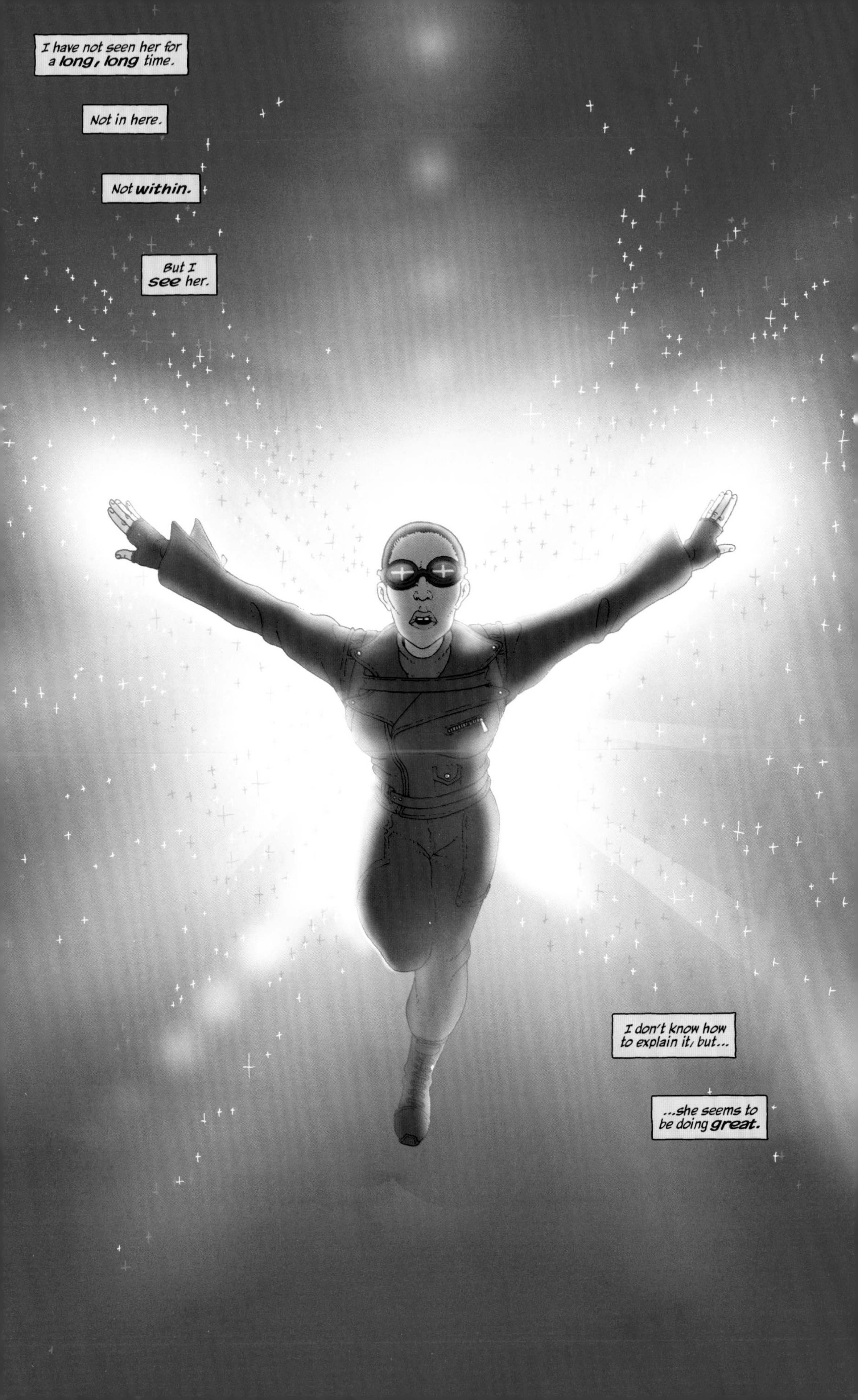
I have not seen her for a long, long time.
Not in here.
Not within.
But I see her.
I don't know how to explain it, but...
...she seems to be doing great.

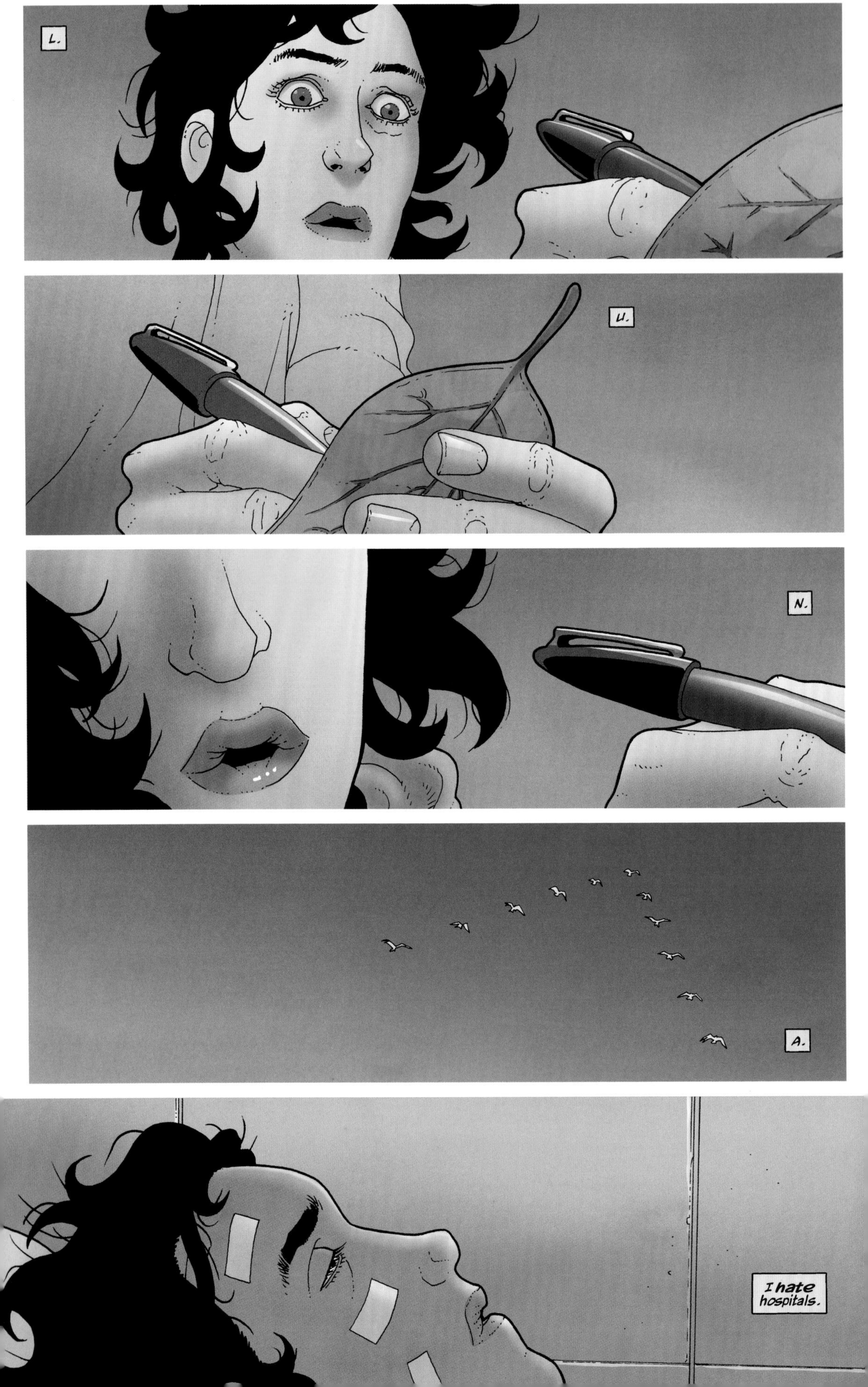
L.
U.
N.
A.
I hate hospitals.

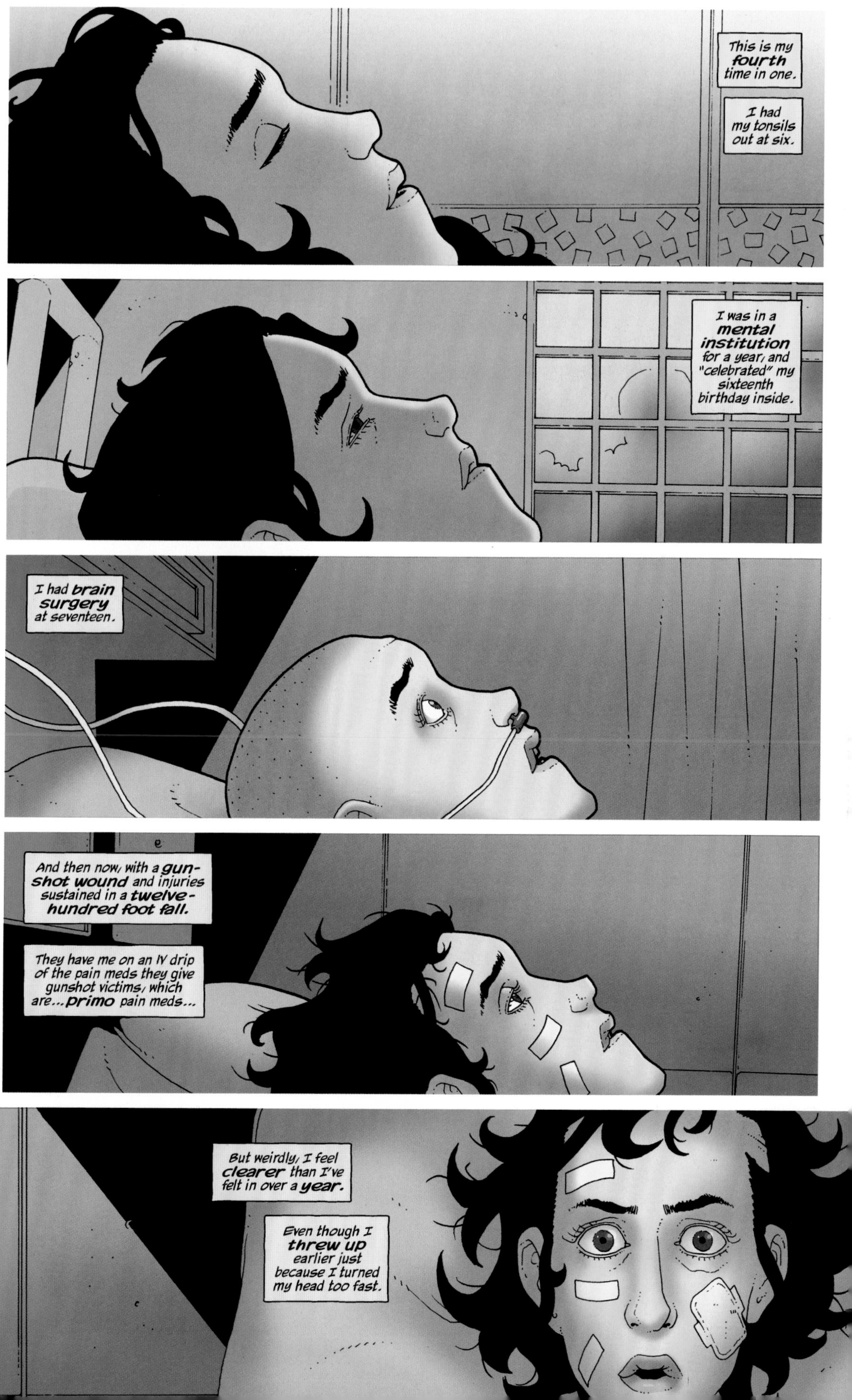
This is my fourth time in one.
I had my tonsils out at six.
I was in a mental institution for a year, and "celebrated" my sixteenth birthday inside.
I had brain surgery at seventeen.
And then now, with a gun-shot wound and injuries sustained in a twelve-hundred foot fall.
They have me on an IV drip of the pain meds they give gunshot victims, which are... primo pain meds...
But weirdly, I feel clearer than I've felt in over a year.
Even though I threw up earlier just because I turned my head too fast.

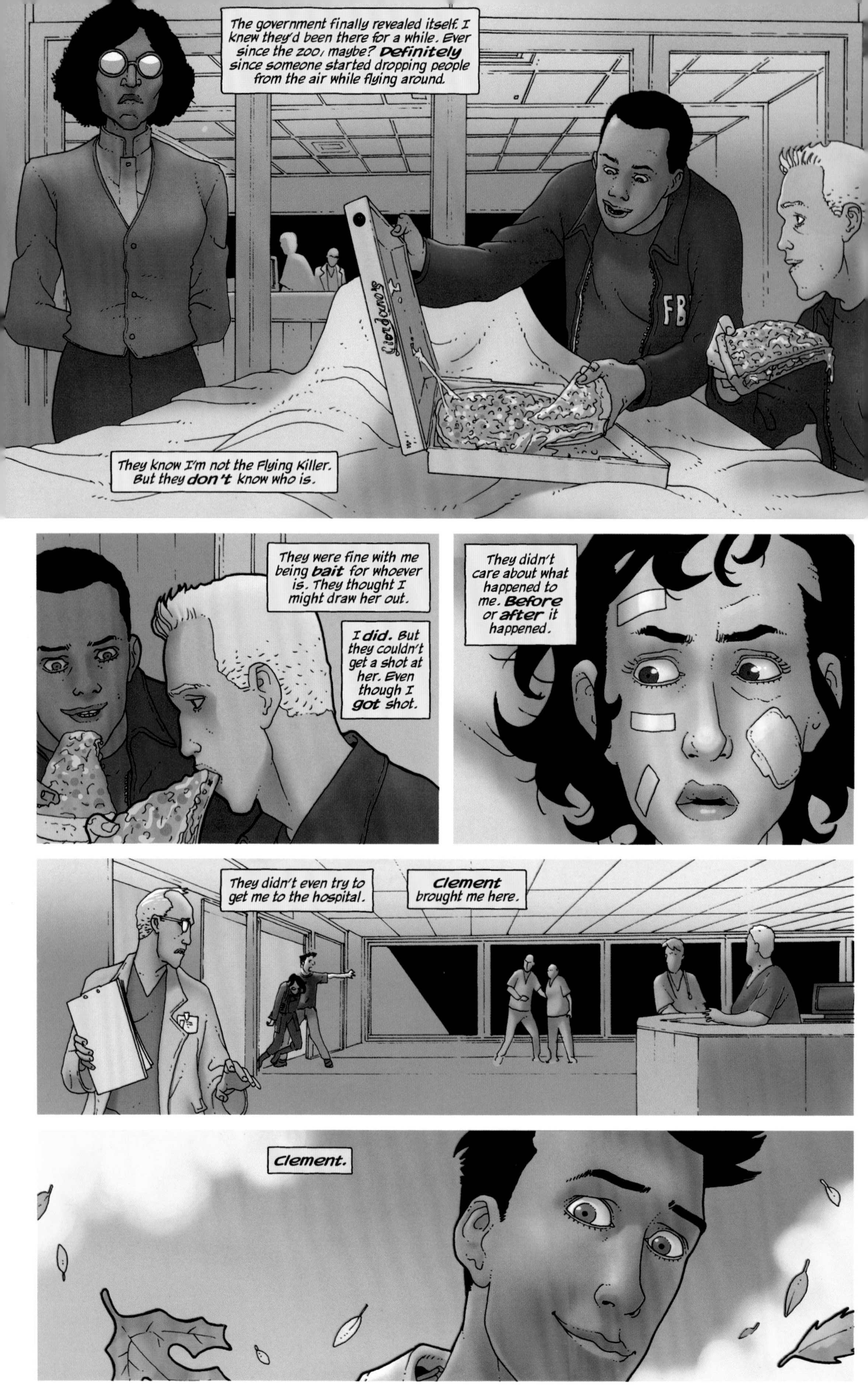
The government finally revealed itself. I knew they'd been there for a while. Ever since the zoo, maybe? Definitely since someone started dropping people from the air while flying around.
They know I'm not the Flying Killer. But they don't know who is.
They were fine with me being bait for whoever is. They thought I might draw her out.
I did. But they couldn't get a shot at her. Even though I got shot.
They didn't care about what happened to me. Before or after it happened.
They didn't even try to get me to the hospital.
Clement brought me here.
Clement.

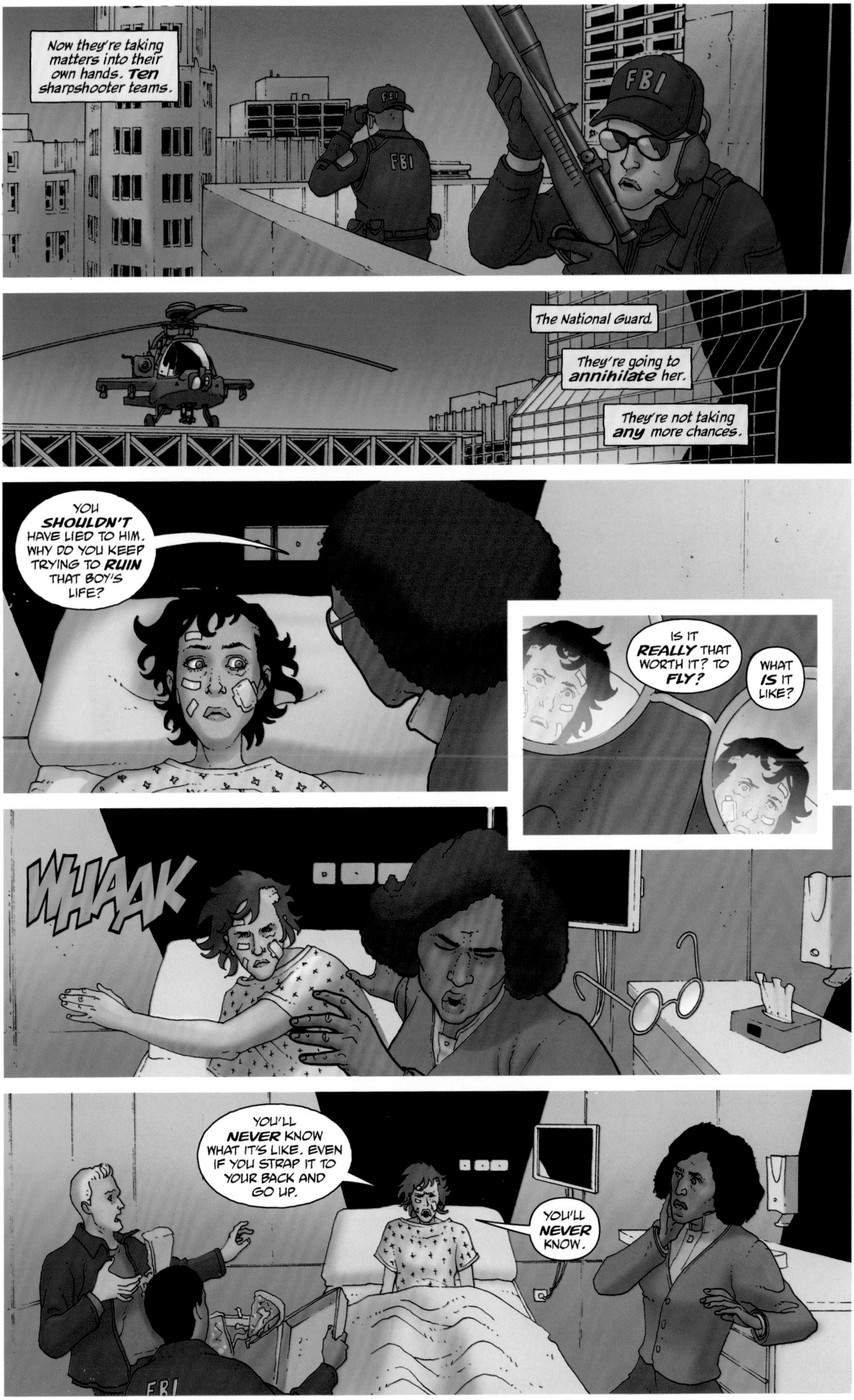
Now they're taking matters into their own hands. Ten sharpshooter teams.
FBI
FBI
FBI
The National Guard.
They're going to annihilate her.
They're not taking any more chances.
YOU SHOULDN'T HAVE LIED TO HIM. WHY DO YOU KEEP TRYING TO RUIN THAT BOY'S LIFE?
IS IT REALLY THAT WORTH IT? TO FLY?
WHAT IS IT LIKE?
WHAAK
YOU'LL NEVER KNOW WHAT IT'S LIKE. EVEN IF YOU STRAP IT TO YOUR BACK AND GO UP.
YOU'LL NEVER KNOW.
FBI

They'll never know.

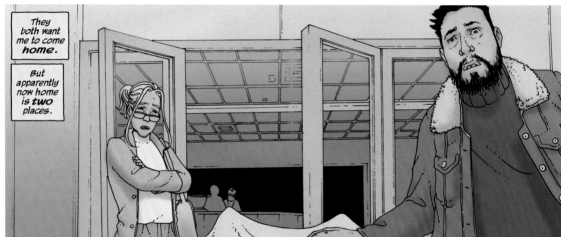

They both want me to come **home**.

But apparently now home is **two** places.

That means **neither** place is home.

I just want them to **leave**.

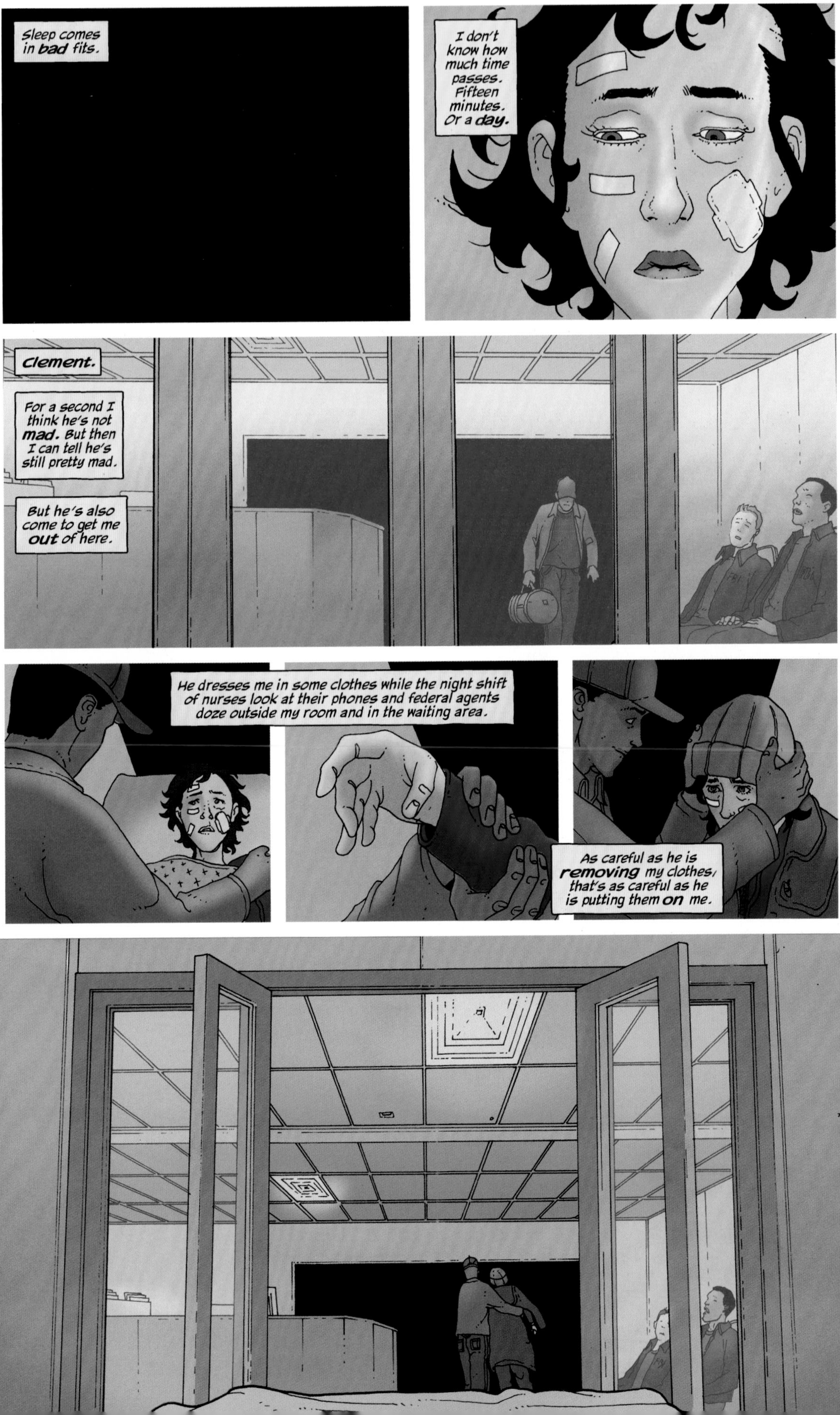

Sleep comes in bad fits.
I don't know how much time passes. Fifteen minutes. Or a day.
Clement.
For a second I think he's not mad. But then I can tell he's still pretty mad.
But he's also come to get me out of here.
He dresses me in some clothes while the night shift of nurses look at their phones and federal agents doze outside my room and in the waiting area.
As careful as he is removing my clothes, that's as careful as he is putting them on me.

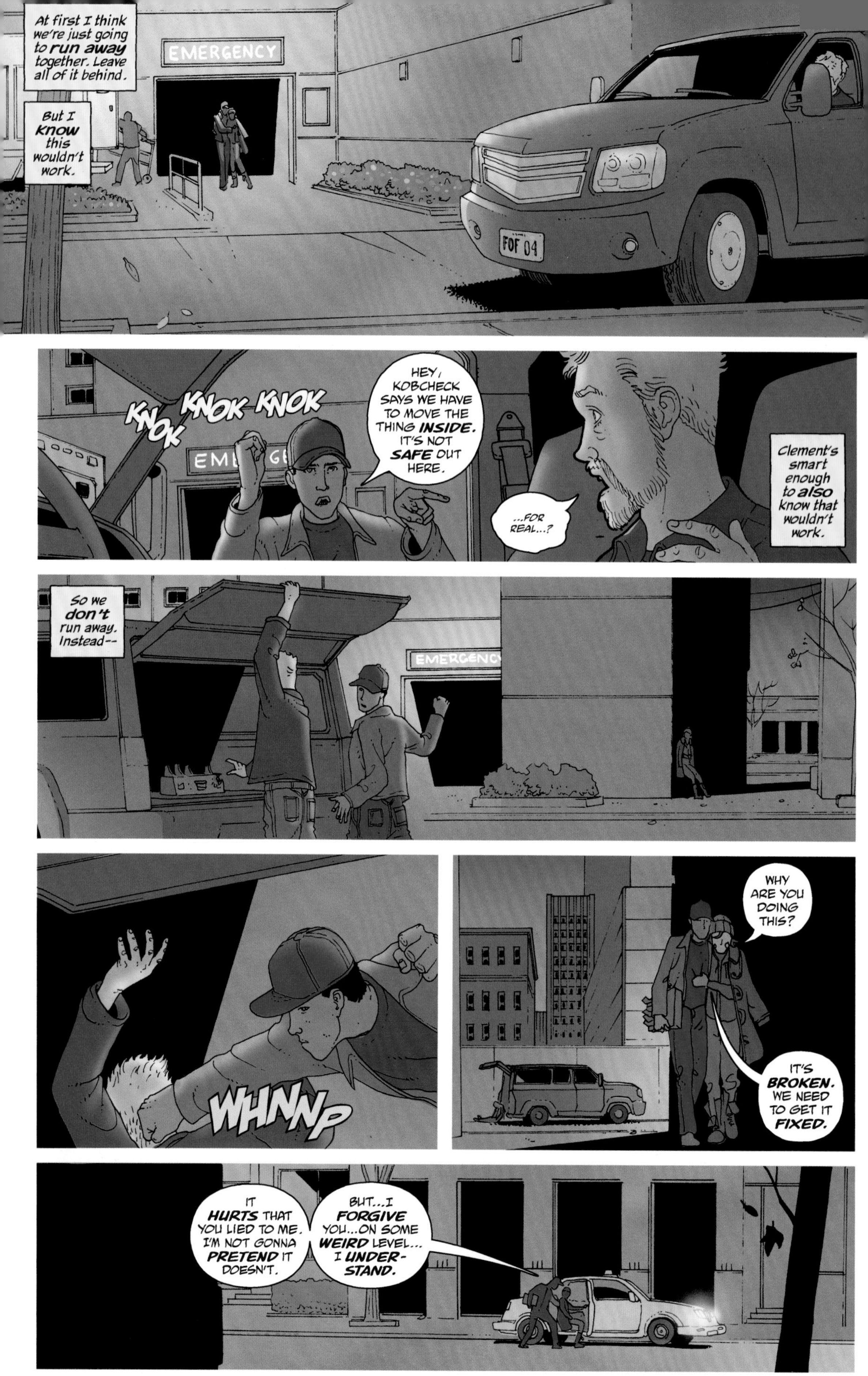
At first I think we're just going to run away together. Leave all of it behind.
EMERGENCY
But I know this wouldn't work.
FOF 04
KNOK KNOK KNOK
HEY, KOBCHECK SAYS WE HAVE TO MOVE THE THING INSIDE. IT'S NOT SAFE OUT HERE.
...FOR REAL...?
Clement's smart enough to also know that wouldn't work.
So we don't run away. Instead--
EMERGENCY
WHNNP
WHY ARE YOU DOING THIS?
IT'S BROKEN. WE NEED TO GET IT FIXED.
IT HURTS THAT YOU LIED TO ME. I'M NOT GONNA PRETEND IT DOESN'T.
BUT...I FORGIVE YOU...ON SOME WEIRD LEVEL... I UNDERSTAND.

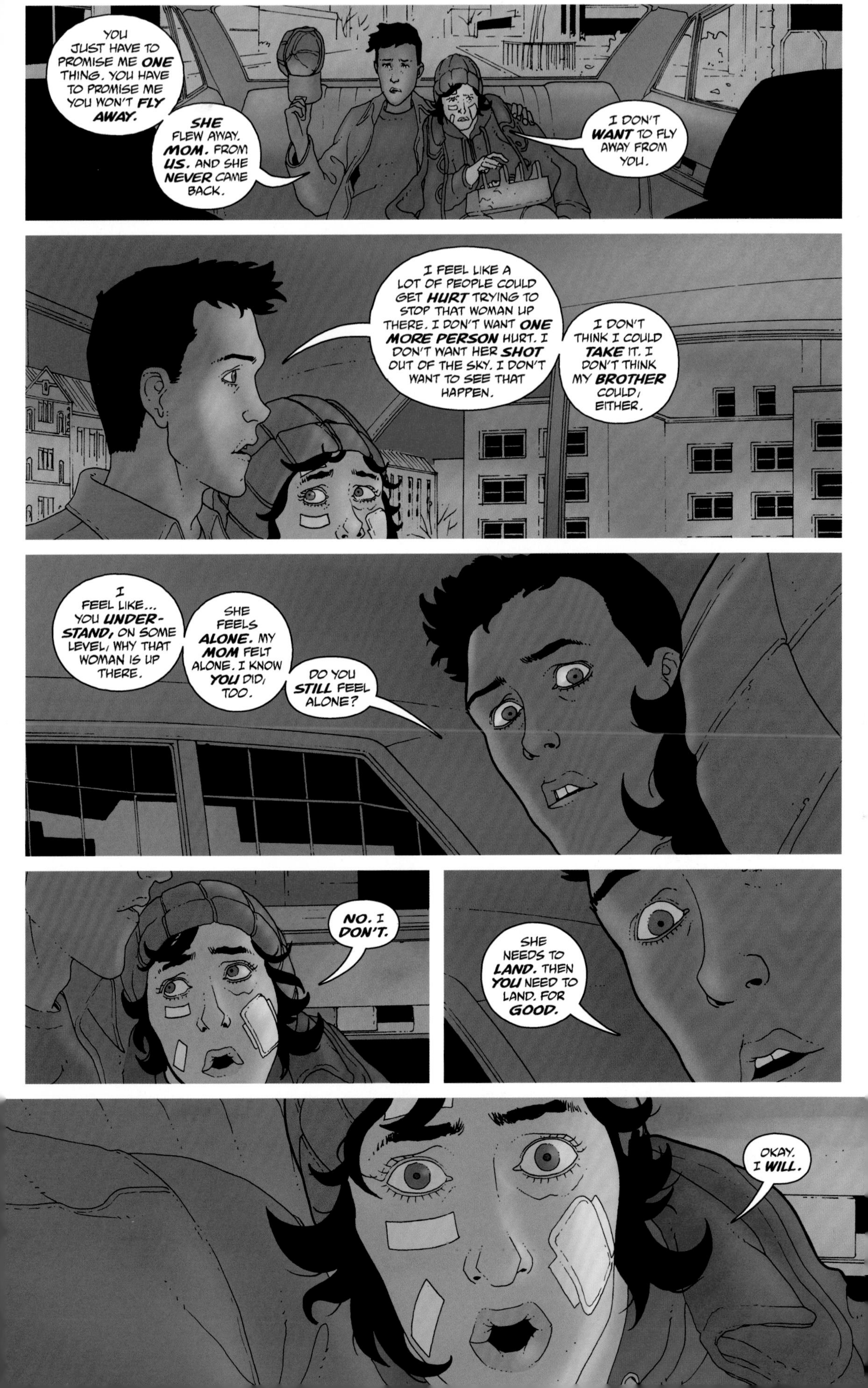

YOU JUST HAVE TO PROMISE ME ONE THING. YOU HAVE TO PROMISE ME YOU WON'T FLY AWAY.
SHE FLEW AWAY. MOM. FROM US. AND SHE NEVER CAME BACK.
I DON'T WANT TO FLY AWAY FROM YOU.
I FEEL LIKE A LOT OF PEOPLE COULD GET HURT TRYING TO STOP THAT WOMAN UP THERE. I DON'T WANT ONE MORE PERSON HURT. I DON'T WANT HER SHOT OUT OF THE SKY. I DON'T WANT TO SEE THAT HAPPEN.
I DON'T THINK I COULD TAKE IT. I DON'T THINK MY BROTHER COULD, EITHER.
I FEEL LIKE... YOU UNDER-STAND, ON SOME LEVEL, WHY THAT WOMAN IS UP THERE.
SHE FEELS ALONE. MY MOM FELT ALONE. I KNOW YOU DID, TOO.
DO YOU STILL FEEL ALONE?
NO. I DON'T.
SHE NEEDS TO LAND. THEN YOU NEED TO LAND. FOR GOOD.
OKAY. I WILL.

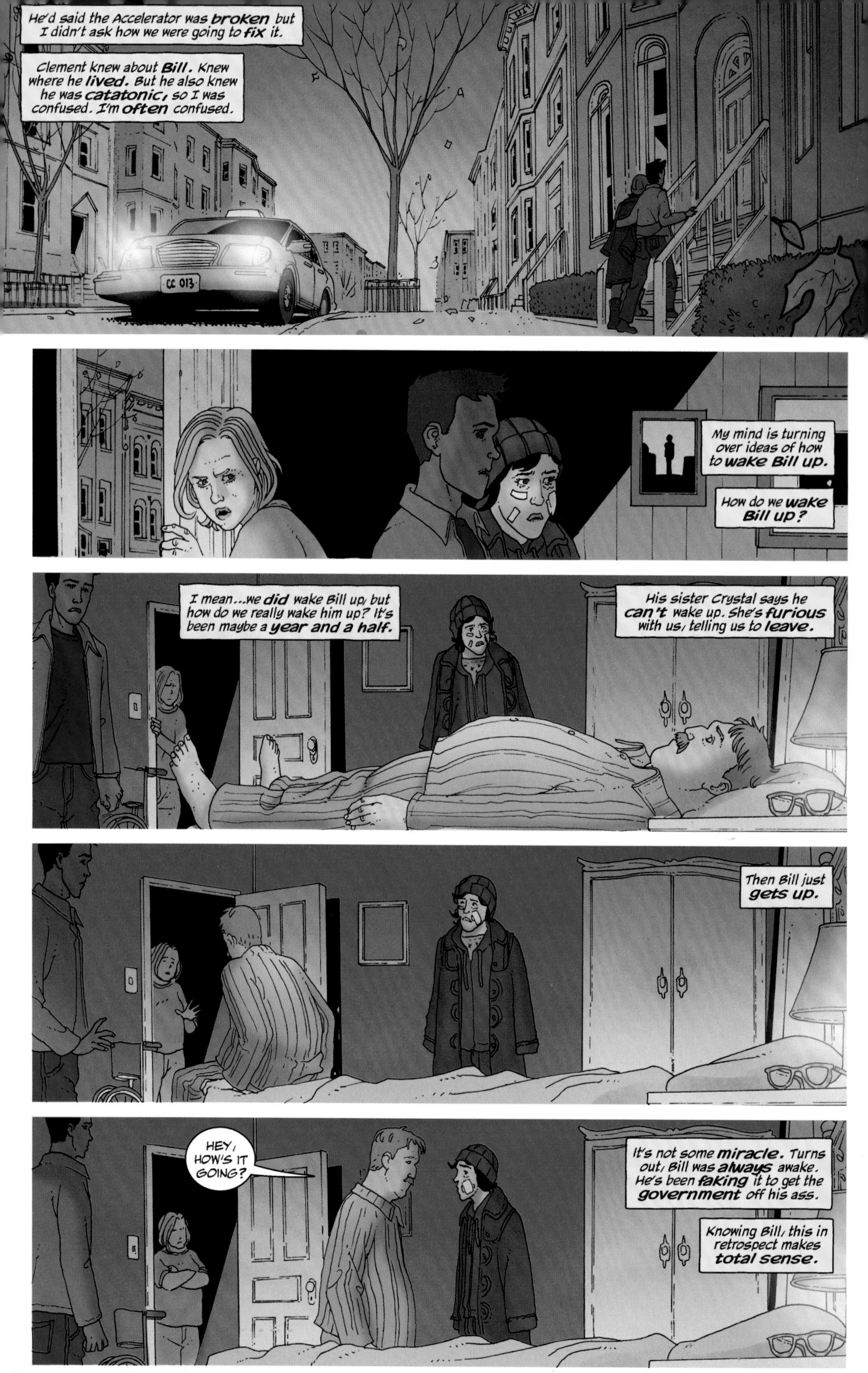
He'd said the Accelerator was broken but I didn't ask how we were going to fix it.
Clement knew about Bill. Knew where he lived. But he also knew he was catatonic, so I was confused. I'm often confused.
CC 013
My mind is turning over ideas of how to wake Bill up.
How do we wake Bill up?
I mean...we did wake Bill up, but how do we really wake him up? It's been maybe a year and a half.
His sister Crystal says he can't wake up. She's furious with us, telling us to leave.
Then Bill just gets up.
HEY, HOW'S IT GOING?
It's not some miracle. Turns out, Bill was always awake. He's been faking it to get the government off his ass.
Knowing Bill, this in retrospect makes total sense.

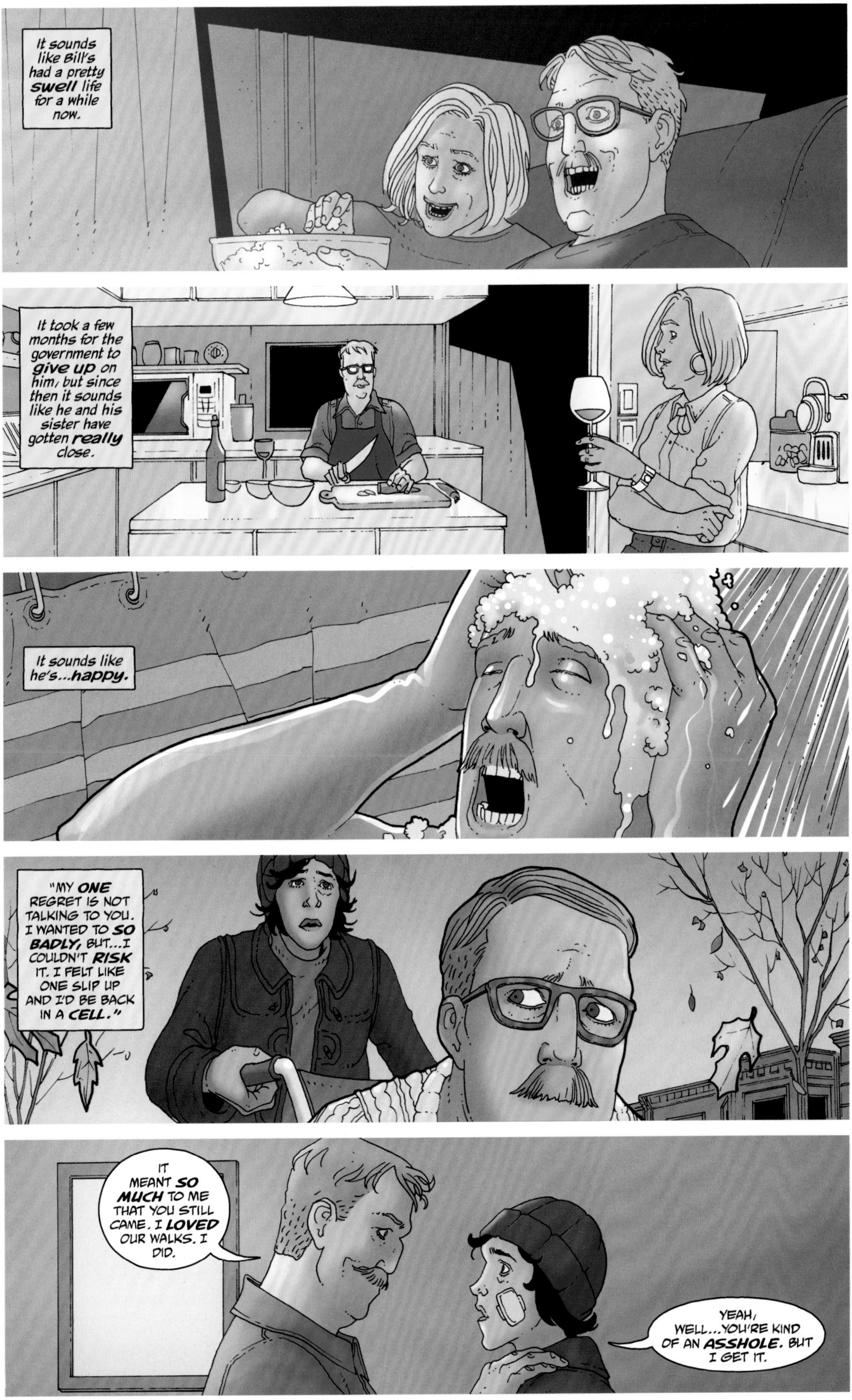
It sounds like Bill's had a pretty swell life for a while now.
It took a few months for the government to give up on him, but since then it sounds like he and his sister have gotten really close.
It sounds like he's...happy.
"MY ONE REGRET IS NOT TALKING TO YOU. I WANTED TO SO BADLY, BUT...I COULDN'T RISK IT. I FELT LIKE ONE SLIP UP AND I'D BE BACK IN A CELL."
IT MEANT SO MUCH TO ME THAT YOU STILL CAME. I LOVED OUR WALKS. I DID.
YEAH, WELL...YOU'RE KIND OF AN ASSHOLE. BUT I GET IT.

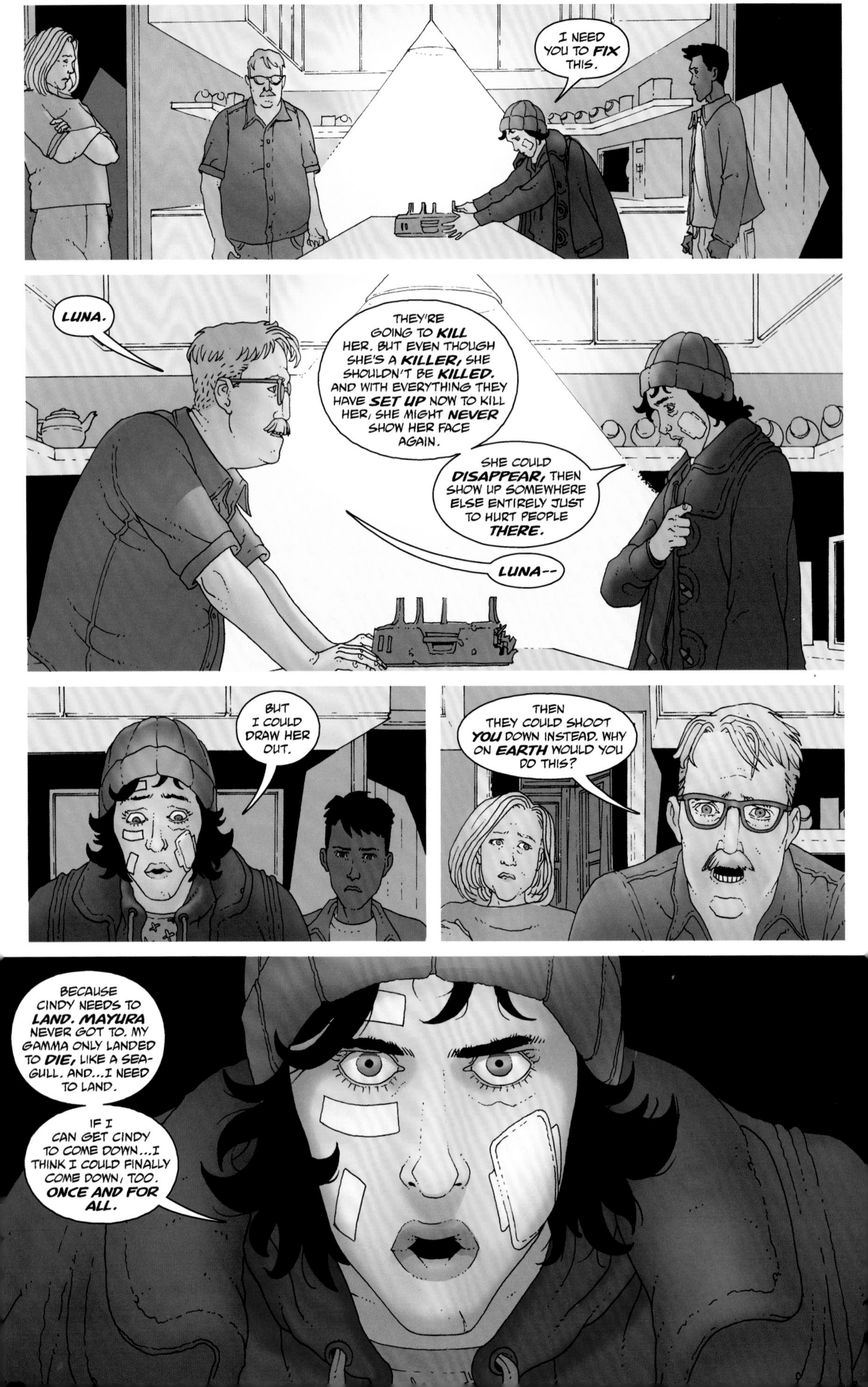
I NEED YOU TO FIX THIS.
LUNA.
THEY'RE GOING TO KILL HER. BUT EVEN THOUGH SHE'S A KILLER, SHE SHOULDN'T BE KILLED. AND WITH EVERYTHING THEY HAVE SET UP NOW TO KILL HER, SHE MIGHT NEVER SHOW HER FACE AGAIN.
SHE COULD DISAPPEAR, THEN SHOW UP SOMEWHERE ELSE ENTIRELY JUST TO HURT PEOPLE THERE.
LUNA--
BUT I COULD DRAW HER OUT.
THEN THEY COULD SHOOT YOU DOWN INSTEAD. WHY ON EARTH WOULD YOU DO THIS?
BECAUSE CINDY NEEDS TO LAND. MAYURA NEVER GOT TO. MY GAMMA ONLY LANDED TO DIE, LIKE A SEA-GULL. AND...I NEED TO LAND.
IF I CAN GET CINDY TO COME DOWN...I THINK I COULD FINALLY COME DOWN, TOO. ONCE AND FOR ALL.

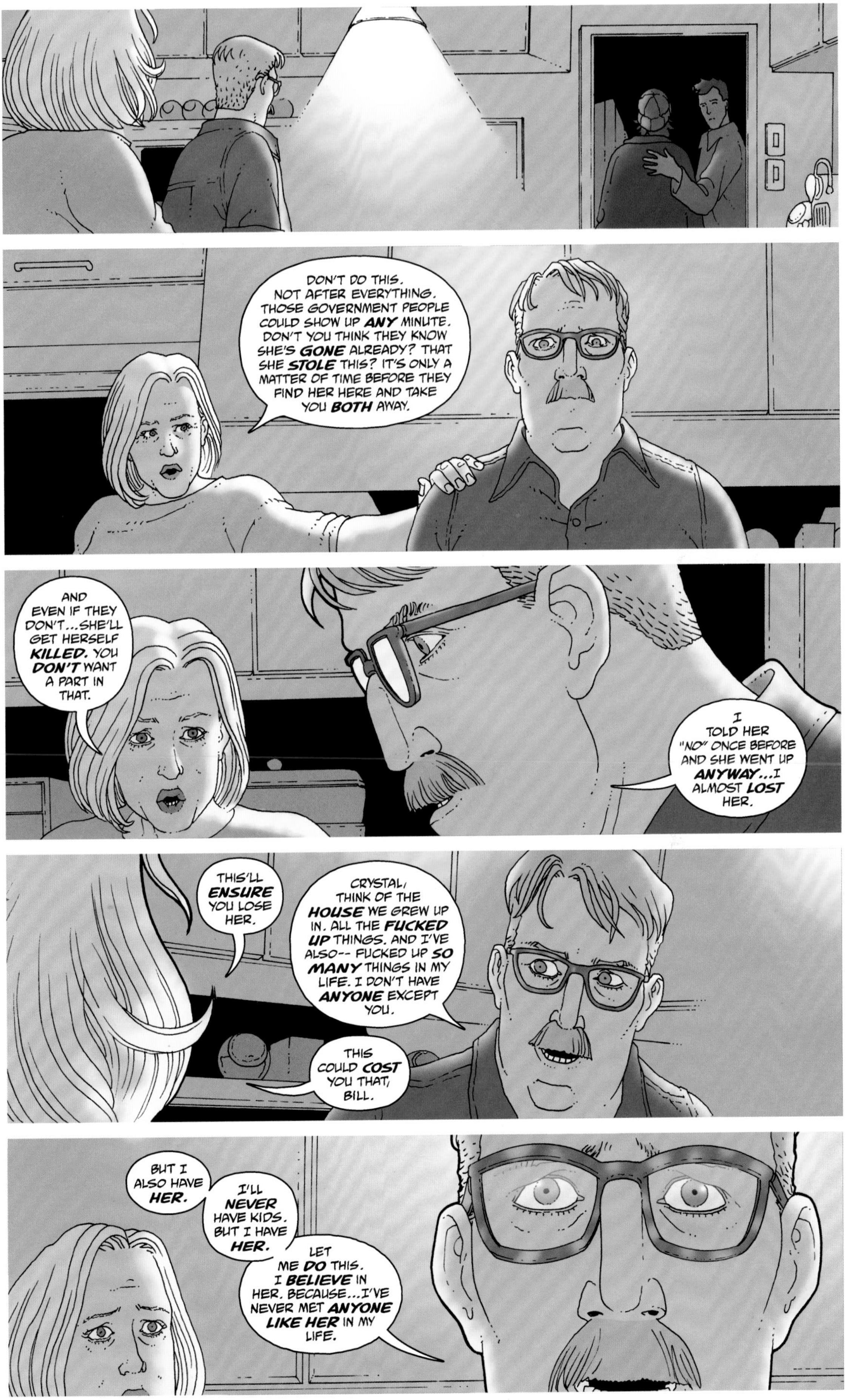
DON'T DO THIS. NOT AFTER EVERYTHING. THOSE GOVERNMENT PEOPLE COULD SHOW UP ANY MINUTE. DON'T YOU THINK THEY KNOW SHE'S GONE ALREADY? THAT SHE STOLE THIS? IT'S ONLY A MATTER OF TIME BEFORE THEY FIND HER HERE AND TAKE YOU BOTH AWAY.
AND EVEN IF THEY DON'T...SHE'LL GET HERSELF KILLED. YOU DON'T WANT A PART IN THAT.
I TOLD HER "NO" ONCE BEFORE AND SHE WENT UP ANYWAY...I ALMOST LOST HER.
THIS'LL ENSURE YOU LOSE HER.
CRYSTAL, THINK OF THE HOUSE WE GREW UP IN. ALL THE FUCKED UP THINGS. AND I'VE ALSO-- FUCKED UP SO MANY THINGS IN MY LIFE. I DON'T HAVE ANYONE EXCEPT YOU.
THIS COULD COST YOU THAT, BILL.
BUT I ALSO HAVE HER.
I'LL NEVER HAVE KIDS. BUT I HAVE HER.
LET ME DO THIS. I BELIEVE IN HER. BECAUSE...I'VE NEVER MET ANYONE LIKE HER IN MY LIFE.

I have a plan.
I don't want to get killed.
I just want all of this to end.
My pain meds are wearing off.
There's a lot of pain.
There's been so much pain for so much time.

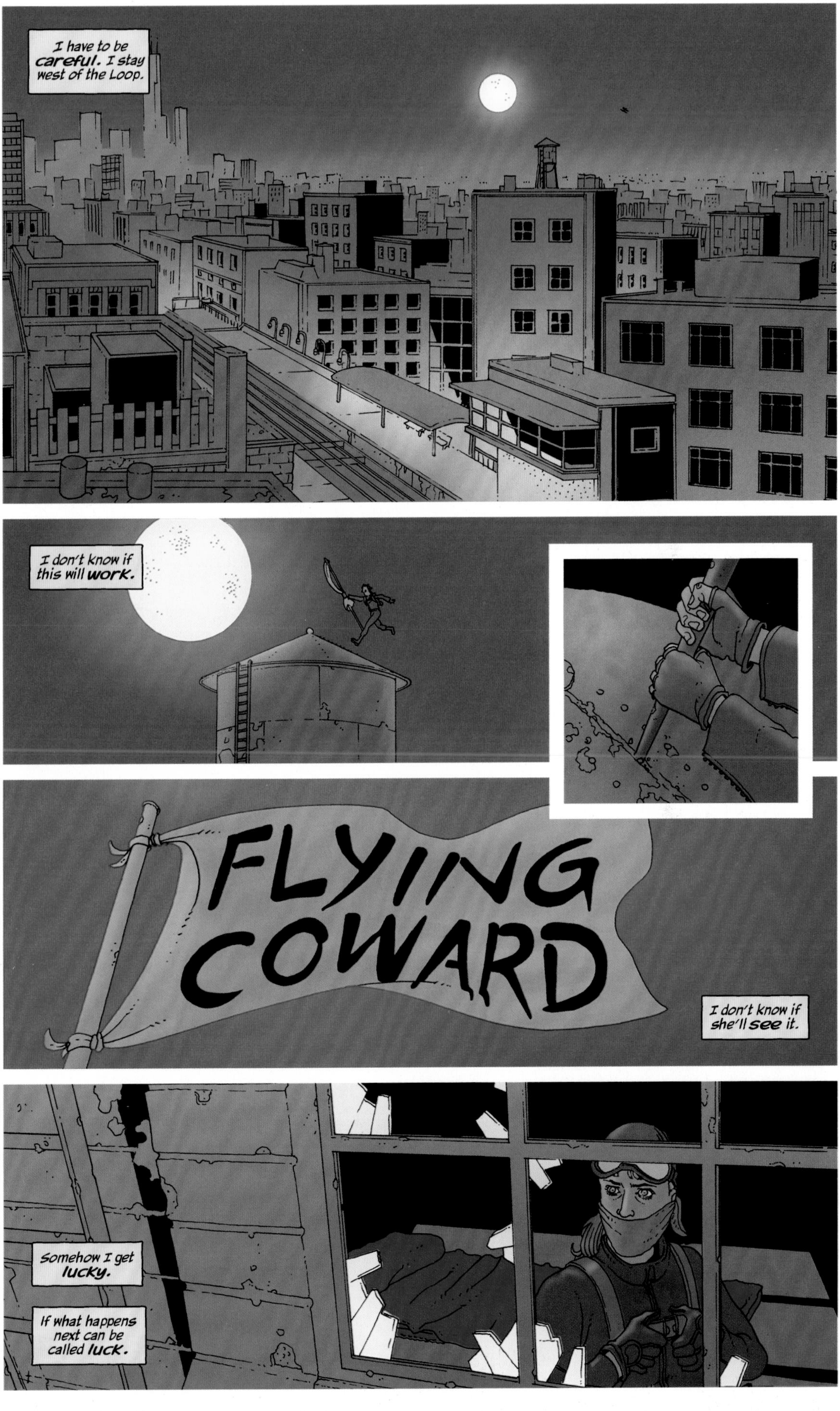

I have to be careful. I stay west of the Loop.
I don't know if this will work.
FLYING COWARD
I don't know if she'll see it.
Somehow I get lucky.
If what happens next can be called luck.

I only have a *few* seconds.

FLYING COWARD

As best I can understand-- with all my *Dysexecutive Dysfunction,* with all the *pain medicine,* with all the *pain,* with my brain being just the one I ended up with when I was born--those few seconds are *now.*

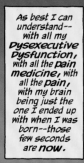

I borrowed Bill's sister's *stun gun.*

You can never be *too careful* in the city.

In this moment, I remember some *book* from sophomore year English class.

I didn't really pay attention and I don't think I really *read* the book.

I was too busy thinking about the *Flying Woman* that kept showing up all over the city.

But in this moment I remember there was something in the book about *best laid plans.*

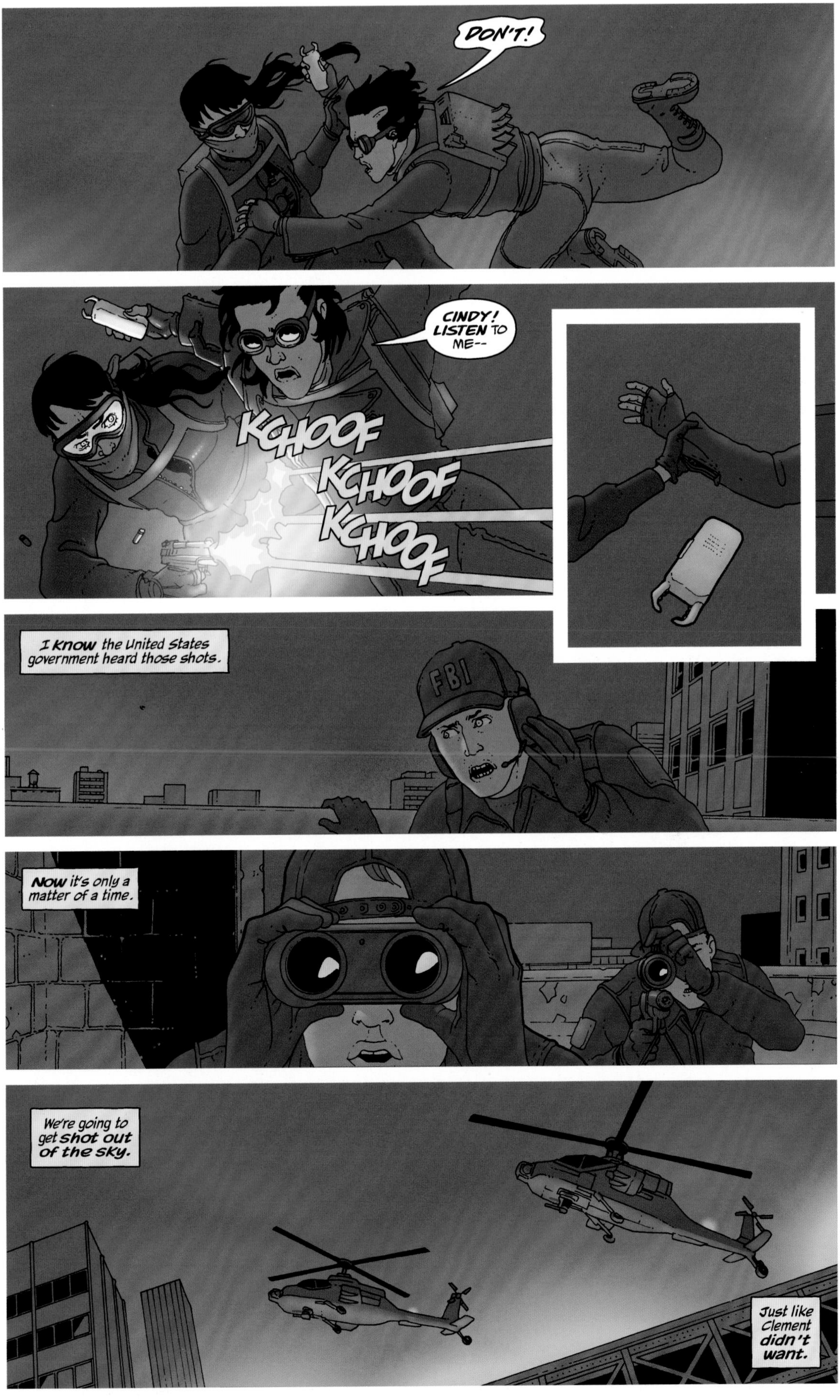
DON'T!
CINDY! LISTEN TO ME--
KCHOOF
KCHOOF
KCHOOF
I KNOW the United States government heard those shots.
FBI
NOW it's only a matter of a time.
We're going to get shot out of the sky.
Just like Clement didn't want.

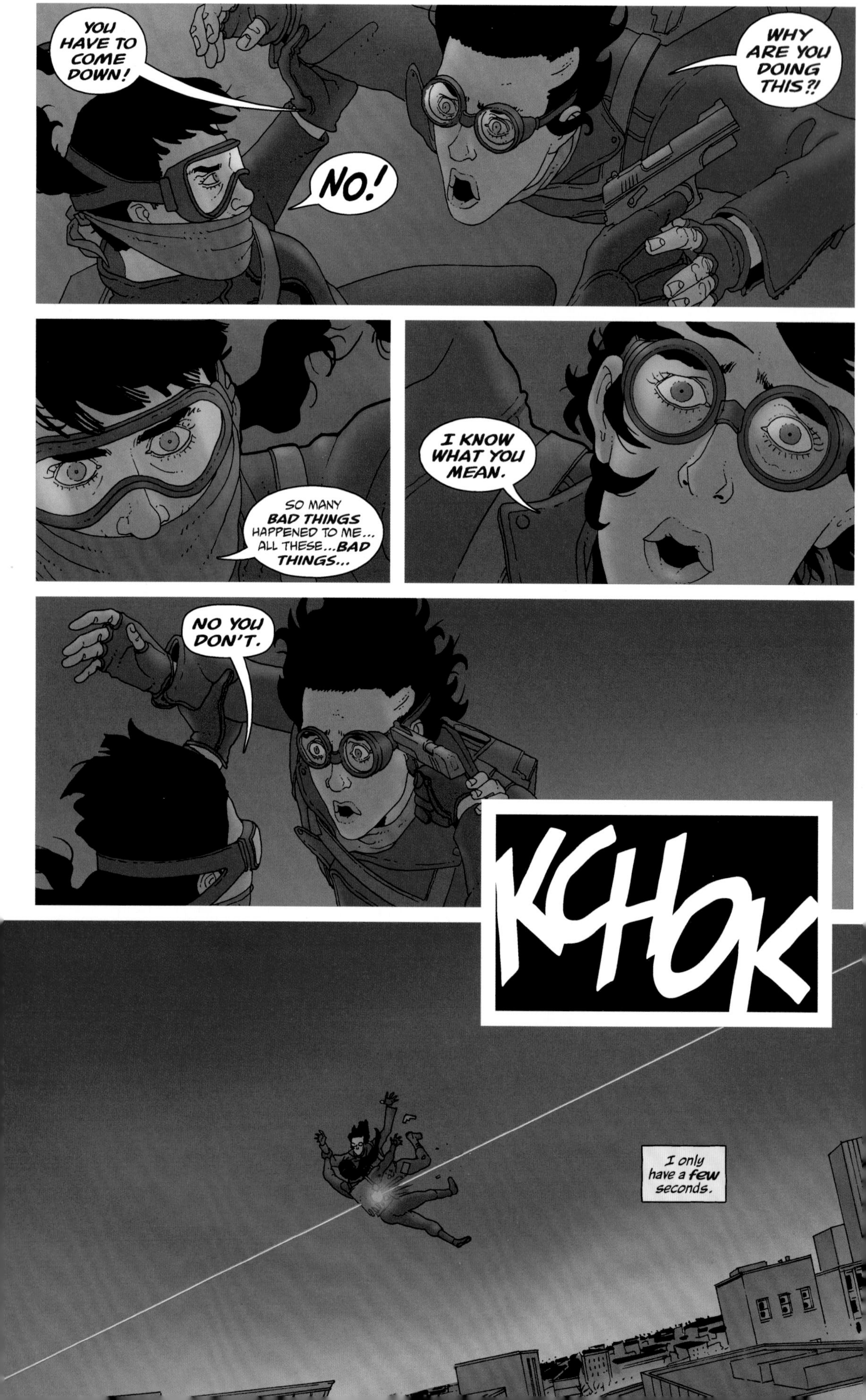
YOU HAVE TO COME DOWN!
WHY ARE YOU DOING THIS?!
NO!
SO MANY BAD THINGS HAPPENED TO ME... ALL THESE...BAD THINGS...
I KNOW WHAT YOU MEAN.
NO YOU DON'T.
KCHOK
I only have a few seconds.

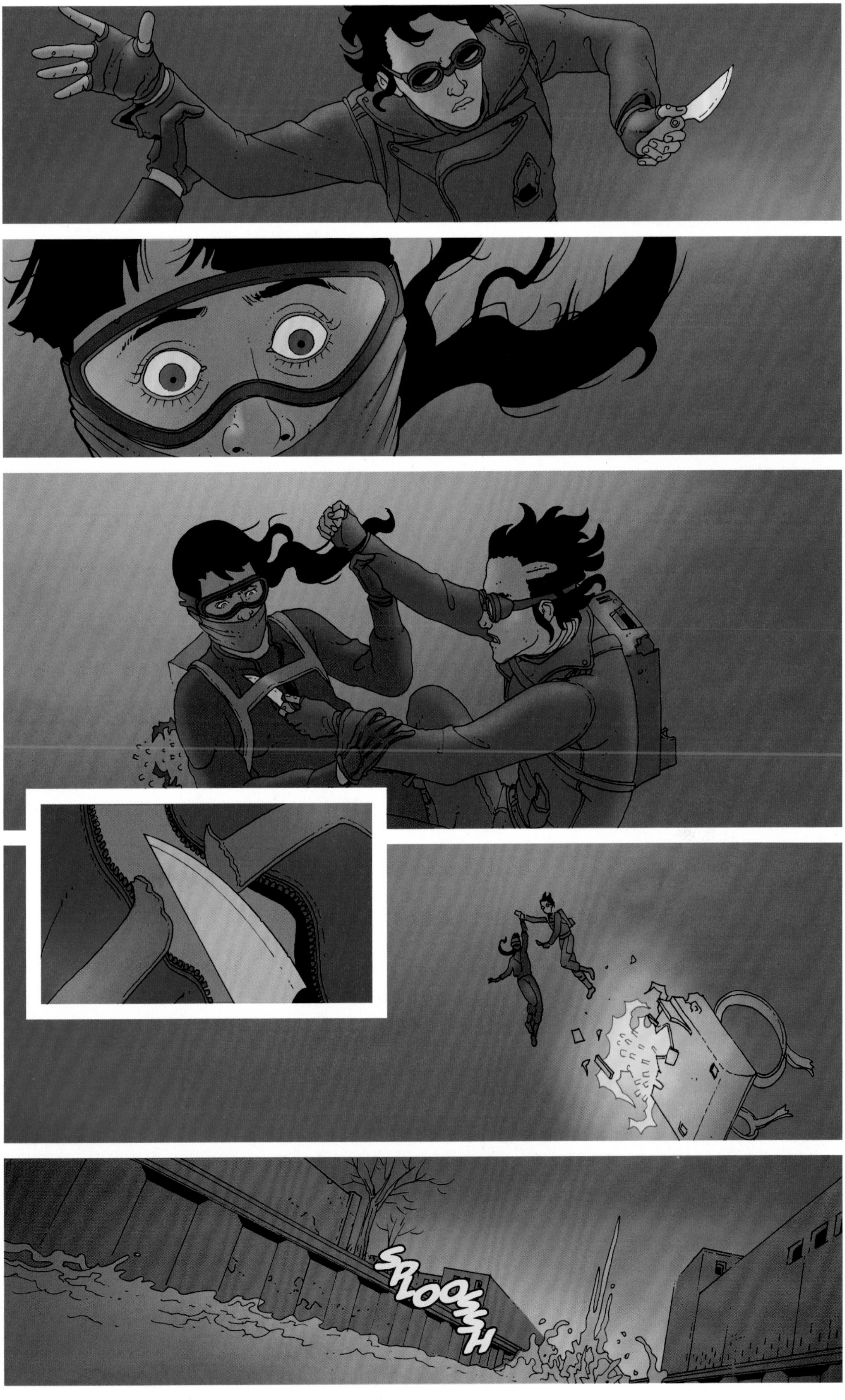
SPLOOSH

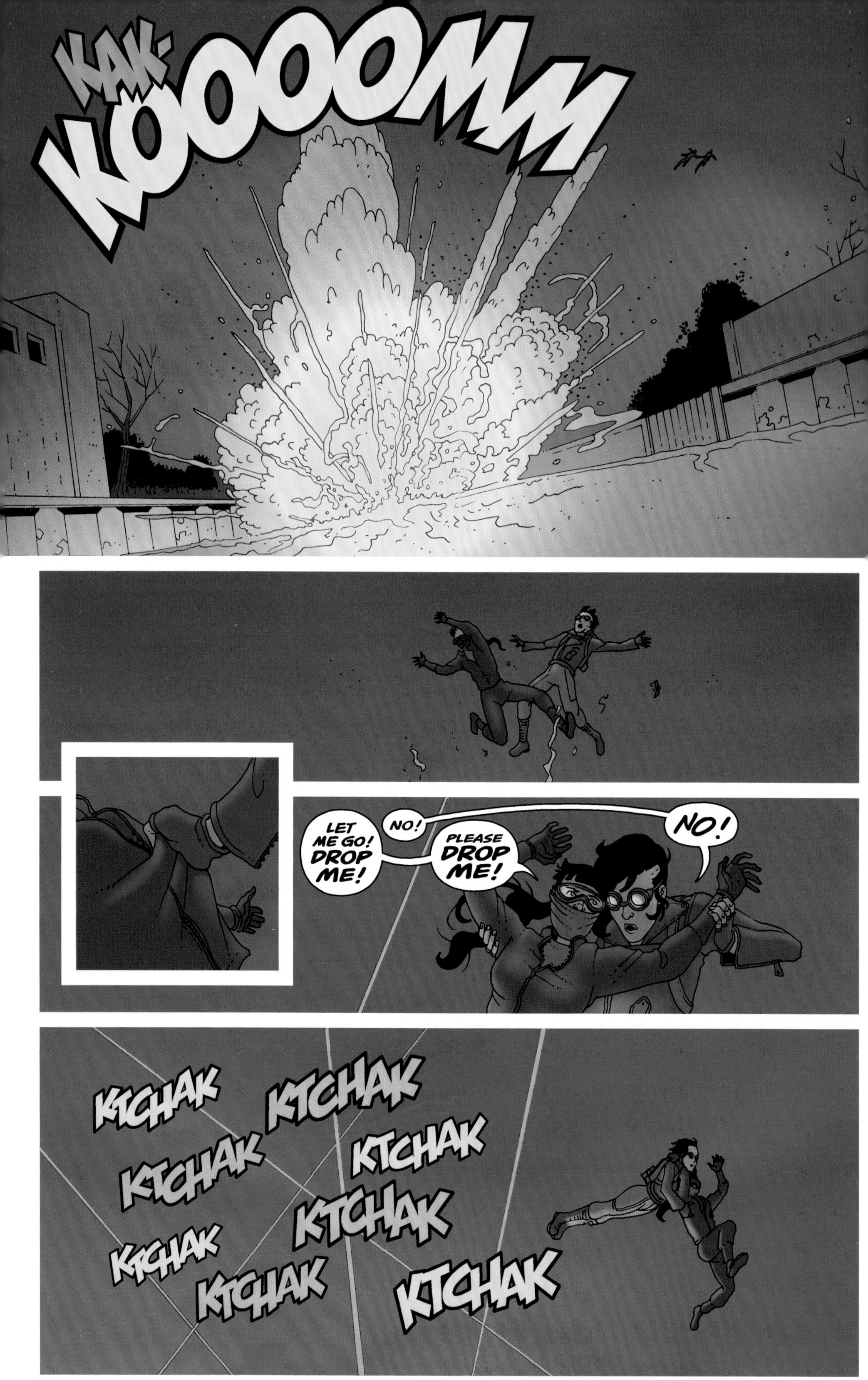
KAK-KOOOOMM
LET ME GO! DROP ME!
NO!
PLEASE DROP ME!
NO!
KTCHAK
KTCHAK
KTCHAK
KTCHAK
KTCHAK
KTCHAK
KTCHAK
KTCHAK

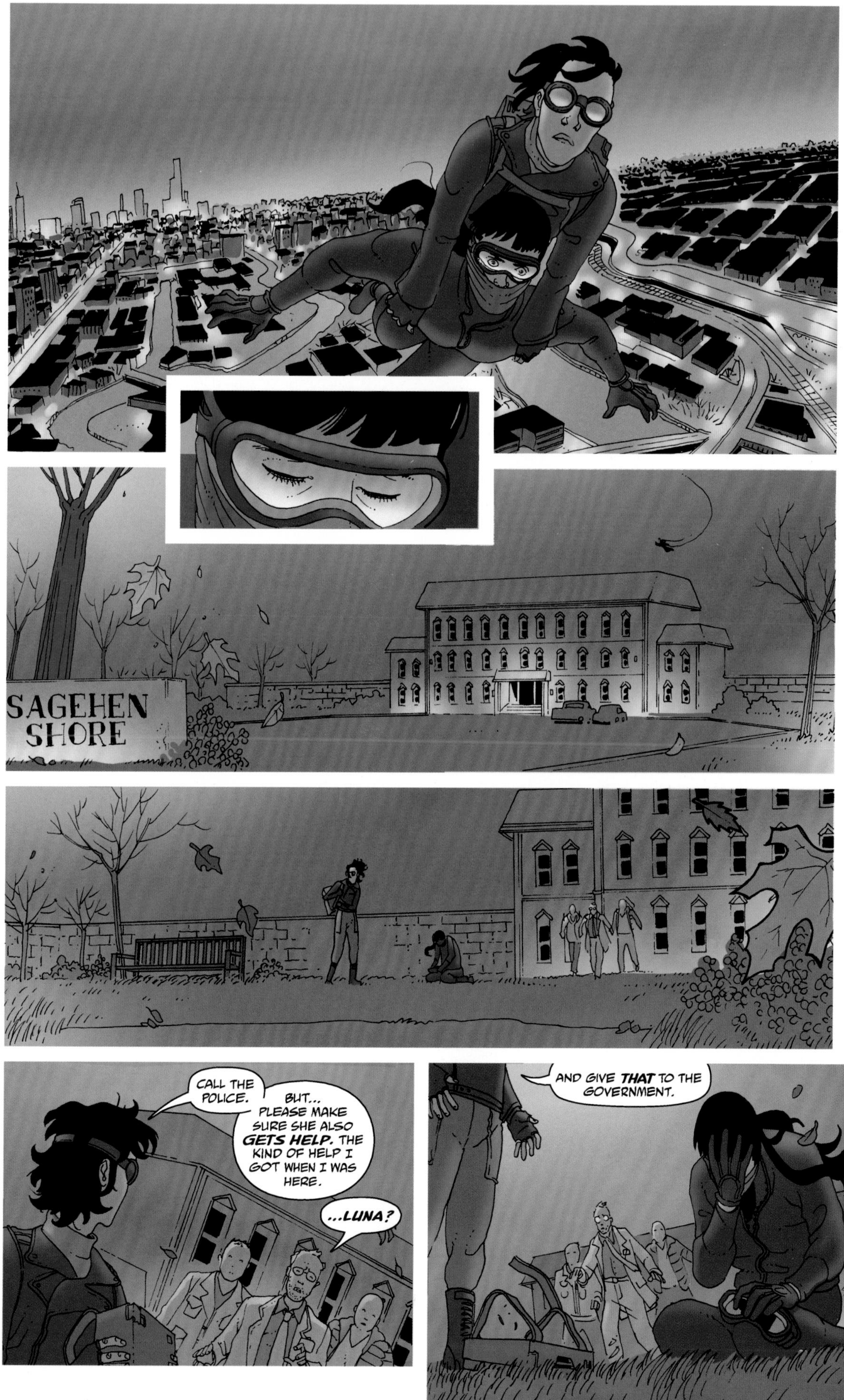
SAGEHEN SHORE
CALL THE POLICE.
BUT... PLEASE MAKE SURE SHE ALSO GETS HELP. THE KIND OF HELP I GOT WHEN I WAS HERE.
...LUNA?
AND GIVE THAT TO THE GOVERNMENT.

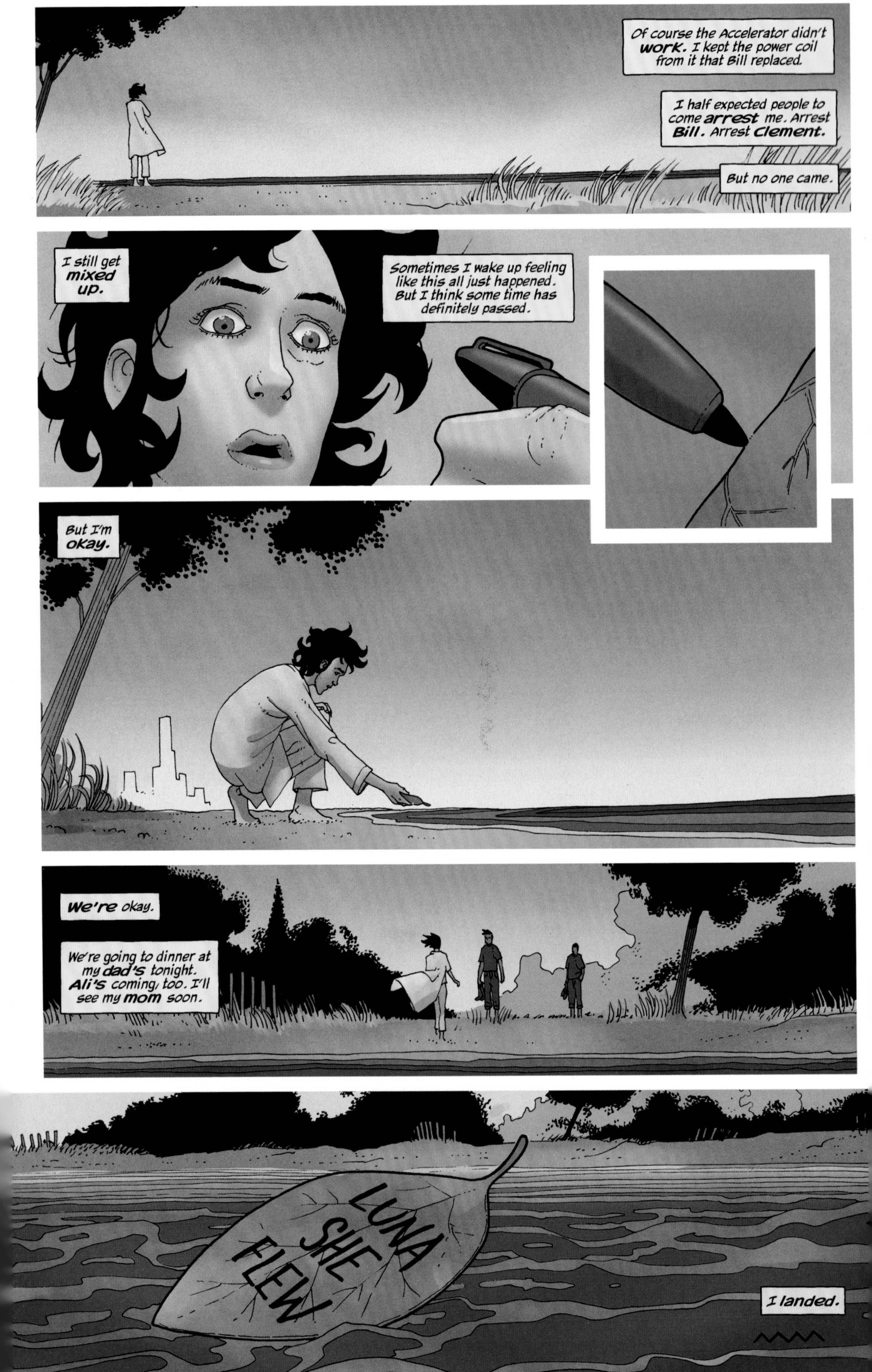
Of course the Accelerator didn't work. I kept the power coil from it that Bill replaced.
I half expected people to come arrest me. Arrest Bill. Arrest Clement.
But no one came.
I still get mixed up.
Sometimes I wake up feeling like this all just happened. But I think some time has definitely passed.
But I'm okay.
We're okay.
We're going to dinner at my dad's tonight. Ali's coming, too. I'll see my mom soon.
LUNA SHE FLEW
I landed.

Mayura Howard
Bill Meigs
Kido Brewster
Dana Church
Cindy ???

me.

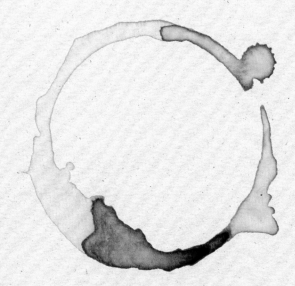

Here are the
thumbnails Martín
did for Chapter One
......

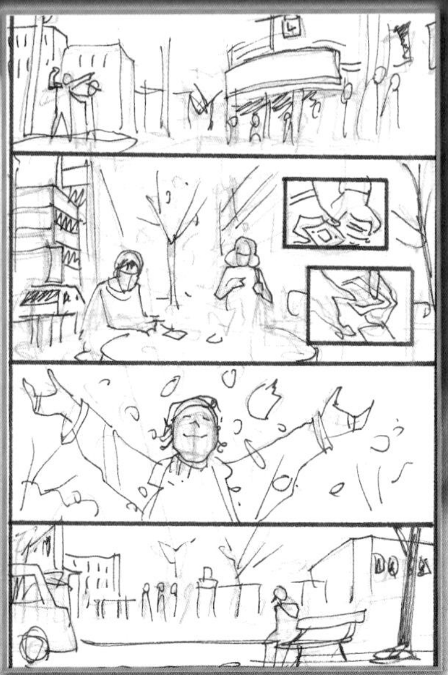

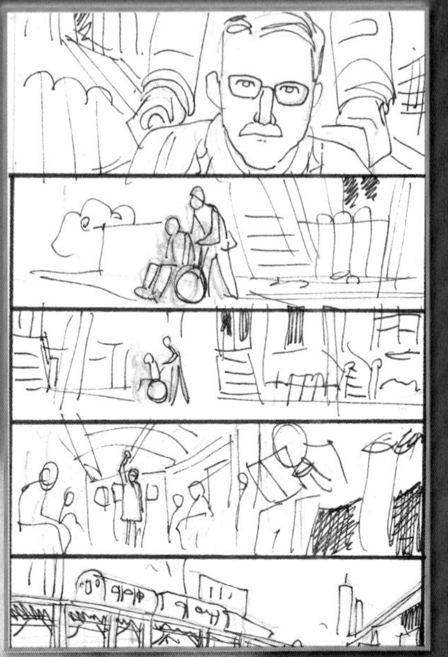

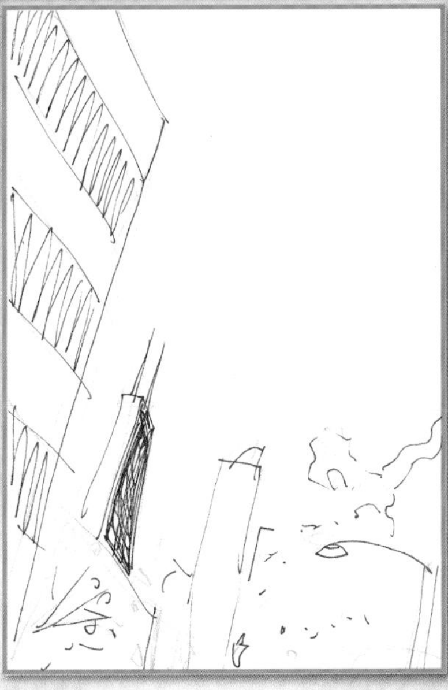

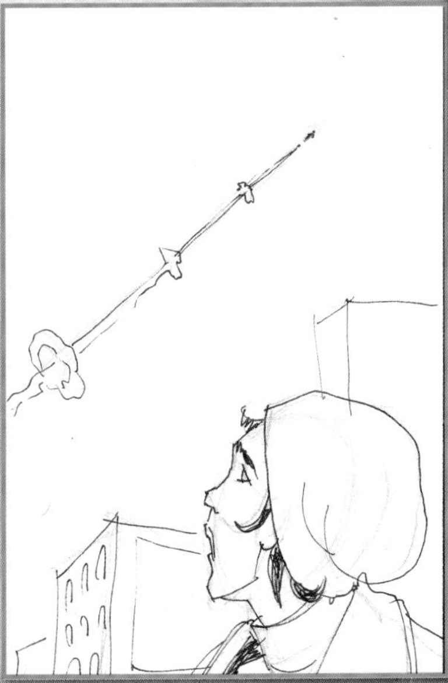

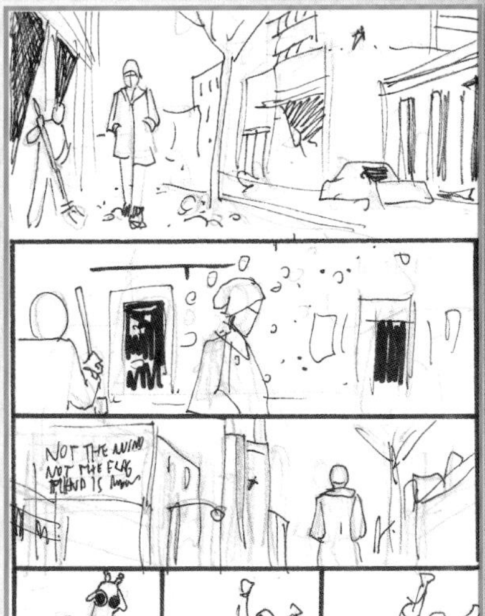
NOT THE WIND
NOT THE FLAG

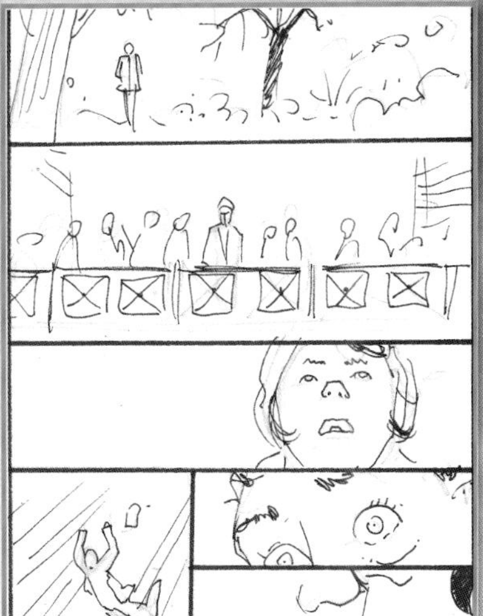

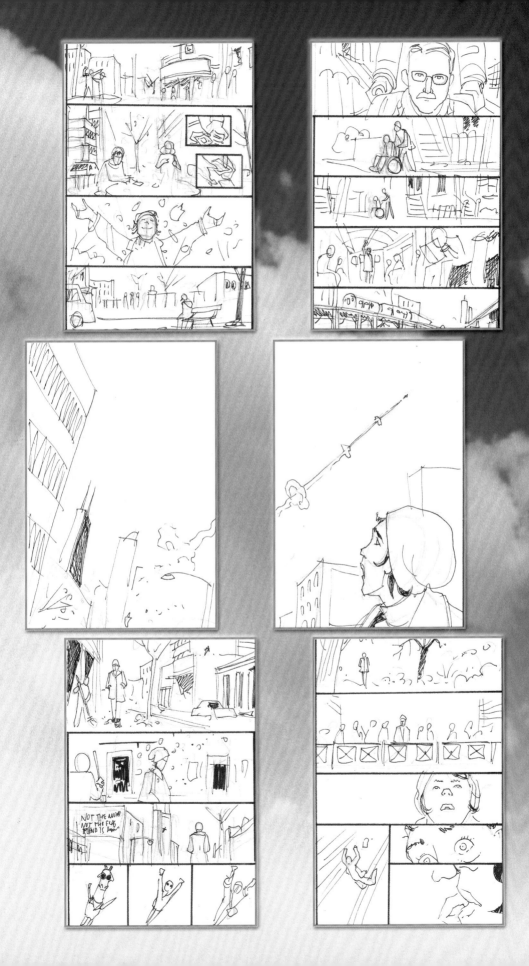

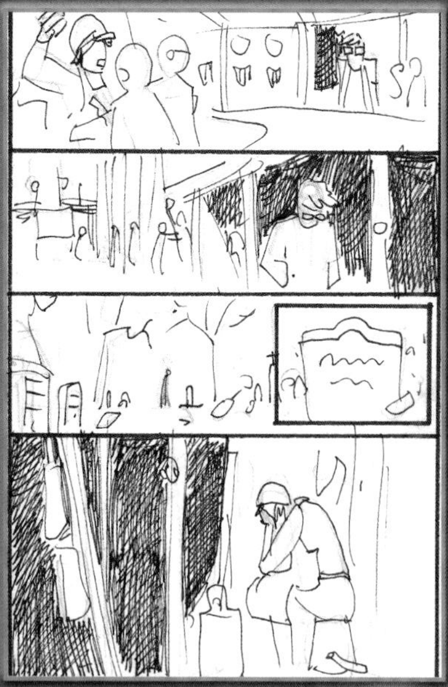

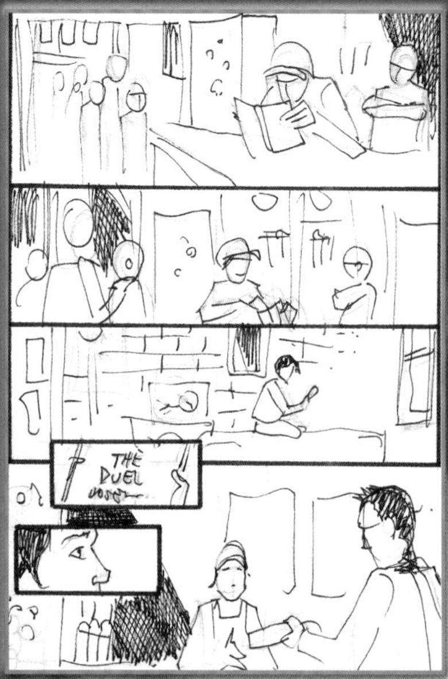
THE DUEL

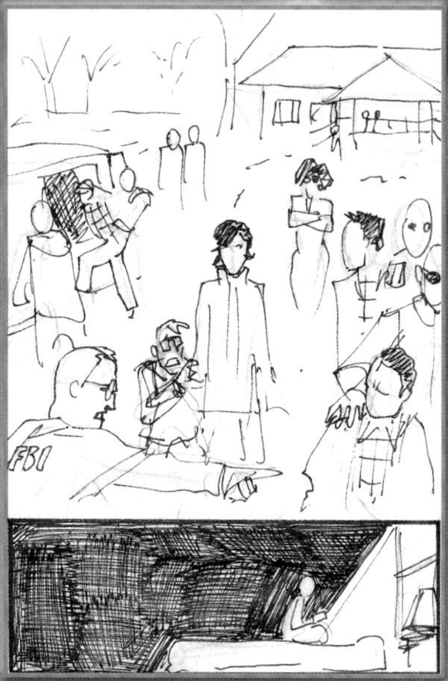
FBI

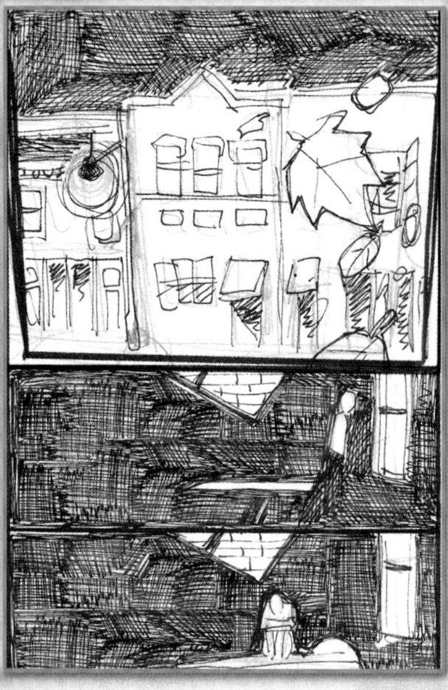

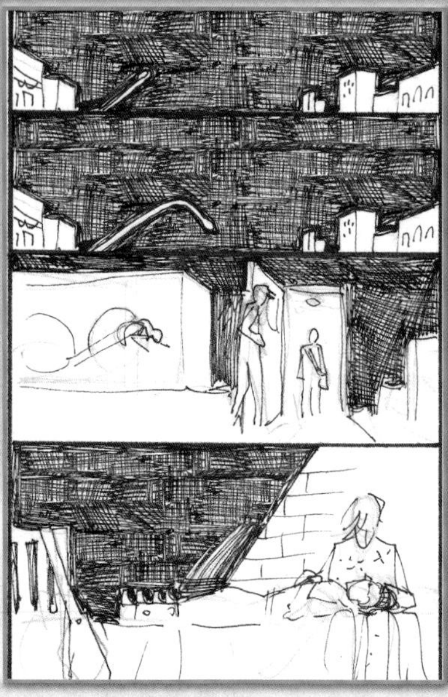

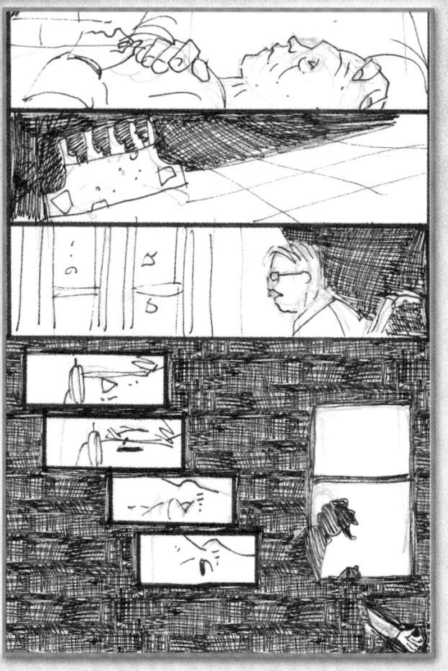

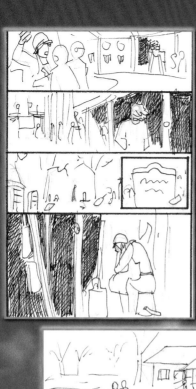

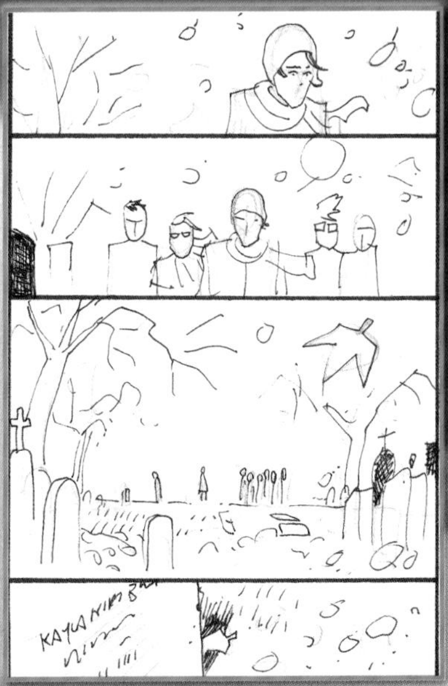
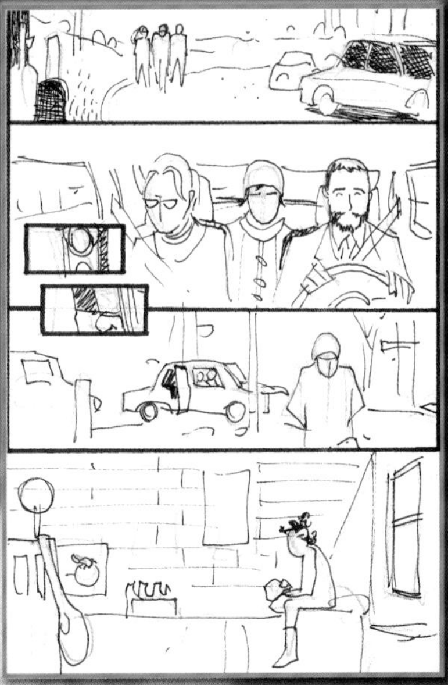
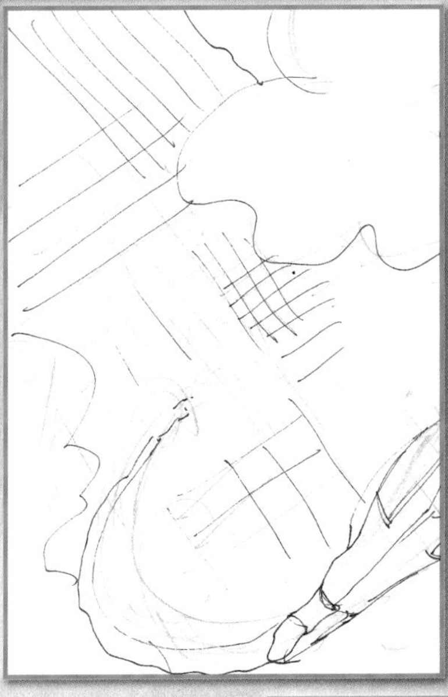
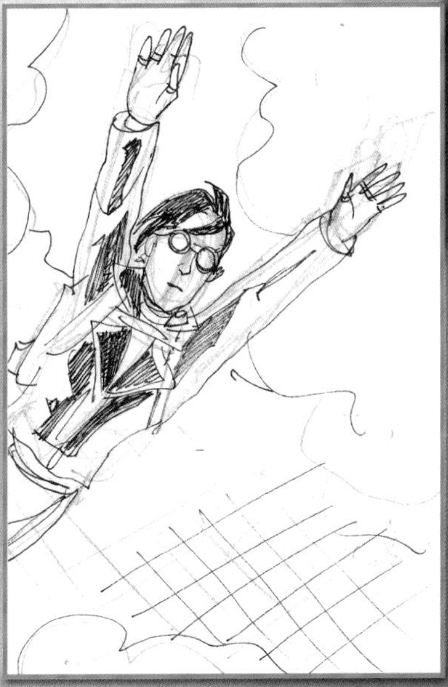
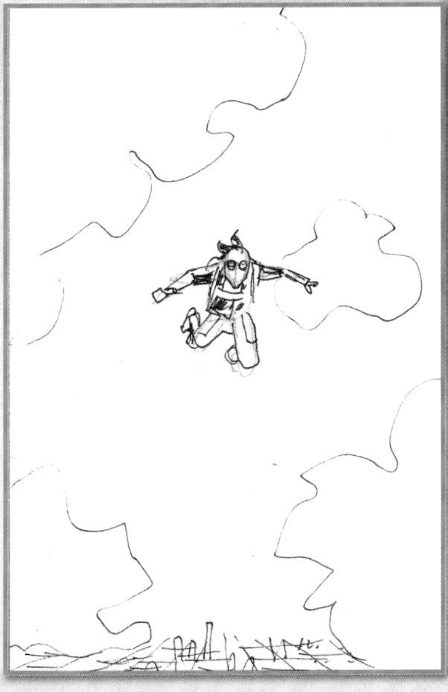

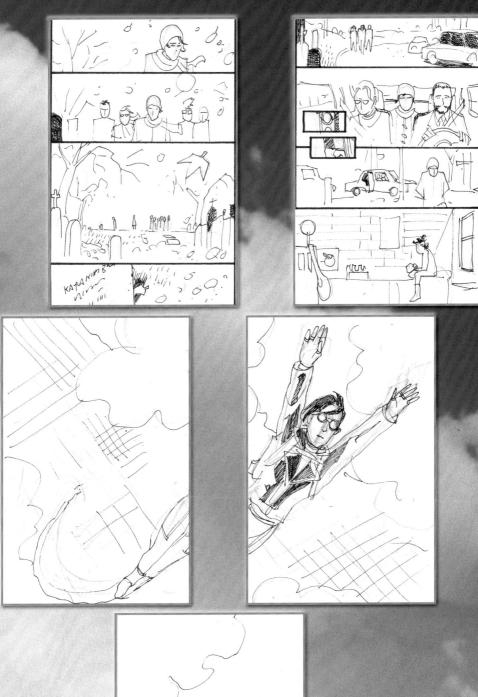

Makes it look easy,
doesn't he?
It's not.

How Martín Morazzo creates an original Luna!

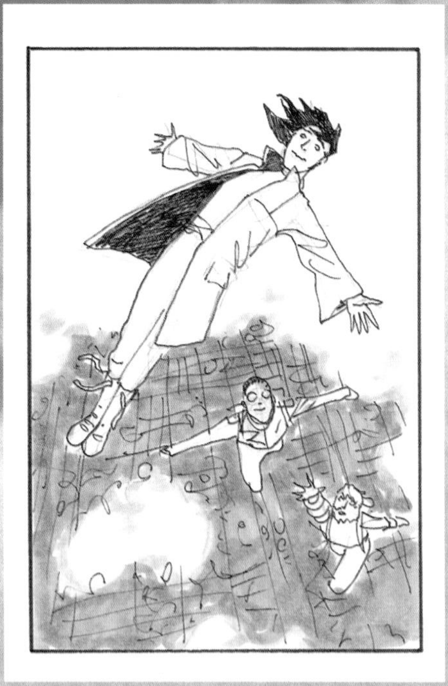

Initial Sketch

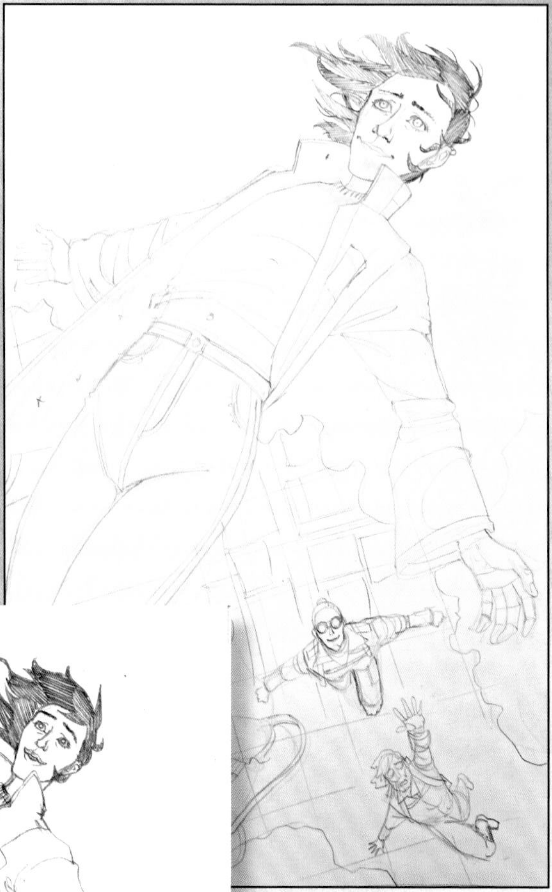

First-Round Pencils

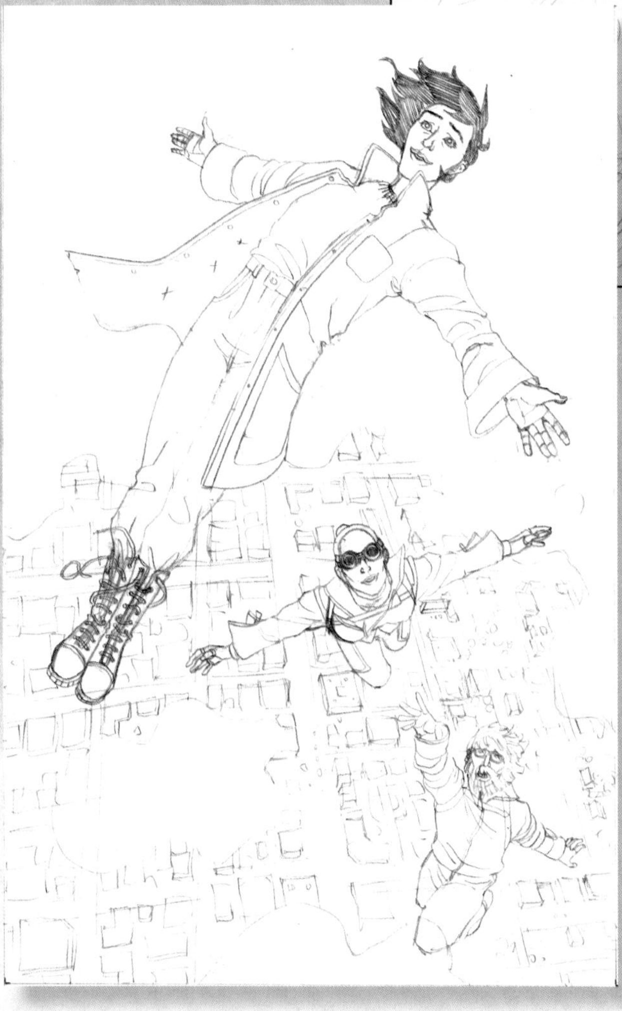

Final Pencils

The Finished Piece

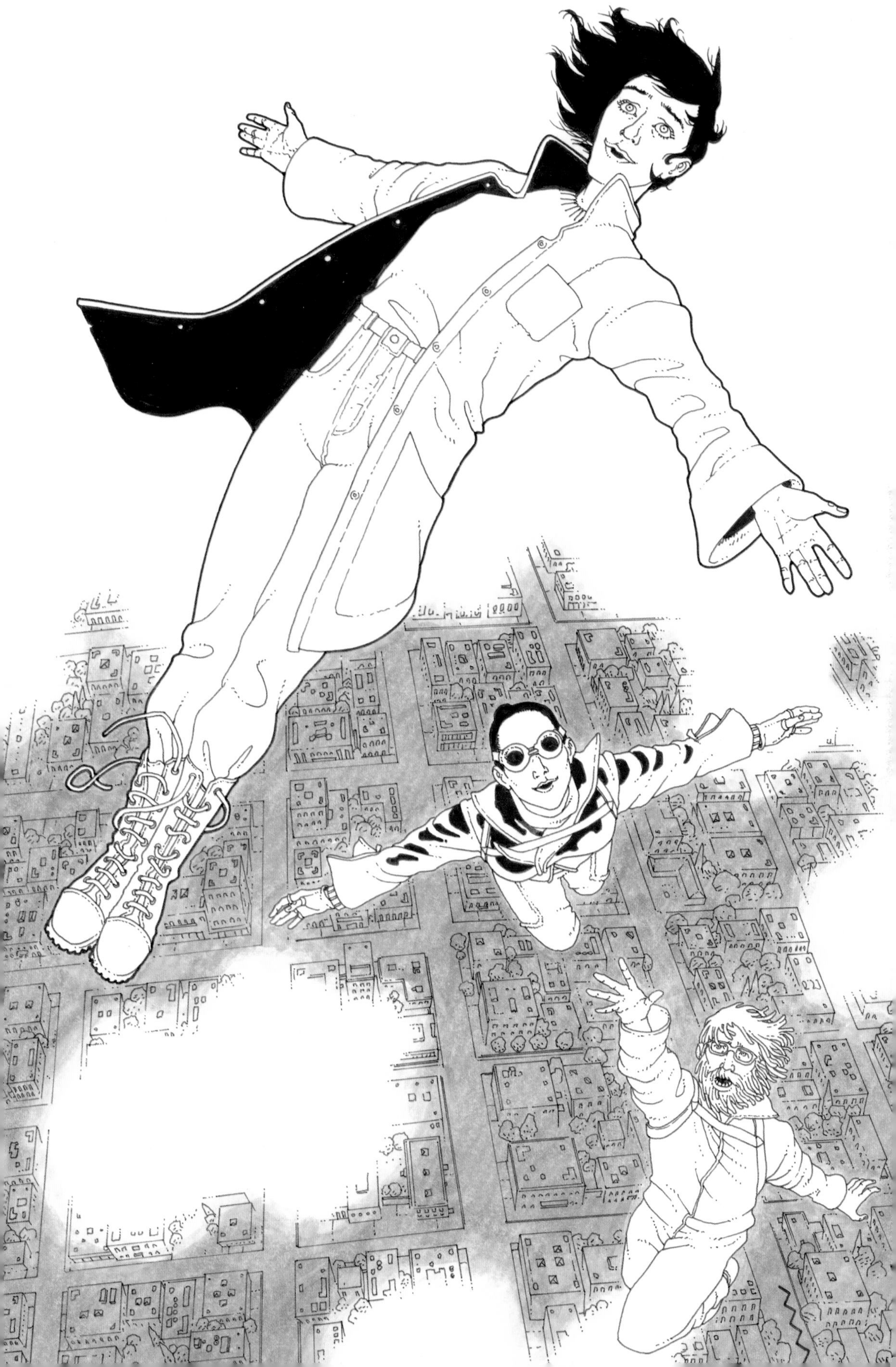

What can I say about *Luna?*

We all love her—I mean, the She Could Fly team, for sure, and probably you, the reader, too—like she is part of our family, maybe a daughter, or a sister.

I think that's probably because, despite the obvious fact that she's a fictional character, she feels so real, so here. We suffered for her, cried with her, and fought alongside her— it is impossible not to feel close to her.

We owed it to Luna to complete her story, especially with how volume 2 ended. And now that we've finished the book, and you have it in your hands, we finally have this moment to feel happy for her, knowing something bright awaits her, with her loved ones.

So now I think of her as being totally at peace—as she is in this sketch—and I don't know about you, but I feel peaceful too. We already miss her... but I know we'll be calm now, just like her, knowing that she, finally, has landed.

— Martín Morazzo

Flying can't last forever.

Nothing stays airborne permanently.

From the first pages of this story, Luna wanted to fly. For me, the idea of "flying" for our characters—especially Luna and the original Flying Woman before her, Mayura Howard—represented the ineffable, the seemingly impossible. Call it "happiness," call it "peace of mind," call it "balance," call it whatever you want... that's what Luna desperately needed.

Many times it felt so far out of her reach that it seemed to reside somewhere way up within the mysteries of the sky. In this final part of her story, she finally got a chance to search for it up there. I'll admit I can't profess the exactitudes of what got her back home, on the ground. Perhaps she learned that to go down, she had to first go up. Maybe whatever she found in the air allowed her to land. Or, there aren't any solid answers at all.

No journey is a straight line, in any direction. We fly. We fall. We can see for miles and we get lost in clouds. We experience the thrill of weightlessness, buck at the terror of collapse, and feel the relief of steady footing. We catch people, sometimes we don't, and sometimes we let them go ourselves.

Ultimately, I wanted Luna to be okay in the end, at least for a while, because... well, because I want to be okay. I want all of us to be. We can never know for sure. All we can do is look within, look without, look up... peer into the light of day and dark of night and try to discern the specks and the dots in the sky and do our best to make sense of them.

Are they birds? Are they planes?

Is it someone I know?

Is it me?

— Christopher Cantwell

BERGER BOOKS ™

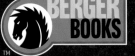

ENIGMA:
The Definitive Edition

Michael Smith's world is turned inside-out with the unfathomable, in-the-flesh arrival of his favorite comic book character, Enigma; a host of twisted villains—and the liberating truth about his own sexual identity.

This lavish edition of the bizarre and groundbreaking LGBTQ+ series features new introductions by the creators, and is packed with 50 pages of never-before-seen extras including development art and behind-the-scenes notes into the making of this celebrated story.

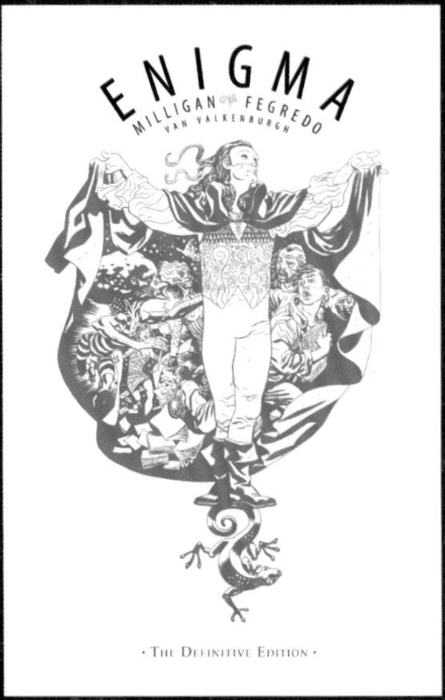
ENIGMA
MILLIGAN FEGREDO
VAN VALKENBURGH
• The Definitive Edition •

POST YORK

In a New York City drowned in its past, Crosby fights not just to survive... but to fully *live*.

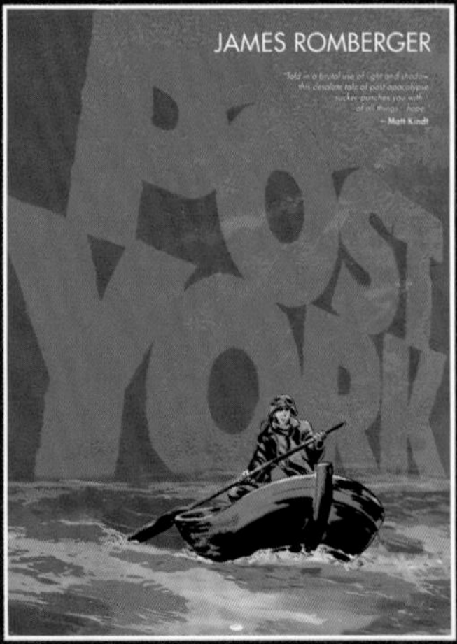
JAMES ROMBERGER
POST YORK

RUBY FALLS

Big secrets in a small town. Lana Blake obsessively chases down the cold case of a infamously progressive "disappeared" woman in this neo-noir thriller.

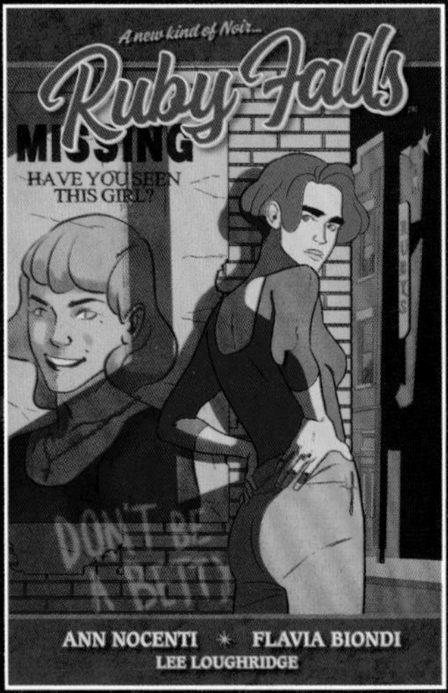
A new kind of Noir...
Ruby Falls
MISSING
HAVE YOU SEEN THIS GIRL?
ANN NOCENTI ✶ FLAVIA BIONDI
LEE LOUGHRIDGE

ANTHONY BOURDAIN'S HUNGRY GHOSTS

One night, chefs gather to outscare each other with tantalizing tales of fear and food — but will they survive?

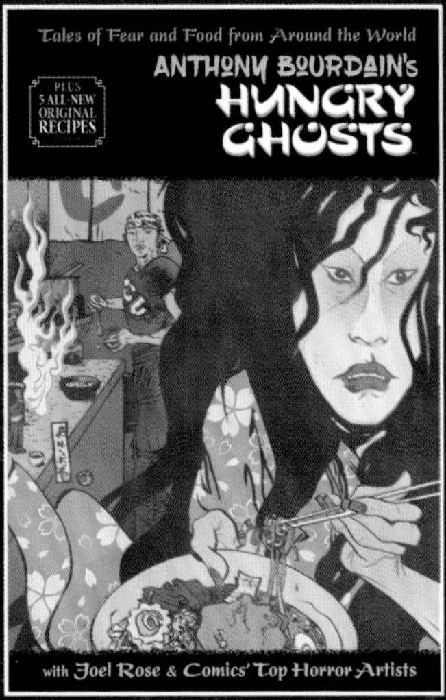
Tales of Fear and Food from Around the World
ANTHONY BOURDAIN'S
HUNGRY GHOSTS
PLUS 5 ALL-NEW ORIGINAL RECIPES
with Joel Rose & Comics' Top Horror Artists

THE GIRL IN THE BAY

A supernatural coming-of-age mystery begins in 1969, when Kathy Sartori is murdered—only to reawaken in 2019, where another version of herself has lived a full life. And her "killer" is about to strike again.

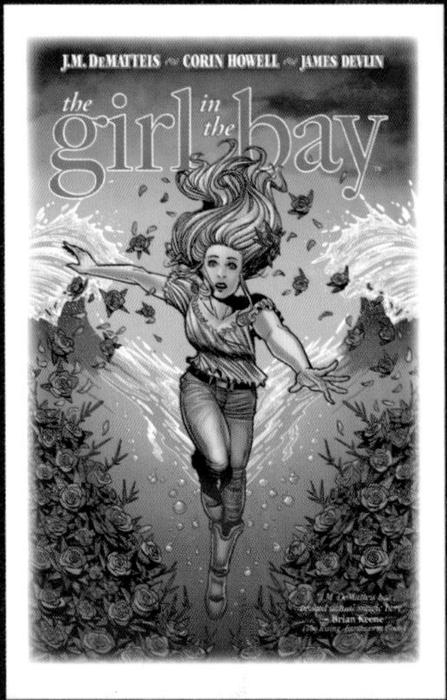
J.M. DeMATTEIS CORIN HOWELL JAMES DEVLIN
the girl in the bay

OLIVIA TWIST

In a dystopian future London, teenage Olivia Twist will discover great power... and just how much it costs.

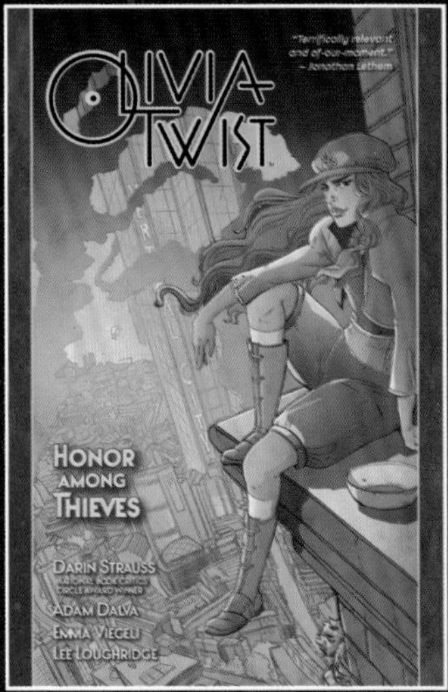
OLIVIA TWIST
HONOR AMONG THIEVES
DARIN STRAUSS
ADAM DALVA
EMMA VIECELI
LEE LOUGHRIDGE

When an alien falls in love with a human, a journalist stumbles into the story of a lifetime, but reporting it just might destroy planet Earth.

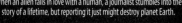

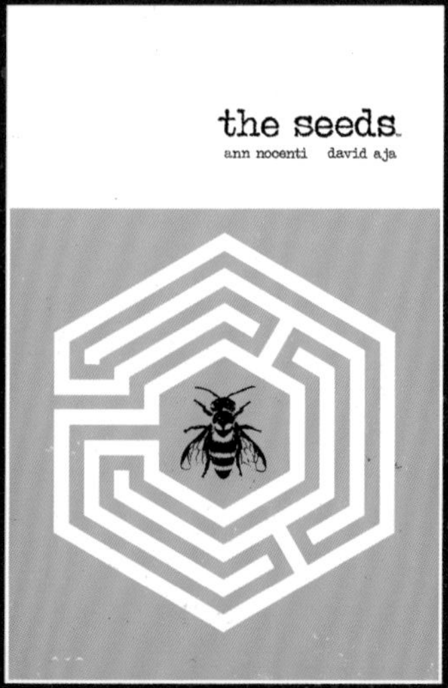
the seeds.
ann nocenti david aja

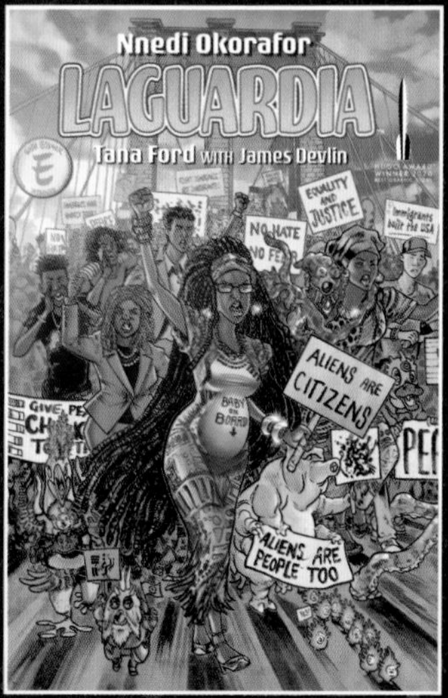
Nnedi Okorafor
LAGUARDIA
Tana Ford WITH James Devlin
EQUALITY AND JUSTICE
NO HATE
ALIENS ARE CITIZENS
ALIENS ARE PEOPLE TOO

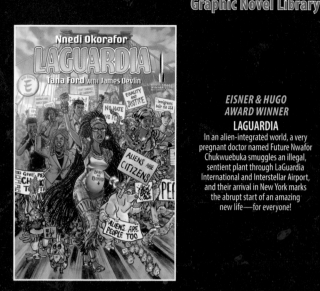

EISNER & HUGO AWARD WINNER

LAGUARDIA

In an alien-integrated world, a very pregnant doctor named Future Nwafor Chukwuebuka smuggles an illegal, sentient plant through LaGuardia International and Interstellar Airport, and their arrival in New York marks the abrupt start of an amazing new life—for everyone!

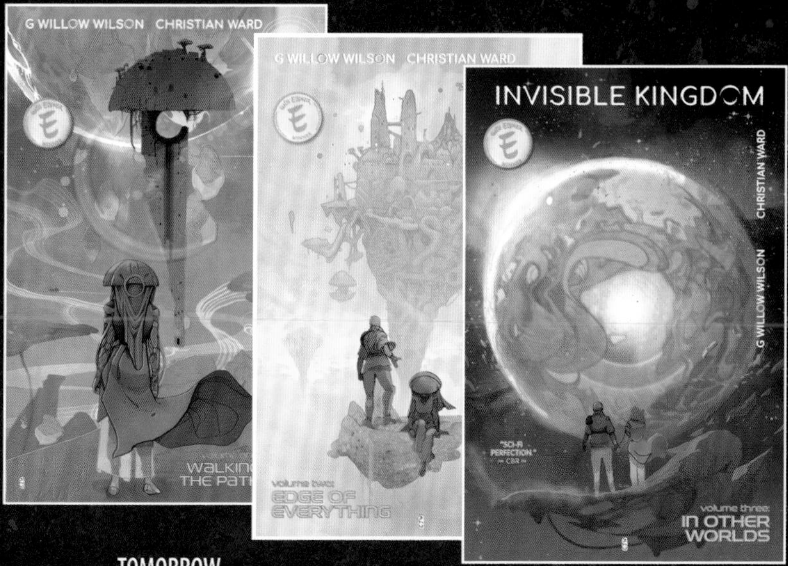
G WILLOW WILSON CHRISTIAN WARD
G WILLOW WILSON CHRISTIAN WARD
INVISIBLE KINGDOM
CHRISTIAN WARD
G WILLOW WILSON
"SCI-FI PERFECTION." — CBR
volume two: EDGE OF EVERYTHING
volume three: IN OTHER WORLDS

EISNER AWARD WINNER

INVISIBLE KINGDOM Vol. One

A young religious acolyte and a dogged freighter pilot uncover an inconceivable conspiracy between a world's major religion and the mega corporation that controls society.

INVISIBLE KINGDOM Vol. Two

With only part of the truth blown open and bigger secrets looming, will Vess and Grix become stronger —or shatter apart?

INVISIBLE KINGDOM Vol. Three

The breathtaking tale of the *Sundog* concludes, and Vess and Grix are faced with a new choice: love...or destruction.

TOMORROW

Desperate twins Oscar and Cira must find their way home after a species-jumping computer virus wipes out all adults.

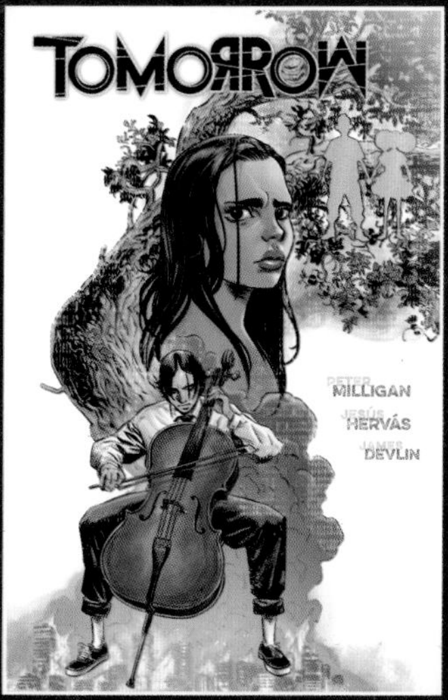
TOMORROW
PETER MILLIGAN
JESÚS HERVÁS
JAMES DEVLIN

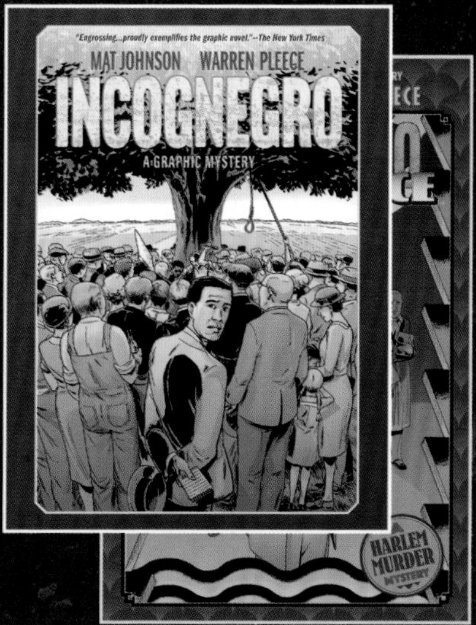
"Engrossing...proudly exemplifies the graphic novel."—The New York Times
MAT JOHNSON WARREN PLEECE
INCOGNEGRO
A GRAPHIC MYSTERY
HARLEM MURDER MYSTERY

INCOGNEGRO: A GRAPHIC MYSTERY

Zane Pinchback goes "incognegro" to investigate his brother's arrest in a fast-paced exploration of race and identity.

INCOGNEGRO: RENAISSANCE

Our race-bending protagonist penetrates a world where he feels stranger than ever before.

Dare to explore more of the weird world of Christopher Cantwell?

Step into the big-box horror of **EVERYTHING** and the tiny town of Holland, Michigan, where something wonderful has arrived: the superstore Everything.

But when people's psyches—and soon, entire lives— start to be viciously manipulated by the store and its mission of 'happiness', wonderful turns sinister.

It's up to the few who can resist Everything's strange pull to shut down the nightmare... **before it takes control entirely.**

"This book bubbles with energy and inventiveness."
—JEFF LEMIRE

EVERYTHING

Christopher Cantwell

I.N.J. Culbard

Shirley

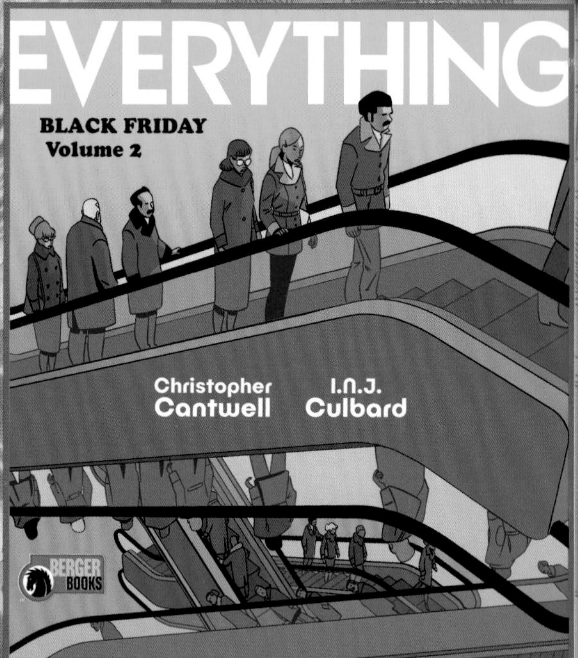

EVERYTHING

BLACK FRIDAY
Volume 2

Christopher Cantwell   **I.N.J. Culbard**

BERGER BOOKS

"This book bubbles with energy and inventiveness."
—JEFF LEMIRE

"A wonderfully bizarre, human, and ominous comic about true Happiness... This is a great book."
—GERARD WAY, *The Umbrella Academy*

...and only from